CANADIAN PUBLIC POLICY

Selected Studies in Process and Style

W0230187

Studies of public policy in Canada are traditionally narrow, focusing on a particular policy area or jurisdiction without giving consideration to the significant procedural commonalities that can be identified across the public policy spectrum. *Canadian Public Policy* provides the first comprehensive, theoretically informed, empirical evaluation of the development of public policy in Canada. It represents the culmination of a fifteen-year program of large-scale primary research into Canadian policymaking by Michael Howlett, an internationally recognized public policy expert.

Each of the chapters investigates one stage of the policy process – including agenda setting, policy formulation, decision making, policy implementation, and policy evaluation – in the Canadian context. The volume is book-ended by an introductory section setting out the logic of the policy cycle model, and a conclusion summarizing the research program and results. Investigating how Canadian experiences can inform and contribute to existing policy models, this unique volume will be a fixture in the Canadian public policy literature for years to come.

MICHAEL HOWLETT is Burnaby Mountain Professor in the Department of Political Science at Simon Fraser University.

Canadian Public Policy

Selected Studies in Process and Style

MICHAEL HOWLETT

UNIVERSITY OF TORONTO PRESS
Toronto Buffalo London

Printed in Canada

ISBN   978-1-4426-4406-9 (cloth)
ISBN   978-1-4426-1241-9 (paper)

Printed on acid-free, 100% post-consumer recycled paper with
vegetable-based inks.

Publication cataloguing information is available from
Library and Archives Canada

University of Toronto Press acknowledges the financial assistance to its
publishing program of the Canada Council for the Arts and the Ontario
Arts Council.

Canada Council   Conseil des Arts
for the Arts   du Canada

ONTARIO ARTS COUNCIL
CONSEIL DES ARTS DE L'ONTARIO

50 YEARS OF ONTARIO GOVERNMENT SUPPORT OF THE ARTS
50 ANS DE SOUTIEN DU GOUVERNEMENT DE L'ONTARIO AUX ARTS

University of Toronto Press acknowledges the financial support of the
Government of Canada through the Canada Book Fund for its publishing
activities.

"It is what we prevent, rather than what we do that counts most in Government."

William Lyon Mackenzie King

Contents

List of Figures   ix
List of Tables   xi
Acknowledgments   xv

Part One: Introduction

1 Introduction   5
2 Policy Development as Decision-Making Process   12

Part Two: The Policy Process in Canada

3 Agenda Setting – Predictable and Unpredictable Policy Windows:
   Institutional and Exogenous Correlates of Canadian Federal Agenda
   Setting   37
4 Policy Formulation: Do Networks Matter? Linking Policy Network
   Structure to Policy Outcomes: Evidence from Four Canadian Policy
   Sectors 1990–2000   65
5 Decision Making – Analysing Multi-Actor, Multi-Round Public
   Policy Decision-Making Processes in Government: Findings from
   Five Canadian Cases   91
6 Policy Implementation: Managing the "Hollow State": Procedural
   Policy Instruments and Modern Governance   118
7 Policy Evaluation – Policy Advice in Multilevel Governance
   Systems: Sub-National Policy Analysts and Analysis   133

Part Three: Conclusion

8 Conclusion – Policy Analytical Capacity and Evidence-Based Policy-
    Making: Lessons from Canada   153

Notes   171
References   179
Permission Credits   221

List of Figures

Figure 1   A Spectrum of Policy-Making Types   19
Figure 2   A Model of Policy Window Types   41
Figure 3   Spectral Density of Acid Rain Mentions   43
Figure 4   Spectral Density of Capital Punishment Mentions   44
Figure 5   Spectral Density of Constitutional Mentions   44
Figure 6   Spectral Density of Drug Mentions   45
Figure 7   Spectral Density of Native Mentions   45
Figure 8   Spectral Density of Nuclear Mentions   46
Figure 9   Cross-Correlation Functions of Native and Constitutional
            Hansard Issue Mentions   51
Figure 10   Cross-Correlation Functions of Nuclear and Acid Rain
            Hansard Issue Mentions   51
Figure 11   Cross-Correlation Functions of Drug and Capital
            Punishment Hansard Issue Mentions   52
Figure 12   Caseplot of Issue Density   54
Figure 13   Coherency of Density and Elections   55
Figure 14   Nuclear Issue Mentions in Hansard   59
Figure 15   Acid Rain Mentions in Hansard   59
Figure 16   Capital Punishment Mentions in Hansard   60
Figure 17   Constitutional Mentions in Hansard   60
Figure 18   Drug Issue Mentions in Hansard   61
Figure 19   Native Issue Mentions in Hansard   61
Figure 20   Budgets and Mini-Budgets   62
Figure 21   Throne Speeches   62
Figure 22   General Elections   63
Figure 23   First Ministers' Conferences   63
Figure 24   Unemployment Rate   64

Figure 25 Violent Crime Rate   64
Figure 26 Actor Policy Activity for Five Canadian Cases – By
          Year   101
Figure 27 Governmental and Non-Governmental Actor Activity by
          Issue Area and Year   103
Figure 28 A Spectrum of Substantive Policy Instruments   122
Figure 29 A Spectrum of Procedural Policy Instruments   128
Figure 30 Aspects of Political Analytical Capacity   163

List of Tables

Table 1   An Early Model of National Policy Styles   20

Table 2   Basic Agenda-Setting Styles   22

Table 3   Basic Policy Formulation Styles   24

Table 4   An Early Model of Decision-Making Styles   25

Table 5   Basic Decision-Making Styles   27

Table 6   A Taxonomy of Substantive Policy Instruments   28

Table 7   A Resource-Based Taxonomy of Procedural Policy
Instruments   29

Table 8   Basic Policy Implementation Styles   30

Table 9   Basic Policy Evaluation Styles   32

Table 10 Auto Correlation of Issue and Correlate Series   47

Table 11 ARIMA Model Identification   48

Table 12 Cross-Correlations: Issues with Media Correlates – Hansard
and Newspapers   49

Table 13 Cross-Correlations: Selected Issues with Objective
Correlates   50

Table 14 Institutional Series Diagnostics   53

Table 15 Cross-Correlation Functions of Issues and Institutions   53

Table 16 A Basic Taxonomy of Policy Change by Mode and Speed of
Change   69

Table 17 An Operationalized Model of Policy Change   72

Table 18 Basic Policy Subsystem Configurations   73

Table 19 Preliminary Operationalizing of Policy Subsystem
Configurations   75

Table 20 Hypothesized Relationship Existing between Policy
Subsystem Configurations and Propensity for Specific Types
of Changes in Policy Outputs   76

Table 21 Subsystem Membership Change by Sector and Organization
Type, 1990–2000   79

Table 22 Policy Change by Sector, 1990–2000   80

Table 23 Subsystem Change by Sector, 1990–2000   80

Table 24 Actual Subsystem Change 1990–2000 and Predicted Policy
Output Changes   81

Table 25 Predicted and Actual Policy Output Changes, 1990–2000   82

Table 26 Basic Decision-Making Styles after Howlett and Ramesh   95

Table 27 Key Dates of Legislative Activity for Five Canadian
Cases   99

Table 28 Range and Variation of Government and NGO Actors
1988–2005   102

Table 29 Actor Type and Issue Support by Round   105

Table 30 Actor Type and Issue Support by Round (per cent)   106

Table 31 Aggregated Types of Actor Activity by Rounds and Issue
Areas (per cent)   108

Table 32 Aggregated Types of Actor Activity by Rounds and Main
Category of Actor (per cent)   109

Table 33 Description of Key Legislative Changes by Issue Area   115

Table 34 Governmental and Non-Governmental Actor Activity by
Issue and Year   116

Table 35 Types of Actor Activity by Rounds   117

Table 36 A Taxonomy of Substantive Policy Instruments   120

Table 37 A Model of Substantive Instrument Choice   123

Table 38 A Resource-Based Taxonomy of Procedural Policy
Instruments   126

Table 39 A Model of Procedural Instrument Choice   130

Table 40 Length of Time   138

Table 41 Education   139

Table 42 Degree Subject Area   140

Table 43 Previous Work Experience   141

Table 44 Number of Post-Secondary Policy Courses Completed   142

Table 45 Completion of Post-Secondary Policy Analysis Courses   142

Table 46 Completion of Formal Internal Training Courses   142

Table 47 Sources of Post-Employment Training   143

Table 48 Work   144

Table 49 Number of FTEs   145

Table 50 Frequency of Work on Short-Term Issues   145
Table 51 Description of Policy Role(s)   146
Table 52 General Policy Tasks Undertaken   147
Table 53 Specific Analytical Technique(s) Used   148
Table 54 Stages of the Policy Process and Associated Policy
          Failures   160
Table 55 Policy Failures and Management Strategies by Stage of the
          Policy Cycle   161

Acknowledgments

This book draws heavily on data originally collected under a series of three-year research grants from the Social Science and Humanities Research Council of Canada for which I am very grateful. Additional funding was received from BC Work-Study and Summer Challenge grants and from the government of British Columbia. Research under these grants was carried out by Lynda Jovanovich, Leslie Banks, Burt Schoeppe, Russell Williams, Andrea Migone, Karen Lochead, Jonathan Kim, Terri Evans, Jonathan Ferschau, Alexia Touralias, Karla Tate, Anastasiya Salnykova, Brian Yaeck, Hristina Dobreva, Joshua Newman, Mandy Cheema, David Petroziello, Marion Gure, and Malvina Lewandowska. Helpful comments on earlier versions of these articles were received from Susan Phillips, Adam Wellstead, Jeremy Rayner, Alex Netherton, Colin Bennett, Rejean Landry, Rodney Haddow, Chris Dunn, Jae Moon, Gerard Boychuk, Benjamin Cashore, Peter May, Brian Head, Tim Tenbensel, Adam Wellstead, Luc Bernier, Bryan Evans, Wendy Taylor, Coralie Breen, and the participants of the several conferences and workshops where original versions of the chapters were presented, including several meetings of the British Columbia Political Studies Association, the Canadian Political Science Associations, and the International Research Society for Public Management.

CANADIAN PUBLIC POLICY

Selected Studies in Process and Style

PART ONE

Introduction

1 Introduction

Books on Canadian public policymaking as a subject of interest to scholars and practitioners of generic policy processes are few and far between. Some texts exist, of course, but most of these do not attempt to situate contemporary Canadian policymaking practices within the larger literature on policy processes developed over the last half century in the policy sciences and tend to be very descriptive and atheoretical. Many other works exist on the details of particular sectors or areas of interest (from forest policy to welfare, health, and others), but virtually all tend to focus on the idiosyncrasies of the Canadian case and generally do not place Canadian practices within either a comparative perspective or the corpus of work on generic policy processes it has engendered. This is despite the fact that policymaking in Canada has some significant process or procedural commonalities which transcend a purely national perspective and can serve as good case studies from which to advance thinking in the policy sciences.

This book serves as a starting point for such considerations. It examines policymaking in this country using Canadian cases and examples to test how Canadian experiences can inform and develop existing policy models and theories developed, generally, on the basis of careful examination of European and American cases, especially the latter.

The chapters in the book represent the culmination of a fifteen-year program of enquiry into Canadian policymaking. Each main chapter originated in successive three-year Social Science and Humanities Research Council (SSHRC) grants established for the study of a stage of the policy process or "policy cycle." Following the template set out in Howlett, Ramesh, and Perl (2009), the policy process is separated into five stages – agenda setting, policy formulation, decision making, policy implementation, and policy evaluation – and each stage in the cycle is the subject of a single chapter. Chapter 1 sets out the model and its implication for considerations of policy processes and styles, while the final chapter examines the future of policymaking in this country and addresses questions of policy success and failure as the likely results of recent efforts in this country to promote enhanced "evidence-based" policymaking. Together the chapters provide the first comprehensive, theoretically informed evaluation of the workings of each stage of the policy cycle in Canada, based on original large-scale primary survey and other quantitative and qualitative research designed to develop and test contemporary models of policy processes against empirical evidence from the Canadian case.

General Approach

As stated above, the book adopts a policy cycle model and uses this framework to organize the analysis and presentation of materials (Jann and Wegrich 2007). This model breaks down the policy process into five distinct stages or activities which can then be examined individually: agenda setting, where problems first emerge on the government's radar; policy formulation, where various actors attempt to influence the shape and direction of subsequent policies; decision making, where authoritative actors take decisions on ultimate policy content and timing; policy implementation, where administrators and non-governmental actors invoke policy tools to execute decisions; and policy evaluation, where a variety of policy actors attempt, formally and informally, to evaluate the effects of policies and feed this information back into their reform or termination.

Each of these stages or activities has engendered a large literature which has described many commonalities or styles of policymaking found in modern governments and which forms the basis of the corpus of theorization and conceptual development in the policy sciences (Howlett, Ramesh, and Perl 2009). This book examines many of these leading theories and models using evidence gleaned from a number of large-scale empirical studies of Canadian policy content and actor behaviour carried out by the author over the past decade and a half.

Contents

The book is organized around chapters on each stage of the Canadian policy process previously published as award-winning articles in leading Canadian and international academic journals, as well as introductory and concluding material also derived from previously published work in leading journals. As such it provides a unique compendium of studies of the Canadian policy process which, while available individually elsewhere, cannot be found as a whole in any other single source. Its main aim is to bring the results of a large-scale, multi-year research program which are currently scattered over a range of academic publications together in one place.

The book is organized as follows.

First, this chapter serves as a preface describing the fifteen-year research program followed by the author and its originating problematic, methods, and results. It explains the origins of each project which contributed to the present volume and the need to aggregate these individual results into a single collection. It summarizes the research findings and spells out their significance to contemporary policy studies and practices both in Canada and abroad.

Also in the introductory part of the book, Chapter 2 provides an overview of thinking about policy processes and policy styles first published as Howlett (2002b). This chapter sets out the logic of the policy cycle model of the policy process and justifies the five-stage model used in the book. It summarizes the large literature found in the policy sciences dealing with each stage and sets out the gaps in baseline knowledge present in the contemporary comparative policy literature dealing with each.

Part II of the book then begins the task of analysing the nature of each stage of the policymaking process in Canada. Chapter 3 (originally published as Howlett [1998]) deals with agenda setting. This chapter addresses the question of the applicability of John Kingdon's influential theory of agenda setting to Canadian political life. It examines the extent to which agenda setting in Canadian governments is routine or discretionary, predictable or unpredictable, and the extent to which it is influenced by events and activities external to itself. The study uses time series data collected on issue mentions related to native affairs, the constitution, drug abuse, acid rain, the nuclear industry, and capital punishment in parliamentary debates and committees between 1977 and 1992. It compares these series to other time series developed from media mentions, violent crime rates, unemployment rates, budget speeches and speeches from the throne, elections, and first ministers' conferences over the same period in order to assess the impact of such events on public policy agenda setting.

Chapter 4 (first published as Howlett [2002] and nominated for the McMenemy Prize for Best Article in the Canadian Journal of Political

Science in 2002) deals with policy formulation and with the nature and influences of policy network types on policy formulation and policy outcomes. Relatively recent contributions to the policy literature have called into question the utility of the "network" approach to the study of public policymaking, including a challenge to long-held views concerning the impact of the structure of policy subsystems on policy formulation. This chapter uses empirical evidence accumulated from case studies of four prominent Canadian federal policy sectors over the period 1990–2000 to address this issue. It sets out a model that explains policy change as dependent upon the effects of the articulation of ideas and interests in public policy processes, and generates several hypotheses relating different subsystem configurations to propensities for paradigmatic and intra-paradigmatic policy dynamics. It suggests that the identification of the nature of the policy subsystem in a given policy sector reveals a great deal about its propensity to respond to changes in ideas and interests.

Chapter 5 (based on Howlett [2007] and nominated for the McMenemy Prize for Best Article in the Canadian Journal of Political Science in 2007) begins the analysis of complex multi-actor, multi-round decision-making processes in Canadian public policy formation. After setting out the notion of a decision-making style and its constitutive elements, the chapter identifies research into complex multi-actor, multi-round decisions as a serious lacuna in the literature on public policy decision making, despite the fact that this type of decision making is very common in public policymaking circumstances. The chapter advances research in this area through the analysis of several hypotheses raised in recent European studies concerning the conditions under which such processes are likely to successfully conclude in a decision, rather than an impasse. These hypotheses are tested against evidence taken from five cases of multi-round decision making in Canada over the period 1995–2005: amendments to the Indian Act, the creation of species at risk legislation, alterations to the Bank Act, the extension of privacy legislation to the private sector, and efforts to develop a Free Trade of the Americas Agreement (FTAA). Data on actor interactions in these five areas gleaned from online newspaper and media index services reveals that Canadian results do not match those arrived at in European studies, showing both different patterns of governmental and non-governmental activity and less volatility in actor behaviour as rounds evolve over time.

Chapter 6 (first published in Howlett [Canadian Public Administration 2000] and winner of the Hodgetts Prize for Best Article in the journal in 2000) deals with policy implementation. Less empirical than Chapters 3–5, this chapter deals with the situation where modern governments face a paradox in that, theoretically, their bureaucratic capacity for action in terms of knowledge, expertise, budgets, and personnel resources is high, while, at the same time, phenomena such as globalization and democratization have severely undermined their ability to directly control social outcomes. Recent works by Canadian, Dutch, American, British, and French scholars have begun to describe a common set of policy instruments contemporary governments now use to indirectly steer social actors towards their preferred policy options. Unlike traditional "substantive" instruments, which directly affect the delivery of goods and services in society, these "procedural" policy instruments are intended to manage state-societal interactions in order to assure general support for government aims and initiatives. Used on an ad hoc basis in the past, these tools have become an essential feature of modern governance. This chapter advances the study of these procedural policy instruments by developing a taxonomy and outlining the rationale for choosing between particular instrument types.

The final chapter in this part, Chapter 7 (which first appeared as Howlett [2009]), deals with policy evaluation and presents the results of the first large-scale survey of policy analysts in Canada conducted in 2008–2009. Despite the existence of a large body of literature on policy analysis, empirical studies of the work of policy analysts are rare, and in the case of analysts working at the sub-national level in multilevel governance systems, virtually non-existent. Many observers decry the lack of even such basic data as how many policy analysts work in subnational government, on what subjects, and with what effect. This is true in many countries, for example, the United States, Germany, and Canada, all federal systems with extensive sub-national governments but where what little empirical work exists focuses on government at the national level. In most cases, in justifying their observations and conclusions observers rely on only one or two quite dated works, on very partial survey results, or on anecdotal case studies and interview research. This chapter reports the findings of several surveys aimed specifically at examining the background and training of provincial and territorial policy analysts in Canada, the types of techniques they employ in their jobs, and what they do in their work on a day-by-day basis. The resulting profile of sub-national policy analysts presented here reveals several substantial differences between analysts working for national governments and their sub-national counterparts, with important implications for training and for the ability of nations to accomplish their long-term policy goals.

Part III serves as a conclusion to the volume. It contains Chapter 8 (which first appeared as Howlett [2009]), which deals with trends in Canadian public policymaking and with questions about the nature of policy success and failure, the need for enhanced policy capacity to deal with large-scale complex problems such as climate change, and difficulties associated with current government efforts to promote better informed or "evidence-based" policymaking. It argues that evidence-based policymaking represents a contemporary effort to reform or restructure policy processes in order to prioritize evidentiary or data-based decision making. Like earlier efforts in the "policy analysis movement," its aim is to avoid or minimize policy failures caused by a mismatch between government expectations and actual, on-the-ground conditions through the provision of greater amounts of policy-relevant information. A significant factor affecting the ability of policymakers to engage in evidence-based policymaking pertains to both governmental and non-governmental "policy analytical capacity." That is, governments require a reasonably high level of policy analytical capacity to perform the tasks associated with managing the policy process in order to implement evidence-based policymaking and avoid several of the most common sources of policy failures. Recent studies, however, suggest that, even in advanced countries such as Canada, the level of policy analytical capacity found in many governments and non-governmental actors is not high, potentially contributing to both a failure of evidence-based policymaking as well as effectively dealing with many complex contemporary policy challenges.

Each individual chapter in Parts II and III serves in its own right as an effort to advance thinking about the nature of the particular aspects of Canadian public policymaking examined and, taken together, provides the first systematic overview of the Canadian public policy cycle and its operation. The chapters underscore the complexity of policymaking in this country but also the ability to understand these complexities using insights from contemporary comparative policy research and public policy theory. The chapters highlight the key role played by Canadian governments in agenda setting, some intentional and some due to the structures and timelines put into place in the Canadian democratic system; the need to examine policy communities and policy networks and their configuration in specific sectors in order to understand policy formulation and change; the need to better understand complex multi-actor, multi-round decision-making processes and their impact on decision-making; the recent development of an entire edifice of procedural policy instruments to supplement and complement the traditional implementation tools used by governments and the generally poor or limited state of policy analysis found in contemporary government, including Canada. As Part III then argues, this pattern suggests an increasingly complex policy environment in which governments increasingly attempt to use more subtle policy tools to achieve their ends. This change in policy style, it is argued, means all levels of Canadian governments will require additional resources and better trained personnel if they are to retain their historically significant role as policy leaders. This is a necessity if governments do not wish to find themselves increasingly driven by events outside of their control and engaged in error-prone patterns of issue fire fighting rather than the pursuit of the prudent goals of "peace, order and good government" which have characterized Canadian policymaking over the past century and a half.

2 Policy Development as Decision-Making Process

The idea that policy development can be thought of as a series of decision-making processes was first broached systematically in the work of Harold Lasswell (Lasswell 1956, 1971). For Lasswell, the policy development process began with intelligence gathering, that is, the collection, processing, and dissemination of information for those who participate in the decision-making process. It then moved on to the promotion of particular options by those involved in the actual decision. The third stage was one in which those decision makers actually prescribed a course of action. In the fourth stage, the prescribed course of action was invoked; meaning a set of sanctions was developed to penalize those who failed to comply with the prescriptions of decision makers. The policy was then applied by the courts and the bureaucracy and ran its course until it was terminated or cancelled. Finally, the results of the policy were appraised or evaluated against the aims and goals of the original decision makers.

This model was highly influential in the development of the policy sciences. Although not entirely accurate, it helped to advance the policy sciences by expanding the idea of the policy process beyond its traditional confines in the actions of governments and their agencies. It also introduced the notion of the policy process as an ongoing cycle, recognizing that most policies do not have a definite life cycle – moving from birth to death – but rather endlessly reoccur, in slightly different guises, as one policy succeeds its predecessor.

In most recent work, a five-stage model of the policy process has been posited. In this model, "agenda setting" refers to the first stage in the process. This is the earliest stage in a sequence of policy development when a problem is initially sensed by policy actors and a variety of solutions put forward. "Policy formulation" refers to the second stage in the process, in which specific policy options are developed within government. In this stage, the range of plausible choices is narrowed by excluding the infeasible ones, and efforts made by various actors to have their favoured solution ranked highly among the remaining few. "Decision making" refers to the third stage, in which governments adopt a particular course of action or non-action. This can involve the adoption of one, or none, or some combination of the solutions remaining at the end of the estimation stage. In the fourth stage of "policy implementation," governments put their decisions into effect. This involves the use of some combination of the tools of public administration in order to alter the distribution of goods and services in society in a way that is broadly compatible with the sentiments and values of affected parties. Finally, "policy evaluation" refers to the fifth stage in the process, in which the results of policies are monitored by both state and societal actors, often leading to the reconceptualization of policy problems and solutions in the light of experiences encountered with the policy in question (Howlett and Ramesh 2003).

This simplified model provides a general framework for understanding the policy development process and points to several of the key temporal activities and relationships that should be examined in furthering study of the issue. However, it does not answer several key questions such as the actual substance of policy, the number and type of relevant actors involved in the process, the exact manner and sequence in which actual policy development processes occur, and whether there exist basic patterns of development in different issues areas, sectors, or jurisdictions (Sabatier 1992). Empirical studies aimed at answering these questions and generating more detailed models of the policymaking process were conducted in the 1960s and 1970s and generated several competing "schools" or approaches to the subject.

Historical Overview: The Ir/Rationality of Policy Development

Early studies of the policy development process differed considerably in terms of their findings and assumptions about the "rationality" of the process. While a number of studies indicated that policymakers went about their business in a calm, methodical, and precise fashion aimed at optimizing or maximizing policy outcomes, others argued the process was much more byzantine, haphazard, and unpredictable. Several examples of these early works are presented below.

Pure Rational Model

Some early studies of individual policymaking in companies, governments, and organizations conducted largely by students of public and business administration found policymakers attempting to follow a systematic method for arriving at logical, efficient policies. To various extents, they argued that policymakers first established a goal; explored alternative strategies for achieving it; attempted to predict its consequences and the likelihood of each occurring; and then chose the option which maximized potential benefits at least cost or risk (Edwards 1954; Gawthrop 1971; Weiss 1977; Carley 1980).

This model was "rational" in the sense that it prescribed a standard set of procedures for policymaking which were expected to lead in all circumstances to the choice of the most efficient means of achieving policy goals (Jennings 1987; Torgerson 1986). Policymakers were thought of as neutral "technicians" or "managers" who identify a problem and then find the most effective or efficient way of solving it (Elster 1991).

Limited Rationality Models

Further empirical research into policymaking processes, however, soon led to a rethinking of many elements of the *rational model*. Policymakers were often found to be neither neutral nor competent and a second wave of models of the policymaking process tended to argue that this was not accidental, or due to avoidable errors made by policymakers, but an inherent and unavoidable characteristic of the policymaking exercise.

Perhaps the most noted critic of the rational model was the American behavioural scientist Herbert Simon. In a series of books and articles beginning in the early 1950s, he argued there were several hurdles that prevented decision makers from attaining "pure" comprehensive rationality in their decisions (Simon 1955 and 1957). First, Simon noted definite cognitive limits to the decision makers' ability to consider all possible options, which forces them to selectively consider alternatives. Second, Simon argued the model assumed that it is possible for decision makers to know the consequences of each decision in advance, while, in reality, no one can predict the future with any degree of certainty. Third, Simon also noted specific policy options usually entail a bundle of favourable and adverse consequences which makes comparisons among them difficult. Moreover, since the same option can often be efficient or inefficient depending on the circumstances, it is not possible for decision makers to arrive at unambiguous conclusions about which alternative is superior.

Simon concluded from his assessment of the rational model that public decisions in practice did not maximize benefits over costs, but merely tended to satisfy whatever criteria decision makers set for themselves in the instance in question. This *"satisficing"* criterion, as he put it, was a realistic one given the *"bounded rationality"* with which human beings are endowed.

The well-known *incremental model* of policymaking developed by Yale University political scientist Charles Lindblom attempted to capture the elements of a policy process characterized by only limited or "bounded" rationality (Dahl and Lindblom 1953; Lindblom 1951, 1958, and 1959). Lindblom (1979) summarized the elements of his model as consisting of the following "mutually supporting set of simplifying and focusing stratagems":

a. Limitation of analysis to a few somewhat familiar policy alternatives ... differing only marginally from the status quo;
b. An intertwining of analysis of policy goals and other values with the empirical aspects of the problem (that is, no requirement that values be specified first with means subsequently found to promote them);
c. A greater analytical preoccupation with ills to be remedied than positive goals to be sought;
d. A sequence of trials, errors, and revised trials;
e. Analysis that explores only some, not all, of the important possible consequences of a considered alternative;
f. Fragmentation of analytical work to many (partisan) participants in policymaking (each attending to their piece of the overall problem domain).

Lindblom argued that policies were invariably developed through a process of "successive limited comparisons" with earlier policies with which decision makers were most familiar. As he put it in his oft-cited 1959 article, "The Science of 'Muddling Through,'" policymakers worked through a process of "continually building out from the current situation, step-by-step and by small degrees" (Lindblom 1959).

For Lindblom, this was due to two related aspects of the policymaking situation. First, since policymaking requires distribution of limited resources among various participants, it is easier to continue an existing pattern of distribution rather than adopt radically new proposals which alter the established pattern of costs and benefits enjoyed, or borne, by specific actors. Second, the standard operating procedures that are the hallmark of bureaucracy also tended to promote the continuation of existing practices. The methods by which bureaucrats identify options and the methods and criteria for choice are often laid out in advance, which inhibits innovation and perpetuates existing arrangements (Gortner et al. 1987).

The incremental model hence viewed policymaking as a practical exercise concerned with solving problems through trial-and-error processes rather than through the comprehensive evaluation of all possible means of achieving policy goals (Manzer 1984). Decision makers, therefore, did not maximize policy outcomes in the traditional, rational sense, because they considered only a few familiar alternatives for their appropriateness and stopped their search whenever an alternative acceptable to established policy actors was found.

Irrational Models

A very different model was put forward by one of Simon's co-authors, James March, and his Norwegian colleague, Johan Olsen, which asserted that public policymaking was neither a fully nor bounded rational activity, but rather an inherently irrational process. The two authors proposed a so-called *garbage can model* of decision making which denied even the limited notion of rationality accepted by incrementalists (March and Olsen 1979). They started from the assumption that both the rational and incremental models presumed a level of intentionality, comprehension of problems, and predictability of relations among actors that simply did not obtain in reality. Based on studies they conducted into policymaking exercises carried out in universities and similarly constructed large institutions, they argued that policymaking is typically a highly ambiguous and unpredictable process only distantly related to searching for means to achieve goals. Rejecting the instrumentalism that characterized most other models, Cohen, March and Olsen argued that decision opportunities were:

> a garbage can into which various problems and solutions are dumped by participants. The mix of garbage in a single can depends partly on the labels attached to the alternative cans; but it also depends on what garbage is being produced at the moment, on the mix of cans available, and on

the speed with which garbage is collected and removed from the scene. (Cohen, March, and Olsen 1979)

That is, they argued that policy solutions were only very loosely related to policy problems and the process of matching solutions to problems was a largely ad hoc one which depended on various unpredictable elements such as the personalities of the actors involved, their presence or absence in specific decision-making instances, and the temporary alliances and arrangements made between them in specific cases. The garbage can metaphor was used deliberately by March and Olsen to strip away the aura of science and rationality attributed to decision making by earlier theorists. They sought to drive home the point that goals are often unknown to policymakers, as are causal relationships. In their view, actors simply define goals and choose means as they go along in a process which is necessarily contingent and unpredictable.

Problems with Existing Models: False Dichotomies and Corrective Syntheses

As is apparent from the above brief overview, each of these early models was constructed on the basis of certain findings and expectations with respect to the behaviour of policymakers, especially in regard to how policymakers characterized acceptable policy outcomes and acted so as to achieve them (Cahill and Overman 1990). Each was constructed on the basis of some empirical findings, but both the incremental and garbage can models were also established on the basis of a critique of the concepts contained in their predecessors. Hence incremental critics of the rational model argued that it would only generate maximal results if all possible alternatives and the costs of each alternative were assessed before a decision was made, while garbage can critics of incrementalism argued that it assumed a constant set of decision makers who could learn from past experiences. In both cases, empirical evidence to the contrary was cited to bolster arguments made about the unreality of such assumptions.

Defenders of rational models, however, were unwilling to accept the superiority of those alternatives based on limited or restricted notions of rationality. Critics found faults with several aspects of incremental policymaking which, as Forester put it, "would have us cross and recross intersections without knowing where we are going" (Forester 1984). The model was criticized, for example, for being unable to explain large-scale change and innovation (Lustick 1980; Berry 1990; Weiss and Wood-house 1992) and for being undemocratic to the extent that it confined policymaking to bargaining within a select group of senior policymakers (Gawthrop 1971). By discouraging systematic analysis and planning and undermining the need to search for promising new alternatives, it was also said to promote short-sighted decisions which can have adverse consequences for society in the long run (Cox 1992; Hayes 1992). In addition to criticisms of the desirability of decisions made incrementally, the model was also criticized for its narrow analytic usefulness. Yehezkel Dror, for example, noted that incrementalism could only work when there is a great deal of continuity in the nature of problems policies are intended to address and in the means available to address them, something that does not always exist (Dror 1964). Incrementalism was also found to be more characteristic of decision making in a relatively stable environment, rather than in situations that are unusual, such as a crisis (Nice 1987) and where large numbers of actors participate in policy development, rather than a few (Bendor 1995).

The garbage can model generated similar criticisms. While it was found by some authors like John Kingdon to be a fairly accurate description of how decisions are made at times in some complex organizations, like legislatures (Kingdon 1984), its generalizability to all instances of policy development was questioned. Gary Mucciaroni for example, argued:

> Perhaps the mode of policy-making depicted by the garbage can model is itself embedded in a particular institutional structure. Put another way, the model may be better at depicting decision-making in certain polities than in others. It may be more useful for describing policy-making in the United States, where the institutional structure is fragmented and permeable, participation is pluralistic and fluid, and coalitions are often temporary and ad hoc. By contrast, policy-making in other countries takes place among institutions that are more centralized and integrated, where the number of participants is limited and their participation is highly structured and predictable ... (where this occurs) ... the result has been a process described as "stable predictable, orderly," "rationalistic," "deliberative" and "planned" quite unlike the garbage can model's image of decision making that is more open, fluid and ad hoc. (Mucciaroni 1992: 466–7)

In addition, it was argued that the model did not well explain the existence of fairly long-term patterns in policymaking and exaggerated

Figure 1: A Spectrum of Policy-Making Types

Synoptic-------	Strategic-------	Disjointed-------	Simple-------	Blundering
		Incremental	Incremental	

[*Proactive* ----------------   ------ *to* --------   ------------------ *Reactive*]

Adapted from Charles E. Lindblom and D. K. Cohen, *Usable Knowledge: Social Science and Social Problem Solving*, New Haven: Yale University Press, 1979.

the gap existing between problems and solutions in most instances (Mucciaroni 1992). These limitations led many analysts to continue to look for alternative models of policymaking processes. Some suggested that the shortcomings of existing models could be overcome by combining elements from each in a new synthetic model. One such effort, for example, suggested that optimal decision making would consist of both a cursory search ("scanning") for alternatives as suggested by incrementalism, followed by a detailed probe of the most promising alternative, as suggested by the rational model (Etzioni 1967). However, most efforts took to heart the idea put forward by Lindblom late in his career, that a spectrum of policymaking styles existed (Smith and May 1980). These ranged from "synoptic" or rational-comprehensive decision making to "blundering," that is, simply following hunches or guesses without any real effort at systematic analysis of alternative strategies. The spectrum put forward by Lindblom and Cohen in 1979 is illustrated in Figure 1.

While Lindblom did not specify under what circumstances a specific option might be used, other authors have since suggested that the manner with which a policy problem or issue would be developed tends to be established on a relatively permanent basis and can usefully be thought of as a policy "style" (Freeman 1985; Coleman 1994). Richardson, Gustafsson, and Jordan (Richardson et al. 1982), for example, defined a policy style as a typical process of policy development characterized by the interaction between (a) the government's approach to problem solving and (b) the relationship between government and other actors in the policy process. Using these two variables, they argued that a limited number of large-scale, typically national, styles could be identified (see Table 1 below).

Table 1. An Early Model of National Policy Styles

Relationship Between Government and Society	Dominant Approach to Problem Solving	
	Anticipatory	Reactive
Consensus	e.g. German "Rationalist Consensus" Style	e.g. British "Negotiating Style"
Imposition	e.g. French "Concertation" Style	e.g. Dutch "Negotiation and Conflict" Style

Source: Adapted from Richardson, Gustafsson, and Grant Jordan (1982).

Several studies applied this concept with great facility to policymaking in various nations and sectors (Vogel 1986; Tuohy 1992). However, others found that few governments were consistently active or reactive; nor did any government always work through either consensus or imposition. Rather than think of policy styles as existing at the national level, they argued that a focus on the *sectoral* level would be more accurate and more productive (Freeman 1985).

Elements of a Policy Style

In this section, the results of studies undertaken into the types of styles prevalent at each stage of the policy cycle are presented. Combining the style found to exist at each stage of the policy development process, it will be argued, generates a useful picture of the overall policy style found in any sector in a jurisdiction.

Agenda-Setting Styles

In the formal study of agenda setting, a distinction is often made between the *systemic* or unofficial public agenda and the *institutional* or formal official agenda. The systemic agenda "consists of all issues that are commonly perceived by members of the political community as meriting public attention and as involving matters within the legitimate jurisdiction of existing governmental authority" (Cobb and Elder 1972). This is essentially a society's agenda for discussion of public problems, such as crime or health care, water quality or wilderness preservation.

The formal or institutional agenda, on the other hand, consists of only a limited number of issues or problems to which attention is devoted by policy elites (Kingdon 1984; Baumgartner and Jones 1991).

Each society has literally hundreds of issues which some citizens find to be matters of concern and would have the government do something about. However, only a small proportion of the problems on the public or systemic agenda are actually taken up by policy actors actively involved in policy development. In other words, the public agenda is an agenda for discussion while the institutional agenda is an agenda for action, indicating that the formal policy process dealing with the problem in question has begun.

Over thirty years ago, the American political scientists Cobb, Ross, and Ross developed a model of typical agenda-setting styles. In their analysis, they argued that three basic patterns of agenda setting could be discerned, distinguished by the origins of the issue as well as the resources used to facilitate their inclusion on the agenda.

In the *outside initiation* pattern "issues arise in nongovernmental groups and are then expanded sufficiently to reach, first, the public [systemic] agenda and, finally, the formal [institutional] agenda" (Cobb, Ross, and Ross 1976). In this case, issues are first initiated when some part of the public articulates a grievance and demands its resolution by the government. The aggrieved groups attempt to expand support for their demand, a process which may involve submerging the specific complaint within a more general one and the formation of alliances across groups. Finally, these groups lobby, contest, and join with others in attempting to get the expanded issue onto the formal agenda. If they have the requisite political resources and skills and can outmanoeuvre their opponents or advocates of other issues and actions, they can often succeed in having their issue enter the formal agenda. Thus, as Cobb, Ross, and Ross summarize it:

> The outside initiative model applies to the situation in which a group outside the government structure 1) articulates a grievance, 2) tries to expand interest in the issue to enough other groups in the population to gain a place on the public agenda, in order to 3) create sufficient pressure on decision makers to force the issue onto the formal agenda for their serious consideration. (Cobb, Ross, and Ross 1976: 132)

The *mobilization* case is quite different and describes "decision-makers trying to expand an issue from a formal to a public agenda." In this model, issues are simply placed on the formal agenda by the government with no necessary preliminary expansion from a publicly recognized grievance. There may be considerable debate within government over the issue, but the public may well be kept in the dark about the policy and its development until its formal announcement. The policy may be specified in some detail or it may just establish general principles whose specification will be worked out later.

In the third, *inside initiation*, pattern, influential groups with special access to decision makers initiate a policy and do not necessarily want it expanded and contested in public. This can be due to technical as well as political reasons. In this model, initiation and specification occur simultaneously as a group or government agency enunciates a grievance and specifies some potential solution to the problem. Expansion is restricted to specialized groups or agencies with some knowledge or interest in the subject. Entrance is virtually automatic due to the privileged place of those desiring a decision. According to Cobb, Ross, and Ross:

> Proposals arise within governmental units or in groups close to the government. The issue is then expanded to identification and attention groups in order to create sufficient pressure on decision makers to place the item on the formal agenda. At no point is the public greatly involved, and the initiators make no effort to get the issue on the public agenda. On the contrary, they try to keep it off. (Cobb, Ross, and Ross 1976: 136)

From the above discussion, it should be apparent that two of the most critical factors in identifying a typical pattern of agenda setting in any policy area are the level and extent of public involvement and support for government action (May 1991), and the response or "pre-response" of the state in directing, mediating, and accommodating this activity (Majone 1989). The resulting agenda-setting styles are set out in Table 2 below. As this table shows, a fourth agenda-setting style, *consolidation*,

Table 2. Basic Agenda-Setting Styles

	Nature of Public Support	
Initiator of Debate	High	Low
Societal Actors	*Outside Initiation*	*Inside Initiation*
State	*Consolidation*	*Mobilization*

exists in addition to the three identified by Cobb, Ross, and Ross. In this last style, state actors may initiate debate on an issue which has high public support and simply consolidate this support in moving the issue on for further development.

Policy Formulation Styles

Studies of policy formulation have also emphasized the importance of the kinds of actors interacting to develop and refine policy options for government (Freeman 1955; Linder and Peters 1990). But unlike agenda setting, where the public is often actively involved, in policy formulation the relevant policy actors are restricted to those who not only have an opinion on a subject, but also have some minimal level of knowledge of the subject area, allowing them to comment, at least hypothetically, on the feasibility of options put forward to resolve policy problems.

Scholars over the years have developed a variety of taxonomies to help identify the key actors in these *policy subsystems*, what brings them together, how they interact, and what effect their interaction has on policy development (Jordan 1981, 1990a, 1990b; Jordan and Schubert 1992). Most of these distinguish between a larger set of actors with some knowledge of the policy issue in question, and a smaller set in which actors not only have requisite knowledge, but also have established patterns of more or less routine interactions with each other (Knoke 1993).

Membership in knowledge-based *policy communities* extends to actors such as state policymakers (administrative, political, and judicial), members of non-governmental organizations (NGOs) concerned with the subject, members of the media who report on the subject, academics who follow or research the area, and members of the general public who, for whatever reason, have taken an interest in the subject (Sabatier 1987, 1988). In many issue areas, the policy community also involves members of other organizations such as businesses, labour unions, or various formalized interest groups or professional associations concerned with government actions in the sector concerned. In some cases, international actors such as multinational corporations, international governmental or non-governmental organizations, or the governments of foreign states can also be members of sectoral policy communities (Haas 1992).

A subset of these actors who interact within more formalized institutions and procedures of government is defined as members of *policy networks* (Coleman and Skogstad 1990; Mann and Mayntz 1991; Pross 1992). These policy networks include representatives from the

Table 3. Basic Policy Formulation Styles

	Policy Network Membership	
Policy Community Idea Sets	Few	Many
Few	*Status Quo Options*	*Marginal/Incremental Options*
Many	*Contested Alternative Options*	*Radical Alternative Options*

community, but are "inner circles" of actors who effectively hold the power to veto many policy options as untenable or infeasible.

In this view, the likely results of policy formulation are contingent upon the nature and configuration of the policy community and network in the specific sector concerned. A key variable that many observers have argued affects the structure and behaviour of policy networks is their number of members, which affects aspects of networks such as their level of integration and the types of interactions members undertake (Atkinson and Coleman 1989 and 1990; Coleman and Skogstad 1990; Van Waarden 1992). What is important for policy communities, on the other hand, is not the number of participants in the community but the number of relatively distinct "idea sets" which exist within it. This affects the nature of conflict and consensus which exists in the community and, as a result, affects the behaviour of community actors (Schulman 1988; Haas 1992; MacRae 1993; Smith 1993; Hessing and Howlett 1997).

The type and nature of options which come forward to governments from the policy formulation phase is affected by the interaction of networks and communities (Smith 1993 and 1994; Howlett and Rayner 1995; Howlett and Ramesh 1998; Howlett 2002a). Table 3 presents a model of policy formulation styles based on the manner in which different types of policy networks and communities interact.

In open subsystems where networks have many members and communities share many idea sets, it can be expected that a propensity for new, radical alternatives to the status quo may be generated in the policy formulation process. In closed subsystems, where networks have few members and communities are dominated by a single idea set, on the other hand, a status quo orientation will emerge in the policy options developed and put before decision makers. In subsystems where only a few actors make up the network but communities are open to new ideas, significant alternatives to the status quo may emerge from the formulation process, but usually over the opposition of network members. In subsystems where many actors deal with few ideas, marginal or incremental options tend to develop.

Decision-Making Styles

In some of their early writings, Lindblom and his co-authors held out the possibility that incremental decision making could coexist with efforts to achieve more "rational" decisions. Thus Braybrooke and Lindblom, for example, argued that four different styles of decision making could be discerned, depending upon the amount of knowledge at the disposal of decision makers and the amount of change the decision involved from earlier decisions (Braybrooke and Lindblom 1963). This generated the two-by-two matrix shown in Table 4.

In Braybrooke and Lindblom's view, the overwhelming majority of decisions were likely to be taken in an incremental fashion, involving minimal change in situations of low available knowledge. However, three other possibilities existed, with the rational model emerging as one possibility and two styles – "revolutionary" and "analytic" – also existing as infrequently used alternatives. Although it was somewhat tautological to utilize "amount of change" as a variable to help explain the degree of change each decision-making style entailed, as a description of commonly occurring decision-making styles this type of model was quite useful. Other authors, like Graham Allison, also developed similar models of distinct decision-making styles (Allison 1969, 1971), but also did not specify in any detail the variables which led to the adoption of a particular style (Bendor and Hammond 1992).

Table 4. An Early Model of Decision-Making Styles

Amount of Change Involved	Level of Available Knowledge	
	High	Low
High	*Revolutionary*	*Analytic*
Low	*Rational*	*Disjointed Incremental*

Attempting to improve upon these models, John Forester argued that there were at least five distinct decision-making styles associated with a variety of decision-making conditions and contexts (Forester 1984, 1989). Forester began from the position that "what is rational for administrators to do depends on the situations in which they work." That is, the decision-making style and the type of decisions made by decision makers varied according to issue and institutional contexts. As he put it in a 1984 article:

> Depending upon the conditions at hand, a strategy may be practical or ridiculous. With time, expertise, data, and a well-defined problem, technical calculations may be in order; without time, data, definition, and expertise, attempting those calculations could well be a waste of time. In a complex organizational environment, intelligence networks will be as, or more, important than documents when information is needed. In an environment of inter-organizational conflict, bargaining and compromise may be called for. Administrative strategies are sensible only in a political and organizational context. (Forester 1984: 25)

Forester suggested that decision making was affected by the number of agents involved in a decision; their organizational setting; how well a problem is defined; the information available on the problem, its causes, and consequences; and the amount of time available to decision makers to consider possible contingencies and their present and anticipated consequences. The number of agents can expand and multiply almost to infinity; the setting can include many different organizations and can be more or less open to external influences; the problem can be ambiguous or susceptible to multiple competing interpretations; information can be incomplete, misleading, or purposefully withheld or manipulated; and time can be limited or artificially constrained and manipulated.

Recasting Forester's variables allows the development of a simple but effective model of decision-making styles present in the policy development process. "Agent" and "setting," for example, can be thought of as elements of how decision makers are situated vis-à-vis policy subsystems, while the notions of the "definitional," "information," and "time" resources can all be seen as relating to the types of constraints placed upon decision makers. Using these dimensions, the model of styles found in Table 5 can be generated.

Table 5. Basic Decision-Making Styles

Severity of Constraints	Complexity of the Policy Subsystem	
	High	Low
High	*Incremental Adjustment*	*Satifycing Search*
Low	*Optimizing Adjustment*	*Rational Search*

In this model, decision makers situated in complex subsystems are expected to undertake adjustment strategies while those dealing with simple configurations of actors and ideas will be more prone to undertake search-type strategies. The nature of the decision criteria, on the other hand, varies with the severity of the informational, time, and other resource constraints under which decision makers operate. Hence decision makers faced with high constraints will tend to favour satisficing over optimization; itself an outcome more likely to occur in situations of low constraint.

Policy Implementation Styles

Generally speaking, comparative implementation studies have also shown that governments tend to develop specific implementation styles in areas which they regulate (Hawkins and Thomas 1989; Kagan 1991; Knill 1998; Howlett 2002c). These styles combine various kinds of instruments into a more or less coherent whole which is consistently applied in particular sectors. More specifically, such styles combine at least one major type of procedural policy instrument with at least one major type of substantive instrument.

Substantive instruments are those directly providing goods and services to members of the public or governments. They include a variety of tools or instruments relying on different types of governing resources for their effectiveness (Tupper and Doern 1981; Woodside 1986; Salamon 1989; Vedung 1997; Peters and Van Nispen 1998). A useful way to classify these (see Table 6 below) is according to the type of governing resource upon which they rely: nodality or information; authority, treasure, or financial resources; or administrative or organizations resources (Hood 1986).

Table 6. A Taxonomy of Substantive Policy Instruments

Principal Use	Governing Resource			
	Nodality	Authority	Treasure	Organization
Effectors	*advice training*	*licences user charges regulation certification*	*grants loans tax expenditures*	*bureaucratic administration public enterprises*
Detectors	*reporting registration*	*census-taking consultants*	*polling, policing*	*record-keeping surveys*

Source: Adapted from Hood (1986).

Procedural instruments are different from substantive ones in that their impact on policy outcomes is less direct. Rather than affect the delivery of goods and services, their principal intent is to modify or alter the nature of policy processes at work in the implementation process (Howlett 1996a; in't Veld 1998). A list of these instruments is provided in Table 7.

Why a particular combination of procedural and substantive instruments is used in particular sectors is a key question. In the case of substantive instruments, Linder and Peters argued that the features of the policy instruments themselves are important for selection purposes because some instruments are more suited for a task at hand than others. They noted that instrument choice was not simply a technical exercise, however, and that variables such as political culture and the depth of its social cleavages, the organizational culture of the concerned agencies and the nature of their links with clients and other agencies all had a major impact on setting the context in which instrument selection occurred (Linder and Peters 1989).

This analysis suggested that the choice of policy instruments is shaped by the characteristics of the instruments, the nature of the problem at hand, past experiences of governments in dealing with the same or similar problems, the subjective preference of the decision makers, and the likely reaction to the choice by affected social groups. However, in attempting to explain a consistent preference for the use of particular instruments over a wide range of contexts, the influence of the first three somewhat idiosyncratic variables can be discounted. More significant for such purposes are the preferences of state decision makers and

Table 7. A Resource-Based Taxonomy of Procedural Policy Instruments

Principal Use	Governing Resource			
	Nodality	Authority	Treasure	Organization
Positive	education exhortation advertising training	agreements treaties advisory group creation	interest group fundings research and intervenor funding	hearings evaluations institutional- bureaucratic reform
Negative	misleading information propaganda	banning groups and associations	eliminating funding	administrative delay information suppression

the nature of the constraints within which they operate (Bressers and O'Toole 1998). States must have a high level of administrative capacity, for example, in order to utilize authority, treasure, and organization-based instruments in situations in which they wish to affect significant numbers of policy targets. When a state has few of these resources, it will tend to utilize instruments like incentives or propaganda or to rely on existing voluntary, community, or family-based instruments (Howlett and Ramesh 1995). Similarly, a key feature of procedural instrument choice is a government's capacity to manipulate policy subsystems. Undertaken in order to retain the political trust or legitimacy required for substantive policy instruments to be effective (Weber 1958; Stillman 1974; Beetham 1991), procedural policy instrument choice is also affected by the size of the policy target. Whether a government faces sectoral delegitimization or widespread systemic delegitimization, affects the types of procedural instruments a government will employ (Mueller 1973; Habermas 1973, 1975; Mayntz 1975). Putting these two type of instruments and variables together leads to the model of implementation styles found in Table 8.

Governments facing a variety of resource or legitimization problems and dealing with large policy targets use low-cost instruments such as exhortation and the provision of information to policy actors. Faced with lower constraints and similarly large-sized targets, they can use treasure-based tools such as offering subsidies to producers of goods and services and extending similar financial aid to interest groups to help finance their activities and formation. In situations where governments

Table 8. Basic Policy Implementation Styles

	Nature of the Policy Target	
Severity of Constraints	Large	Small
High	*Institutionalized Voluntarism (Exhortation and Information Manipulation)*	*Representative Legalism (Regulation and Financial Manipulation)*
Low	*Directed Subsidization (Financial and Recognition Manipulation)*	*Public Provision with Oversight (Organization and Information Manipulation)*

face small targets under situations of high constraint, they tend to use forms of authoritative instruments – including such substantive tools as regulation and procedural ones such as advisory committees and other forms of manipulating the recognition and representation extended to specific policy actors. Finally, in situations where they face low constraints and the same smaller targets, governments can use tools such as crown corporations and public enterprises and direct institutional manipulations such as restructuring government ministries and agencies and the networks of relations which accompany them.

Policy Evaluation Styles

The last stage of the cycle is policy evaluation. For many early observers, policy evaluation ideally consisted of assessing whether a public policy was achieving its stated objectives and, if not, what could be done to eliminate impediments to their attainment. Thus David Nachmias defined policy evaluation as "the objective, systematic, empirical examination of the effects ongoing policies and public programs have on their targets in terms of the goals they are meant to achieve" (Nachmias 1979, 3f). However, while analysts often resorted to concepts such as "success" or "failure" to conclude their evaluation, as Ingram and Mann cautioned:

> [T]he phenomenon of policy failure is neither so simple nor certain as many contemporary critics of policy and politics would have us believe. Success and failure are slippery concepts, often highly subjective and

reflective of an individual's goals, perception of need, and perhaps even psychological disposition toward life. (Ingram and Mann 1980, 16)

That is, public policy goals are usually not stated clearly enough to find out if and to what extent they are being achieved, nor are they shared by all key policy actors. Moreover, the possibilities for objective analysis are also limited because of the difficulties involved in the attempt to develop objective standards by which to evaluate governments' level of success in dealing with subjective claims and socially constructed problems. Furthermore, the formal, overt goals stated by governments typically gloss an array of "latent objectives" which policy also serves. Thus, for example, while governments may attempt to reduce industrial effluents through raising regulatory standards, they also have an interest in preserving conditions for employment and for economic activity, objectives that can easily conflict with increased regulation (Kerr 1976).

What is significant in the evaluative process is not so much ultimate success and failure, but, as Lindblom correctly anticipated, that policy actors and the organizations and institutions they represent can *learn* from the formal and informal evaluation of policies in which they are engaged. This can lead them to modify their positions in the direction of greater substantive or procedural policy change, or it can lead them to resist any alteration to the status quo (Majone 1989).

Yet policy evaluations do not necessarily result in policy change. That is, while the concept of evaluation suggests an implicit "feedback loop" is an inherent part of the policy cycle, in many cases this loop may not be operationalized (Pierson 1993). This implies that understanding the conditions under which learning occurs or does not occur is critical to understanding and modelling evaluative styles.

A significant variable in this regard is the capacity of an organization to absorb new information. As Cohen and Levinthal argued in the case of the private firm:

the ability to evaluate and utilize outside knowledge is largely a function of the level of prior related knowledge. At the most elemental level, this prior knowledge includes basic skills or even a shared language but may also include knowledge of the most recent scientific or technological developments in a given field. Thus, prior related knowledge confers an ability to recognize the value of new information, assimilate it, and apply it to [commercial] ends. These abilities collectively constitute what we call [a firm's] "absorptive capacity." (Cohen and Levinthal 1990: 128)

Table 9. Basic Policy Evaluation Styles

State	Type of Policy Subsystem	
Administrative Capacity	Open	Closed
High	*Social Learning*	*Lesson Drawing*
Low	*Informal Evaluations*	*Formal Evaluations*

This is not the only significant variable, however, as the organization must also be receptive to new information and capable of its dissemination. Hence, as Cohen and Levinthal also suggested, a second significant variable affecting the potential for administrative learning is the kind of links which exist between administrators and larger policy communities. Table 9 presents a model of evaluative styles based on these two variables.

Only when state administrative capacity is high would one expect any kind of learning to occur. If a relatively closed network dominates the subsystem, however, then this learning is likely to be restricted to some form of "lesson drawing," in which policymakers draw lessons from past uses of policy instruments (Rose 1991; Bennett and Howlett 1992). If the links between the network and the community are more open, one would expect other forms of learning, such as "social learning," in which ideas and events in the larger policy community penetrate into policy evaluations. When state capacity is low, one would expect little learning to occur. If the policy subsystem in such circumstances is dominated by existing networks, one would expect to find formal types of evaluation with little substantive impact on either policy instruments or goals. If the subsystem is more open to members of the policy community, one would expect a range of informal evaluations to occur, but still find little substantive impact on policy outcomes or processes (Howlett and Ramesh 1995).

Conclusion: Policy Development as Policy Style

As Lasswell noted in the 1950s, envisioning policy development as a staged, sequential, and iterative process is a useful analytical and methodological device. Methodologically, such an approach reduces the complexity of public policymaking by breaking down that complexity into a small number of stages and substages, each of which can be investigated alone or in terms of its relationship to any or all of the other stages of the cycle.

Analysing policy development in terms of policy cycles and policy styles is useful for several reasons. Not only does it help to make sense out of the different models put forward earlier in the history of policy studies, such as the rational, incremental, and garbage can models, it also helps to advance studies of these models by specifying the conditions under which such styles could occur. That is, the type of development process specified by each model is shown not to be a universal one, but rather can be seen as a specific combination or set of styles found at each stage of the process, occurring only in the specific circumstances underlying each stage. Analytically, as this chapter has argued, adopting such an approach is also useful as it helps to make sense out of the different approaches to understanding patterns of policy development first developed by Lindblom, March and Olsen, and others. More importantly, it also allows the insight of Richardson and his colleagues that it is possible to observe and model fairly long-term patterns in policy development processes as *policy styles*, and a general model of sectoral policy development styles to be developed.

Although this implies that there are quite a large number of possible policy styles, the discussion above highlights how these will tend to fall into several common types. That is, certain common variables reappear at different stages of the policy cycle and influence the styles found at a number of different stages of the process. The nature of the policy subsystem, for example, is a significant factor affecting the style adopted at several different stages. And, since the nature of a subsystem tends to remain constant over an extended period of time (Baumgartner and Jones 1991; Blom-Hansen 1997; Mortensen 2007), this helps not only to restrict the number of common policy styles, but also to explain their persistence over time. This is also true of administrative capacity, a second variable that reappears in various forms as a determining element of the styles found to exist at particular stages of the policy development process. Examination of these two factors helps identify the specific style present in any given sector and provides a good starting point to understanding the policy process at work in that issue area.

PART TWO

The Policy Process in Canada

3 Agenda Setting – Predictable and Unpredictable Policy Windows: Institutional and Exogenous Correlates of Canadian Federal Agenda Setting

Policy Windows and Policy Theory

Whether there is a systematic pattern through which issues become subjects for government action is of critical importance to students of the policy process and to policy actors both inside and outside government. Interest groups, think tanks, political parties, and other non-governmental actors must all operate and plan their activities in accordance with some notion of which issues are likely to emerge on government agendas and which are not. Governments at all levels, from the sub-national to the international, must also be able to recognize which issues are likely to move successfully from social to official agendas, and vice versa, if they are to have any hope of dealing with the problems of modern governance in a systematic and managed fashion.

Both governmental and non-governmental actors act in accordance with assumptions they make about the factors and variables which drive agenda setting. Interest groups may, for example, adhere to broad general notions of popular democracy in which they expect issues which gain a high public profile to gain access automatically to official agendas (Cobb and Elder 1972). Politicians, on the other hand, may subscribe to a set of process-related beliefs which provides a much larger role for administrative discretion and bureaucratic politics in preventing popular issues from obtaining serious consideration (Allison and Halperin 1972). Whether an interest group expends its funds on legal challenges to administrations, or on public education and media campaigns, for example, will depend on the nature of the assumptions it makes about the actual process of agenda setting characterizing the contemporary policy process.

Whether these assumptions about agenda politics are accurate, therefore, is a critical question, and, in the hope of providing a better understanding of this stage of the policy cycle, students of public policy processes have developed several models which attempt to describe, explain, and predict agenda-setting behaviour (Howlett and Ramesh 1995). Many early models focused on the nature of the actors involved in the process, and the general characterization of agenda-setting "styles" in typical relationships of power and influence existing between significant actors (Cobb, Ross, and Ross 1976; Rochefort and Cobb 1994). These studies tended to support the view that agenda setting in democratic states is largely a matter of governments responding to social pressures, and focused their attention on how the activities of interest groups could facilitate this process. Other studies, however, pointed to a much larger role played by government agencies and a variety of "boundary-spanning" organizations, such as the media, in blocking, filtering, or otherwise affecting the development of public concerns, thus undermining the notion that agenda setting was a relatively simple, one-way transmission process (Downs 1972; Hogwood 1992; Howlett 1996 and 1997).

A wide variety of analysts from a disparate range of fields have endorsed a model of agenda setting first put forward by John Kingdon in his 1984 work on the operation of the federal legislative system in the United States (Kingdon 1984). This model deals with the question of state and non-state influences on agenda setting by focusing on the role played by policy entrepreneurs both inside and outside government in taking advantage of agenda-setting opportunities – policy windows – to move items onto formal government agendas. It suggests that the characteristics of issues (the problem stream) combine with the characteristics of political institutions and circumstances (the politics stream) and the development of policy solutions (the policy stream), leading to the opening and closing of opportunities for agenda entrance. Such opportunities can be seized upon or not, as the case may be, by policy entrepreneurs able to recognize and act upon them.

Kingdon's model of agenda setting is now considered the standard in policy studies. Among other subjects, it has been used to describe and assess the nature of U.S. foreign policymaking (Wood and Peake 1998); the politics of privatization in Britain, France, and Germany (Zahariadis 1995; Zahariadis and Allen 1995); the nature of U.S. domestic anti-drug policy (Sharp 1994); the collaborative behaviour of business and environmental groups in certain anti-pollution initiatives in the United

States and Europe (Lober 1997); and the overall nature of the reform process in Eastern Europe (Keeler 1993). Somewhat surprising, however, none of these efforts has subjected Kingdon's model to empirical analysis. Despite the fact that Kingdon's own work focuses exclusively on the federal level in the United States, many of these studies simply assume that the model can be applied cross-nationally.

Using time series data collected on issue mentions related to native affairs, the constitution, drug abuse, acid rain, the nuclear industry, and capital punishment in federal parliamentary debates and committees over the period 1977–92, this chapter tests the applicability of Kingdon's model to the Canadian case. In so doing, it first refines the notion of a policy window in order to aid the operationalization of this concept. It then tests for their existence in Canada by comparing the record of issue mentions in Parliament to other time series developed from media mentions, violent crime rates, unemployment rates, budget speeches, speeches from the throne, elections, and first ministers' conferences in order to assess the impact such events have upon the agenda-setting process.

Analytical Components of the Policy Streams Model

In order to examine empirically the existence, nature, and influence of policy windows in Canada, one must be able to clarify exactly what this concept entails. In this context, it is important to note that different types of windows were identified by Kingdon and are implicit in his work. The elements of each is set out below, and a taxonomy given to help organize the differences.

The General Policy Streams Model

In his study of U.S. agenda setting, Kingdon argued that this process could best be conceived as one in which more or less fleeting opportunities arose for issues to enter government debate. In the right circumstances, policy windows could be seized upon by key players in the political process in order to gain entrance for particular issues. Policy entrepreneurs play a key role in this process by linking, or "coupling," policy solutions and policy problems with political opportunities (Kingdon 1984: chapters 7 and 8).

Linking these three streams together is a necessary, but not a sufficient, condition for issue entrance. That is, something else is required:

the opening of a policy window. Kingdon suggested that while window openings were sometimes governed by certain fortuitous happenings – including seemingly unrelated external "focusing events," crises or accidents, or the presence or absence of policy entrepreneurs both within and outside governments – at other times they were affected by institutionalized events, such as elections or budgetary cycles.

As Kingdon noted:

> Sometimes, windows open quite predictably. Legislation comes up for renewal on schedule, for instance, creating opportunities to change, expand or abolish certain programs. At other times, windows open quite unpredictably, as when an airliner crashes or a fluky election produces unexpected turnover in key decision-makers. Predictable or unpredictable, open windows are small and scarce. Opportunities come, but they also pass. Windows do not stay open long. If a chance is missed, another must be awaited. (Kingdon 1984: 213)

Ultimately, Kingdon suggested that two principal types of window exist: the "problem" and "political" windows. As he argued, "Basically a window opens because of change in the political stream (for example, a change of administration, a shift in the partisan or ideological distribution of seats … or a shift in national mood); or it opens because a new problem captures the attention of governmental officials and those close to them" (Kingdon 1984: 176). To this initial distinction Kingdon added the idea that windows would also vary in terms of their predictability. While arguing that random events are occasionally significant, he stressed the manner in which institutionalized windows dominate the U.S. agenda-setting process.[1] As he put it: "there remains some degree of unpredictability. Yet it would be a grave mistake to conclude that the processes … are essentially random. Some degree of pattern is evident" (Kingdon 1984: 216). In fact, he argued that many windows open in a more or less predictable, cyclical pattern: "Windows sometimes open with great predictability. Regular cycles of various kinds open and close windows on a schedule. That schedule varies in its precision and hence its predictability, but the cyclical nature of many windows is nonetheless evident" (Kingdon 1984: 193).

Hence the general model established by Kingdon suggests the existence of four possible window types based on the relationship existing between the origin of the window – political or problem – and their degree of institutionalization. Although Kingdon did not provide a

Figure 2: A Model of Policy Window Types

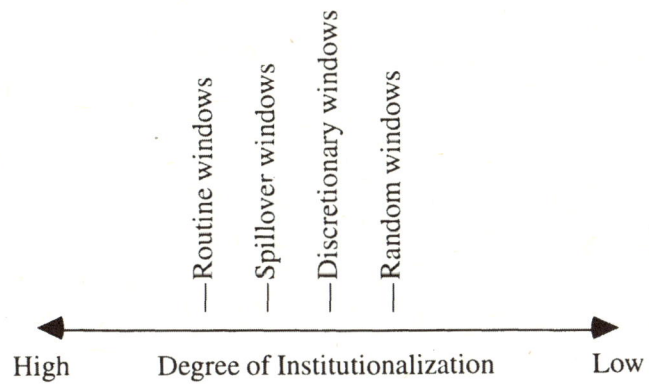

specific nomenclature to describe the four window types, the general outline of each type is discernible from an examination of his work and several of his key sources.[2] The four principal window types identifiable in Kingdon's work are: *routine political windows*, in which institutionalized procedural events dictate predictable window openings; *discretionary political windows*, in which the behaviour of individual political actors leads to less predictable window openings; *spillover problem windows*, in which related issues are drawn into an already open window; and *random problem windows*, in which random events or crises open unpredictable windows.

These basic types of windows and their relationship are set out in Figure 2. In this model, it is the level of institutionalization of a window type which determines its frequency of appearance and hence its predictability. That is, a testable hypothesis related to policy windows is that the most institutionalized types will occur more frequently than the least and hence will have the highest degree of predictability.

In the discussion below, Canadian data are examined in order to assess the frequency of appearance of different types of policy windows. This allows (1) an assessment to be made of the extent to which Kingdon's model can transfer cross-nationally; (2) a determination to be made of the types of variables which typically affect Canadian agenda setting; and (3) an assessment of the extent to which federal agenda setting is predictable or unpredictable. The results of this analysis have

significant implications for both the theory and practice of agenda setting in Canada. That is, they not only provide an empirical examination
of Kingdon's model, but also information of use to both government
and non-governmental policy actors in Canadian agenda setting.

Policy Windows in Canada: Empirical Evidence

The development of a taxonomy of policy window types and the generation of a testable hypothesis related to the frequency of window occurrence allows an empirical examination of Kingdon's model to be made
against the evidence of the actual pattern of issue occurrence in Canada.

In this section, tests are constructed and carried out in order to de-
termine the existence and frequency of occurrence of routine, spillover,
discretionary, and random policy windows in Canada. These examina-
tions rely upon time series data collected on issue mentions in the Canadian federal parliament and how these mentions correlate with each
other, with a variety of institutionalized parliamentary procedures,
with media mentions of those same issues, and with "objective" or exogenous measures of social and economic performance.

For this purpose, issue series were collected for three pairs of related
policy areas. Environmental (acid rain and nuclear power), jurisdictional (native and constitutional), and social (capital punishment and
drug use) issues were selected. The series measured mentions in parliamentary debates, in parliamentary committees, and in newspapers
and periodicals. Series on the occurrence of significant parliamentary
events were generated for budget speeches, speeches from the throne,
first ministers' conferences, and elections. Finally, two series measuring
exogenous social and economic conditions were collected: one containing unemployment rates and the other rates of violent crime throughout the country.

The sources used for each series are set out in Appendix 1. The time
series generated were analysed using a variety of procedures in SY-
STAT and SPSS TRENDS 6.1 (Wilkinson, Hill, and Yang 1992; SPSS
Trends 6.1 [New York 1994]). Case plots of the basic issue and institutionalized series are contained in Appendices 2–4.

Random Policy Windows in Canada

Spectral analysis techniques were used to test for the existence of random windows in Canada.[3] These techniques reconstruct time series data
so as to identify the magnitude and frequency of cyclical oscillations.

Figure 3: Spectral Density of Acid Rain Mentions

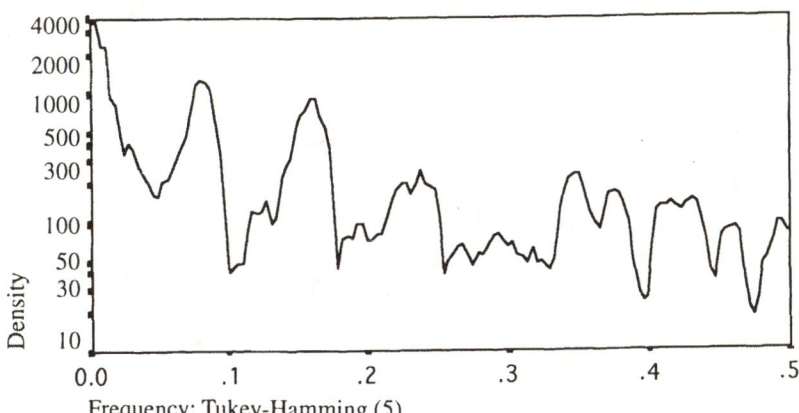

Frequency: Tukey-Hamming (5)

After correcting for possible trend and substituting for missing cases, each time series is transformed using Fourier equations to change patterns of high and low occurrences into fluctuations of magnitude and frequency. A periodogram or similar graphical display is then developed which compares the square of the magnitude to frequency. Sharp spikes at various frequencies reveal cyclical behaviour in the series. For example, a single sharp spike at a low frequency is typical of a more or less regular sinusoidal wave. A tendency towards a flat line (discounting the initial spike at frequency 0 reflecting the general harmonic of the entire series with itself – the "fundamental" frequency) is typical of a random or "white noise" pattern.

If the windows in federal parliamentary institutions for the six issues were in fact unpredictable and random, one would expect a spectral analysis of such mentions to be extremely irregular, approaching a "white noise" pattern. Smoothed logarithmic displays of the periodograms – or "spectral density" plots – for each of the six issue series reveal the shapes in Figures 3–8. These figures reveal that, although the magnitude of the cycles varies, each of the six series exhibited fairly strong cyclical behaviour. Acid rain mentions had an annual and semi-annual cycle; capital punishment a thirty-month and five-month cycle; constitutional issues a semi-annual cycle; drug issue mentions a six- and eight-month cycle; and both native and nuclear issues a four- and six-month cycle. Spectral analyses of committee mentions reveal similar cyclical activity.

Figure 4: Spectral Density of Capital Punishment Mentions

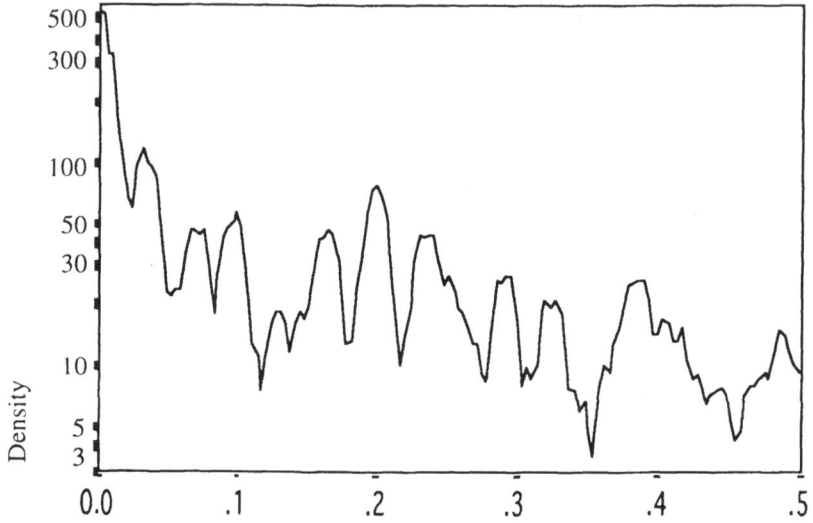

Frequency: Tukey-Hamming (5)

Figure 5: Spectral Density of Constitutional Mentions

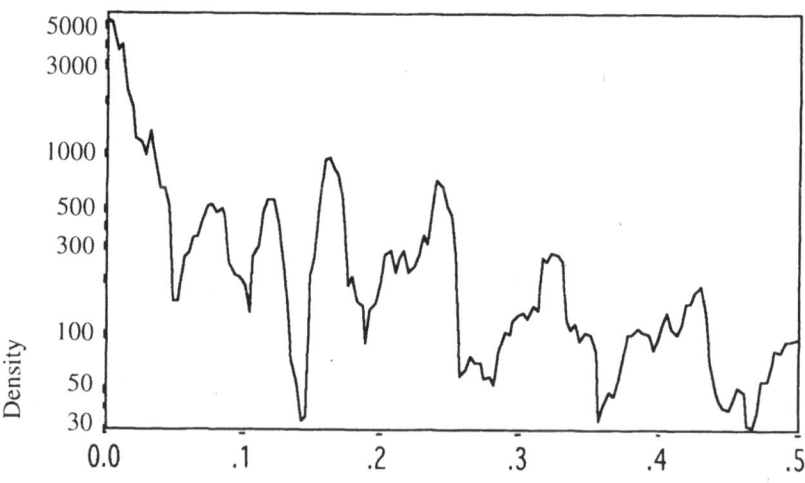

Frequency: Tukey-Hamming (5)

Figure 6: Spectral Density of Drug Mentions

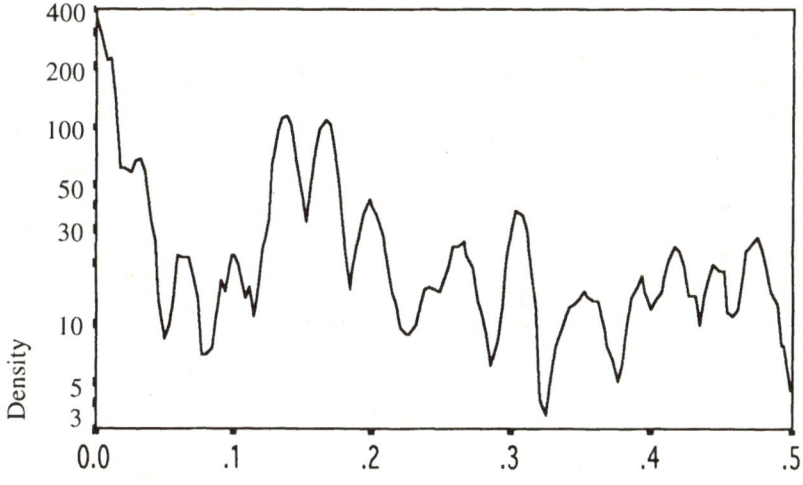

Frequency: Tukey-Hamming (5)

Figure 7: Spectral Density of Native Mentions

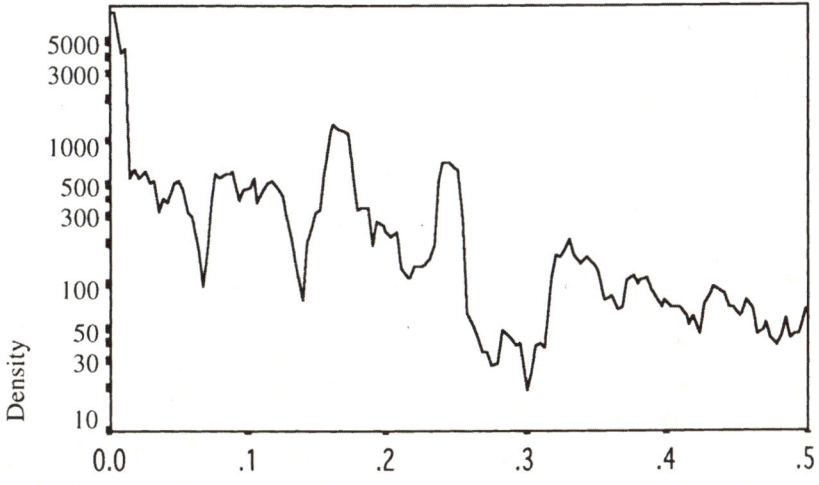

Frequency: Tukey-Hamming (5)

Figure 8: Spectral Density of Nuclear Mentions

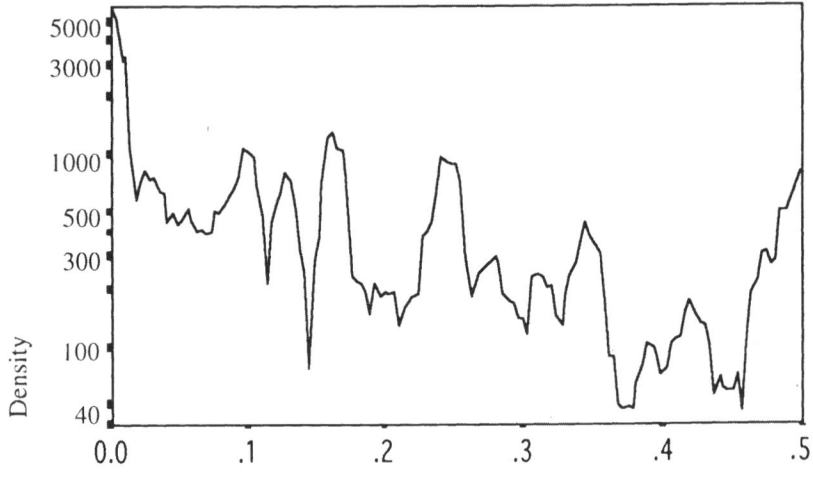

Frequency: Tukey-Hamming (5)

All these figures display the low frequency spikes characteristic of modified sinusoidal cycles, and not the flat line one would expect if issue mentions were random. Therefore, none of these cases provides evidence of the existence of a white noise or random series. While this does not rule out the existence of random windows existing in other areas, it does lend support to the contention that such occurrences are rare.

Discretionary Policy Windows in Canada

The second type of unpredictable policy window is the discretionary (non-spillover) window. In this type, politicians attempt to set the agenda to deal with an idiosyncratic issue, normally selected from among matters already of some public concern. In devising a test for this in Canada, or elsewhere, issue mentions can be correlated with exogenous factors such as media coverage, or more "objective" measures of increasing problem severity – such as increasing unemployment or

Table 10. Auto Correlation of Issue and Correlate Series

	DurbinWatsons	First orderACFs
Hansard		
Nuclear issues	1.327	0.333
Native issues	1.139	0.428
Drug abuse issues	1.281	0.358
Acid rain issues	0.985	0.506
Constitutional issues	1.016	0.491
Capital punishment issues	1.033	0.482
Media		
Nuclear issues	1.088	0.439
Native issues	0.630	0.683
Drug abuse issues	1.604	0.198
Acid rain issues	1.008	0.493
Constitutional issues	0.548	0.722
Capital punishment issues	0.867	0.566
Exogenous		
Unemployment rates	0.100	0.948
Crime rates	0.079	0.945

crime rates, measures whose own causal structure is unrelated to the political process. That is, a test can be developed for the presence of this type of window by examining the relationship between issue mentions and various "objective correlates" of their status as "pressing problems" (Beecher, Lineberry, and Rich 1981; King et al. 1993).

In this case, given the high rates of auto correlation in the series of issue mentions and their "objective correlates" (see Table 10), ARIMA time series methods[4] should be used. In order to control for problems of within-series auto correlation, ARIMA models were identified and a transfer function estimated for each series. After being fitted, the residuals from the modelled series were then cross-correlated.[5] On the basis of an analysis of the auto-correlation functions (ACF) and partial auto-correlation functions (PACF) taken for each series, the MA, trend, and

Table 11. ARIMA Model Identification

	ARIMAparameters		ARIMAparameters
Hansard		Media	
Nuclear issues	0,1,0	Nuclear issues	1,0,0
Native issues	0,1,0	Native issues	1,0,0
Drug abuse issues	2,0,0	Drug abuse issues	0,1,0
Acid rain issues	0,1,0	Acid rain issues	0,1,0
Constitutional issues	1,0,0	Constitutional issues	1,0,0
Capital punishment issues	1,0,0	Capital punishment issues	1,0,0
Exogenous		Exogenous	
Crime rates	1,0,0	Unemployment	1,0,0

AR parameters for each series were estimated and the models set out in Table 11. Cross-correlations functions (CCFs) for the series residuals are in Tables 12 and 13.

The figures in Table 12 provide some evidence that media mentions correlate with issue mentions, but not for all issues, and, most often, not in the direction necessary for media-influenced discretionary windows to exist. For nuclear issues, for example, there is some evidence that Hansard mentions lag newspaper mentions at six-, five-, and one-month intervals, but these CCFs are very weak. There is also weak evidence that rather than lag newspapers, Hansard mentions lead newspapers at three-month intervals. There is only weak evidence of Hansard mentions of native issues lagging newspaper mentions at seven and three months. As was the case with nuclear issues, there is also weak evidence that Hansard mentions do not lag, but lead newspaper mentions at four months. No evidence of Hansard mentions of drug issues lagging newspapers exists, and only a weak Hansard lead at two months is displayed. Acid rain mentions also display Hansard mentions lagging media mentions at three and zero months. Similarly, the highest correlation of all six issue areas (.429) is found with mentions of the constitution and media coverage, at a zero lag. A substantial Hansard lead of three months also exists. The only significantly strong correlation showing the required media lead over parliamentary

Table 12. Cross-Correlations: Issues with Media Correlates – Hansard and Newspapers[a]

Lag	Nuclear	Acidrain	Constitution	Capital Punishment	Native	Drugs
–7	0.024	0.069	0.031	–0.032	0.131	0.066
–6	0.102	–0.006	0.041	0.116	–0.043	–0.170
–5	0.093	–0.060	0.069	–0.011	–0.168	0.038
–4	0.009	–0.143	0.085	0.040	–0.044	–0.028
–3	0.062	0.107	0.035	–0.024	0.169	–0.002
–2	–0.048	0.019	–0.033	0.336	–0.021	0.026
–1	0.100	–0.012	0.217	–0.077	0.036	–0.031
0	–0.037	0.100	0.429	0.232	0.009	0.037
1	–0.092	0.097	0.015	–0.135	–0.046	–0.031
2	0.031	–0.033	–0.218	0.006	–0.095	0.110
3	0.099	–0.048	0.119	0.017	–0.036	–0.008
4	–0.009	–0.027	0.033	–0.025	0.111	–0.016
5	–0.008	–0.093	0.040	–0.092	0.061	–0.043
6	–0.034	0.062	0.017	0.107	0.045	0.012
7	–0.018	–0.029	–0.048	0.021	–0.197	–0.054

[a] Significance level = 0.063.

mentions required to establish the existence of a discretionary window is found in the capital punishment series at two (.336) months, with a sizable correlation also at zero (.232) months.

Table 13 presents the results of CCFs calculated with the "objective correlates" of crime and unemployment rates. Given the nature of the issue series and these exogenous measures, only four variations were examined. These related crime rates to the two social issues of drug and capital punishment mentions, and nuclear and acid rain mentions with unemployment rates in anticipation of some evidence of a jobs-environment trade-off. The data in Table 13 show some evidence of the anticipated relationship between crime rates and drug issue mentions, with drug mentions lagging the crime rate by seven and two months. The links between acid rain and nuclear industry mentions

Table 13. Cross-Correlations: Selected Issues with Objective Correlates[a]

Lag	Drug issues with crime	Capital punishment with crime	Nuclear issues with unemployment	Acid rain issues with unemployment
−7	.213	−.175	.069	.020
−6	−.238	−.092	−.039	−.044
−5	.034	.013	−.012	−.026
−4	.010	.040	−.051	.028
−3	−.058	−.037	.106	.012
−2	.122	.008	−.099	.051
−1	.053	−.062	−.004	−.070
0	.031	.082	−.030	.035
1	−.053	−.003	.011	−.030
2	−.055	.038	.053	.031
3	.115	−.042	.002	.002
4	−.013	.100	−.042	−.019
5	−.043	−.062	.009	−.029
6	.016	−.062	.082	.061
7	−.110	.064	.010	−.042

[a] Significance level = 0.063.

and unemployment are, however, weak, and mostly insignificant, as are those for capital punishment and violent crime rates. Tests on committee mentions also revealed no significant correlations. These results suggest that discretionary windows may exist in some of the six issue areas, but certainly not all. Only capital punishment showed significant media leads over parliamentary mentions, while "objective" exogenous correlates had only a weak influence on drug mentions. These findings support the idea that discretionary windows in which parliamentarians introduce issues of current public concern exist in Canada but are infrequent.

Spillover Windows in Canada

A test for spillover windows can be devised by examining the manner in which mentions of broadly similar issues correlate. In order to

Figure 9: Cross-Correlation Functions of Native and Constitutional Hansard Issue Mentions

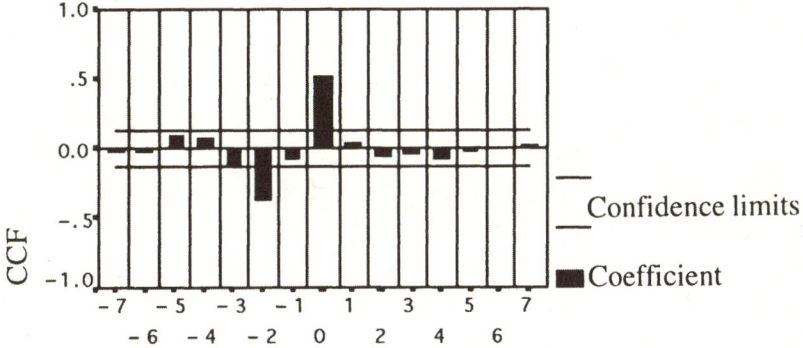

Figure 10: Cross-Correlation Functions of Nuclear and Acid Rain Hansard Issue Mentions

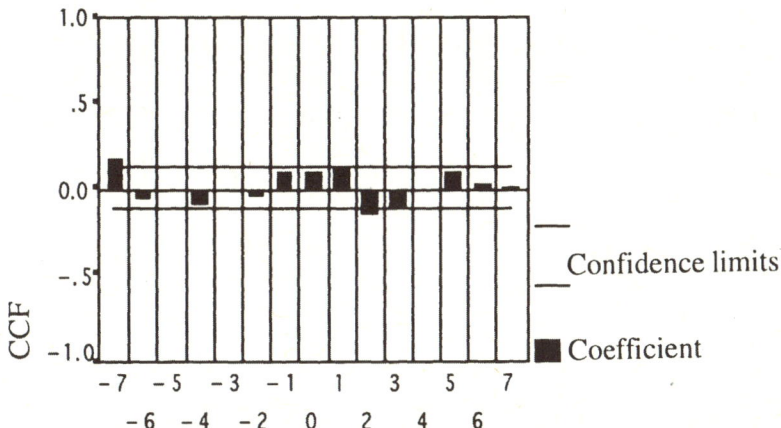

conduct this test, cross-correlation functions of series residuals were used to assess the manner in which the three pairs of related issue series covaried with each other. CCFs for two jurisdictional issues – natives and the constitution; for both environmental issues – acid rain and nuclear issues; and for both social issues – drugs and capital punishment – were calculated. The CCF graphs for these three pairs of series are presented in Figures 9 to 11.

Figure 11: Cross-Correlation Functions of Drug and Capital Punishment Hansard Issue Mentions

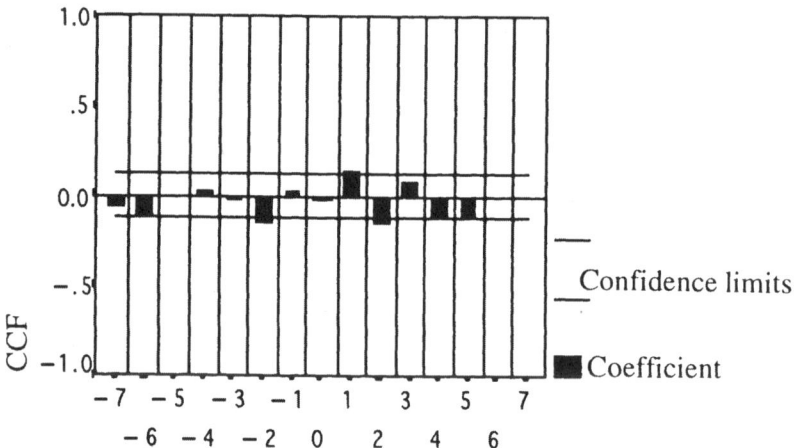

These figures reveal a significant spillover effect in native and constitutional issues, with a substantial CCF of .523 at lag zero. A weaker correlation exists for the two environmental issues, nuclear and acid rain mentions, with a CCF of .103 at lag zero. Drug issues and capital punishment did not display any spillover at lag zero. This latter finding, however, should not be surprising given the finding in the previous section that each of these issues had displayed evidence of the existence of a discretionary window.

Routine Windows

Finally, there is the question of fully institutionalized or routinized windows. In order to test for the existence of such windows, the covariance of the six issues with four institutional series – elections, throne speeches, first ministers' conferences, and budgets – was examined. Table 14 shows the diagnostics developed for these latter series. Since the series for budgets, conferences, and throne speeches display no significant auto correlation, the original series rather than their residuals were used in these tests. Although the election variable displayed some auto correlation, the most difficult problem associated with assessing its effect on issue mentions is that Parliament is not in session during

Table 14. Institutional Series Diagnostics

Series	DurbinWatson	First orderACFs
Budget	1.818	0.089
Conference	1.453	0.273
Throne	1.714	0.143
Election	0.903	0.548

Table 15. Cross-Correlation Functions of Issues and Institutions[a]

Issue	Throne(lag −1)	Conference(lag 0)	Budget(lag 0)
Natives	0.216	0.116	0.176
Constitution	0.140	0.272	0.146
Nuclear	0.171	0.037	0.095
Drugs	0.117	0.140	0.025
Capital punishment	0.150	0.098	0.238
Acid rain	0.122	0.035	0.200

[a] Significance level = 0.072.

the federal election campaign. Since the campaign period extends over forty days and overlapped with three monthly periods, an alternative measure to a cross-correlation function is needed.

Results of CCFs for issue mentions in Hansard and the three non-auto-correlated institutional variables are presented in Table 15. The CCFs for the conference and budget series are for lag zero. The CCFs for the throne speech variable are listed for lag negative one since the House of Commons is not in session for all of the thirty-day period included at lag zero. These data provide evidence of institutional correlates of all issues: all correlate with throne speeches, all except nuclear and acid rain with first ministers' conferences, and all except drug issues with budgets.

The impact of elections can be assessed by examining the coherence[6] of election cycles with those of issue mentions. Rather than examine all six issues separately, a composite measure – issue "density" – was used.[7] The case plot of this new "density" variable – the sum of all six issue mentions – is shown in Figure 12.

Figure 12: Caseplot of Issue Density

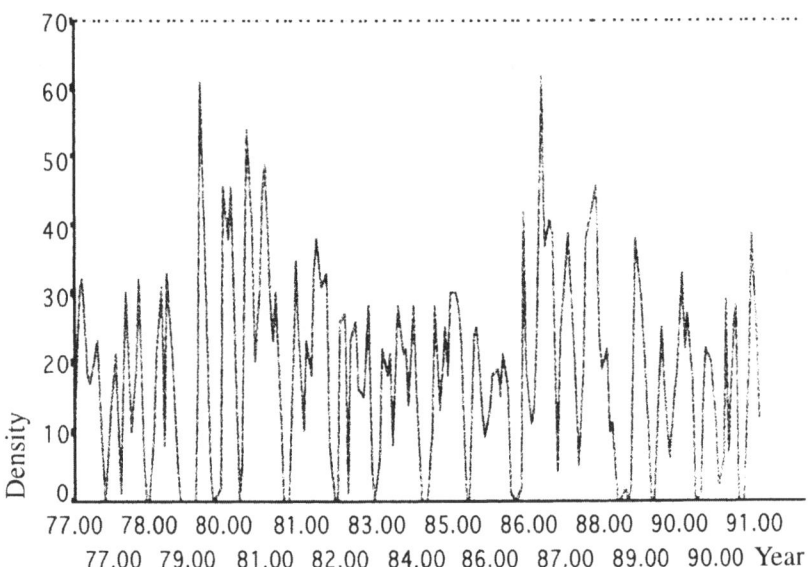

Note: Double mention of some years is caused by representation of monthly data in annual graphical format.

Given the federal elections in 1979–80 and 1984, which coincide closely with the peaks in the caseplot, there is anecdotal evidence that issue density appears to vary with elections. More formally, the coherency graph contained in Figure 13 shows that the covariance of the two series is quite striking. It also shows very strong covariation at frequencies of .13 (twelve months) and .33 (four months) between the two series, although the direction of these relationships is not revealed by this measure. An examination of the CCFs for the two series, however, reveals a .253 lead of density with elections at six months and a .213 lag, suggesting a strong pattern of large issue mentions in the run-up to an election and in the immediate post-election period.

Although many of the institutional correlations are weak, both tests provide evidence of the presence and significance of institutional windows in Canada.

Figure 13: Coherency of Density and Elections

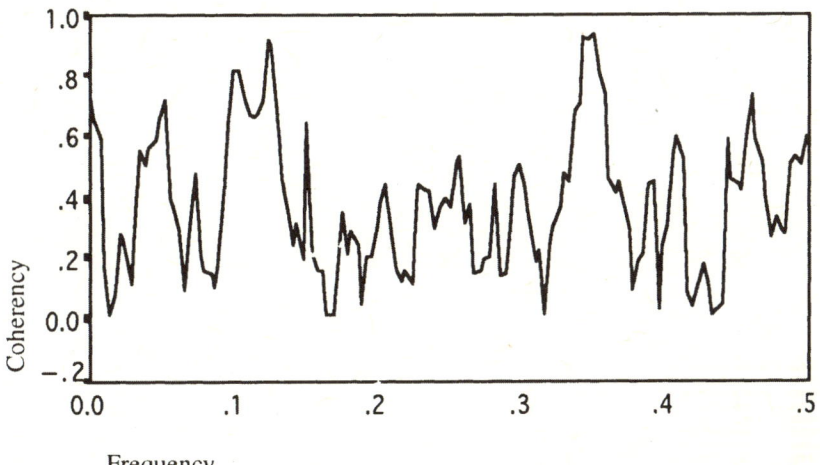

Conclusion

This chapter uses time series ARIMA and Spectral Analysis techniques to evaluate the frequency and occurrence of different types of policy windows in Canada. The tests found evidence that three of the four types of policy windows identified by Kingdon existed in Canada over the period examined, and support for the hypothesized link between level of window institutionalization and frequency of occurrence also exists. Only six cases were used in the study, and hence the results must be interpreted with some care. However, while any conclusions reached must be subjected to further research, the tests revealed that of the four types of policy windows identified at the outset:

– No evidence was found of random windows. This supports the idea put forward by Kingdon that such windows are, in fact, quite rare.
– Some evidence was found that issue mentions of capital punishment in the media led those in Parliament, and that increases in crime rates led drug mentions. These findings support the idea that discretionary windows exist but are not frequent occurrences.

– Strong evidence was found that native and constitutional issue mentions were linked as, to a weaker extent, were acid rain and nuclear issue mentions. This suggests that spillover windows exist and may be quite common.
– Finally, as Kingdon and Walker both suggested, evidence of the impact of institutionalized procedural events was detected in all six issue areas. While this provides evidence of the existence of routine windows, the findings of strong coherence between issue density and elections provided some specific evidence that a pattern of routine openings in the run-up and immediate post-election period exists.

These findings support the appropriateness of the application of Kingdon's theory of agenda setting to the Canadian context. That is, there is evidence that policy windows of different types exist in Canada, and there is evidence that the frequency of occurrence of the window types varies by level of institutionalization – with the most institutionalized types occurring much more frequently than the least institutionalized. These findings have several implications for both the theory and practice of agenda setting in Canada.

On a practical level, the finding that Kingdon's model fits Canada provides an alternative model for policy actors to use to guide their behaviour. That is, both government and non-governmental actors should alter their behaviour to accord with the findings that policy windows vary in frequency. The preponderance of routine windows, for example, means that there is a certain amount of predictability of openings and closings of which government officials and other policy actors should be cognizant when they attempt to influence policymaking. Similarly, the finding of high correlations between issues in spillover windows underlines the fact that, in the right circumstances, issue linkage can provide significant opportunities for policy entrepreneurs. Explicitly analysing agenda setting in terms of the windows model means that policy actors can better plan their own efforts to influence policy,[8] rather than by using implicit or inaccurate models. Window manipulation and agenda control should become part of the vocabulary of policy design and governance in Canada (Leik 1992; de Bruijn and ten Heuvelhof 1995; Klijn 1996).

Theoretically, the finding that Kingdon's model carries cross-nationally is significant in itself, and it also suggests several research directions. That cyclical agenda-setting behaviour related to institutionalized policy windows exists, for example, suggests a reassessment of the existence or non-existence of relatively long-term political cycles in

Canada, and elsewhere, should be made. That is, most studies testing for the existence or non-existence of such cycles (Nordhaus 1975; Hibbs 1977 and 1987; Tufte 1978) have found little evidence that they exist.[9] However, these studies have all relied on *output*-related measures such as increases or decreases in level of public expenditure or public employment to make this assessment.[10] This does not, of course, preclude the possibility suggested here that *input*-related cycles exist. That is, it is quite possible that many issues are raised which, for various reasons, are never implemented; thus policy cycles may exist at the agenda-setting stage but not be linked to output or "implementation" cycles.

The existence of disjointed agenda setting and implementation cycles raises interesting questions about the nature of Canadian policy processes in general. Why is it that items and issues appear on government agendas, then disappear prior to implementation? Is this a reflection of the politics of policy formulation, decision making, implementation, or all three? And what does it tell us about the nature of the ideas and actors involved in these processes? Research into these disjointed policy cycles may shed some light on the larger determinants of the overall policymaking process by revealing the nature of the links existing between its various stages.

While most research into the subject has focused on the micro level in attempting to explain a pattern of blocked policy development (Zelditch et al. 1983; Jones 1994; Howlett and Rayner 1995), longitudinal research should investigate the linkages which may exist between relatively short-term agenda-setting cycles and larger, and longer-term, sociopolitical cycles in influencing transitions between stages. As Andrew MacFarland and others have noted: "There is a tendency for reform cycles in hundreds of issue areas to proceed in phase. In other words, during a given year the political power of producer groups will be relatively high in many issue areas simultaneously, while in another year the political power of countervailing groups and autonomous government will be relatively high in many issue areas" (MacFarland 1991: 264).

While it is beyond the scope of this chapter to comment in any substantial way on this observation, it would not be too surprising to find that relatively short-term agenda-setting cycles are closely linked to medium- and long-term changes in "policy moods" or "sentiments" (Lewis-Beck 1988; Stimson 1991; Suzuki 1992; Durr 1993; Stimson, Mackuen, and Erikson 1995; Adams 1997). Such a finding would help to continue the development of both the understanding and practice of agenda-setting behaviour in Canada and elsewhere by adding a substantive dimension to Kingdon's procedural model.

Appendix 1: Data Sources

Issue mentions related to native affairs, the constitution, drug abuse, acid rain, the nuclear industry, and capital punishment in parliamentary debates and committees over the period 1977–92 were derived from the index to the Debates of the House of Commons (1977–92) provided directly by the index and reference service of the House of Commons in Ottawa, and from the *Index to Journals of the House of Commons of Canada* (1977–92).

Institutional series were developed from a variety of sources. Budget and mini-budget dates were obtained from Canada, Department of Finance, *Budgets and Financial Statements since 1963*. Dates for speeches from the throne were obtained from *The Ottawa Letter*, 13 (42), 204; 13 (93), 534; 14 (41), 272; 14 (68), 476; 16 (49), 391; 16 (97), 802; 17 (93), 753; 18 (102), 824; 19 (15), 111; and 20 (19), 168. Election dates were found in Elections Canada, *Canada's Electoral System: How It Evolved and How It Works* (1988). The dates for first ministers' conferences were found in *The Chicago Tribune*, 29 August 1992, 11; Alberta Federal and Intergovernmental Affairs, *Eighteenth Annual Report to March 31, 1991*, Edmonton, Alberta; Alberta Federal and Intergovernmental Affairs, *Fifteenth Annual Report to March 31, 1988*, Edmonton, Alberta; Canadian Intergovernmental Conference Secretariat, *Federal-Provincial First Minister's Conferences, 1906–1986*, Ottawa, Ontario 1986; Canadian Intergovernmental Conference Secretariat, *Federal-Provincial Conferences on the Constitution, September 1978 to March 1987, List of Public Documents*, Ottawa.

Series developed from media issue mentions were derived from the *Canadian Newspaper Index* (1977–87) covering the *Montreal Star*, *The Globe and Mail* (Toronto), *Toronto Star*, *Vancouver Sun*, and the *Winnipeg Free Press*, the *Canadian Business and Current Affairs* (CBCA) computerized index (1987–92) and the *Canadian Periodical Index*.

The data on violent crime occurrences were obtained as a special series from Statistics Canada, Canadian Centre for Justice Statistics, Ottawa. Missing monthly data for 1982 resulted in the use of the annual average for that year. Unemployment rates were obtained from Statistics Canada, *Labour Force Annual Averages*.

Where possible, each keyword or event appearance was recorded for each source on a daily basis. These daily totals were summed for every thirty-day period over the entire fifteen-year period to provide a record of 183 "monthly" cases for each series. In the case of "standard" series for violent crime and unemployment, monthly data were used.

Appendix 2: Caseplots of Issues

Note: Double mention of some years is caused by representation of monthly data in annual graphical format.

Figure 14: Nuclear Issue Mentions in Hansard

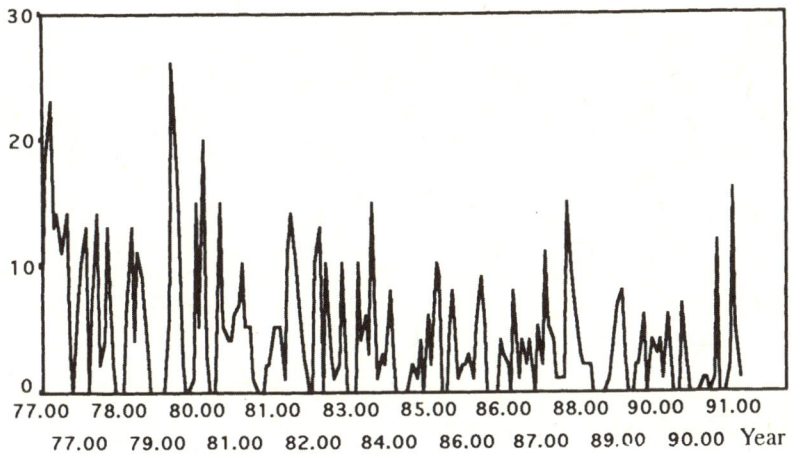

Figure 15: Acid Rain Mentions in Hansard

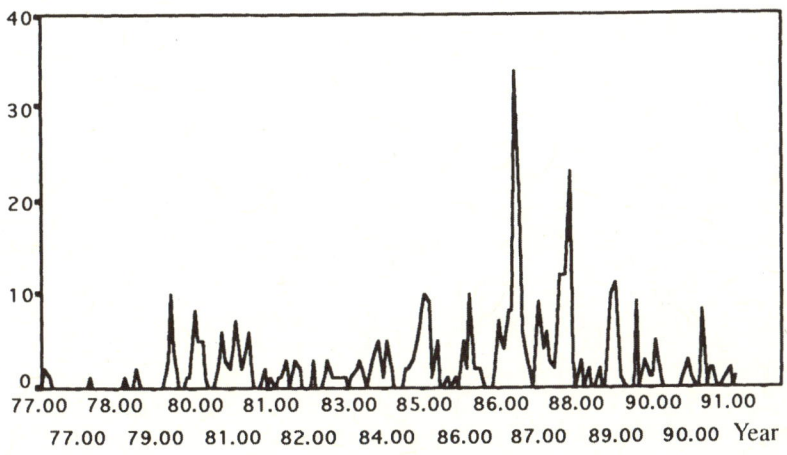

Figure 16: Capital Punishment Mentions in Hansard

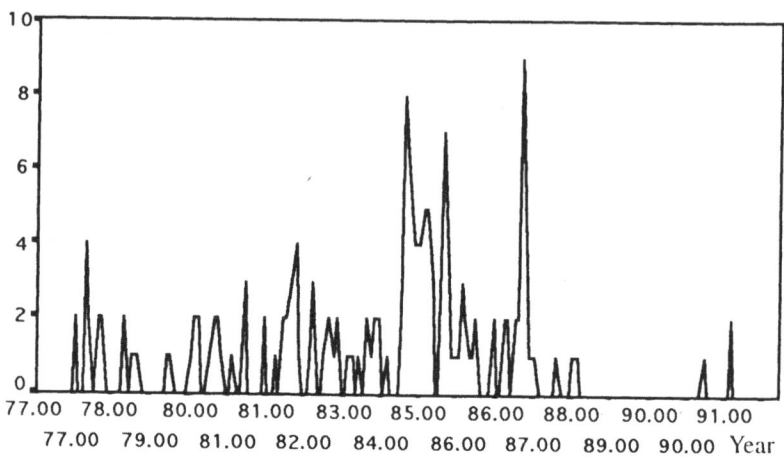

Figure 17: Constitutional Mentions in Hansard

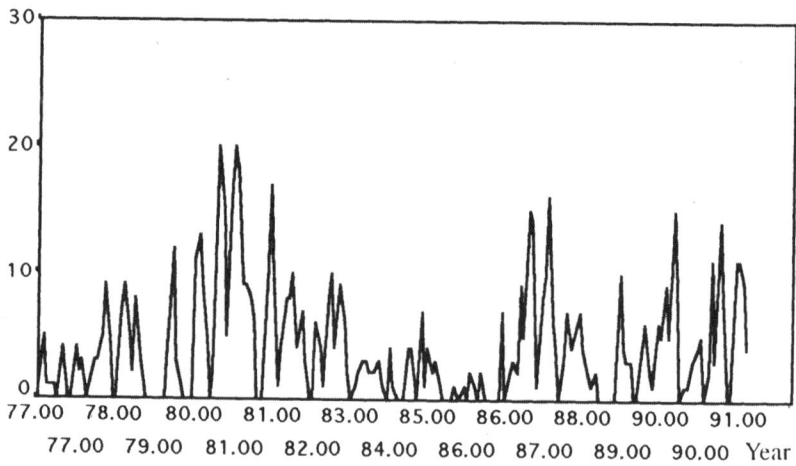

Figure 18: Drug Issue Mentions in Hansard

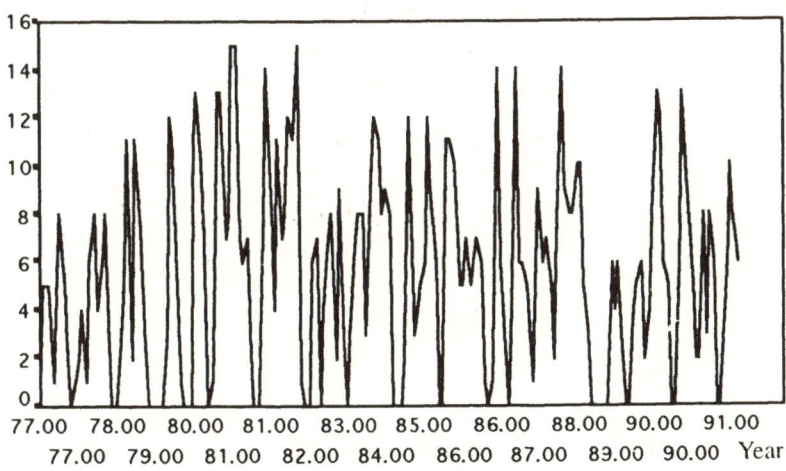

Figure 19: Native Issue Mentions in Hansard

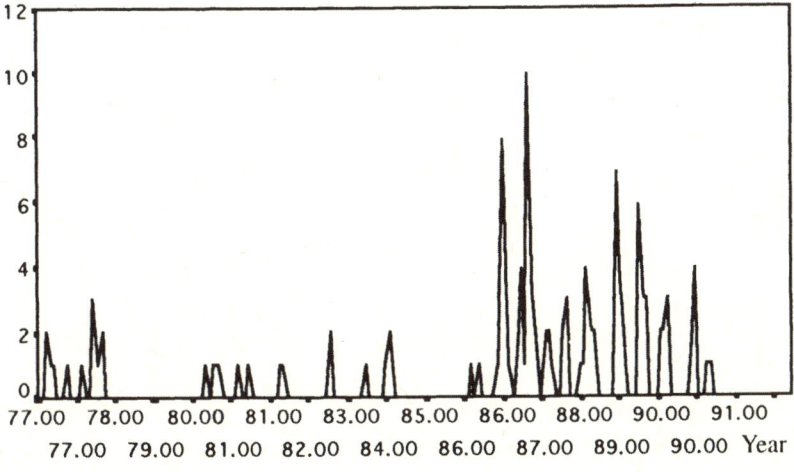

Appendix 3: Caseplots of Institutional Events

Note: Double mention of some years is caused by representation of monthly data in annual graphical format.

Figure 20: Budgets and Mini-Budgets

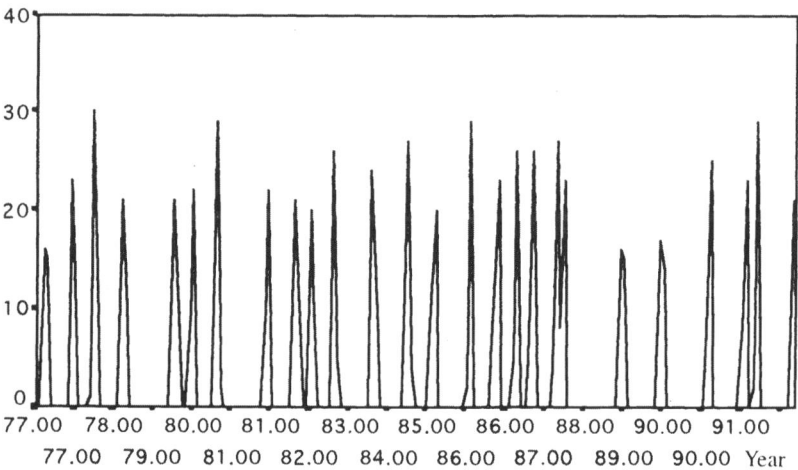

Figure 21: Throne Speeches

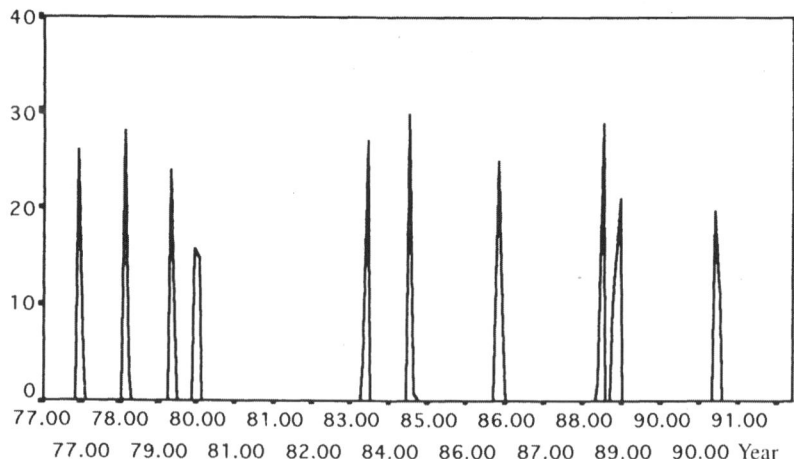

Figure 22: General Elections

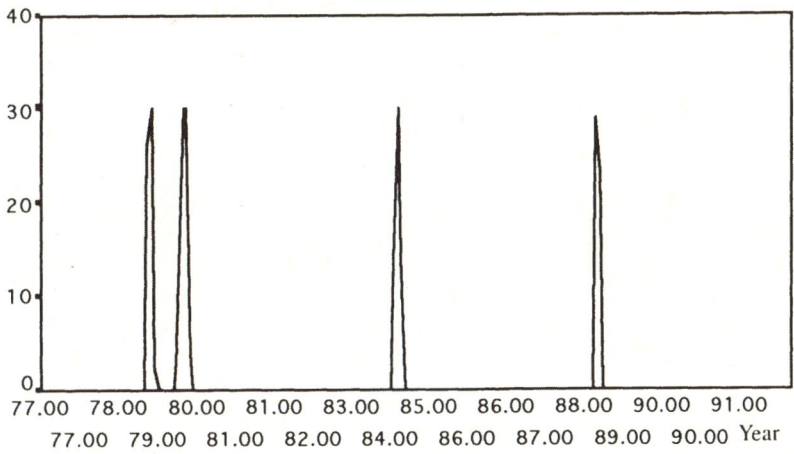

Figure 23: First Ministers' Conferences

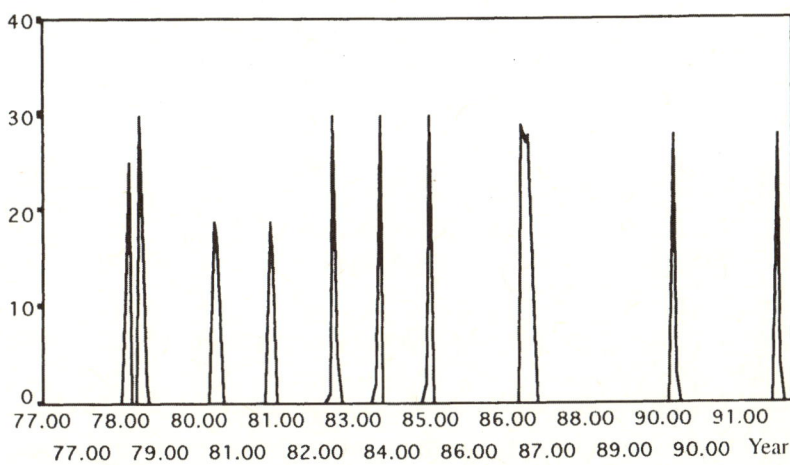

Appendix 4: Caseplots of Objective Correlates

Note: Double mention of some years is caused by representation of monthly data in annual graphical format.

Unemployment Rate

Figure 24: Unemployment Rate

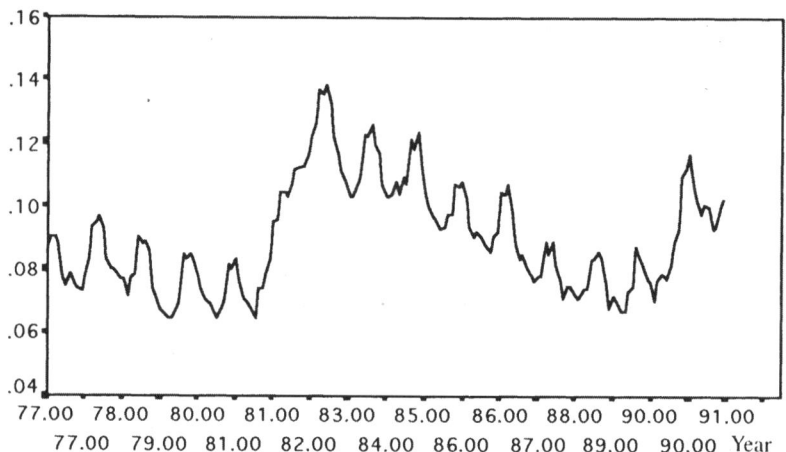

Figure 25: Violent Crime Rate

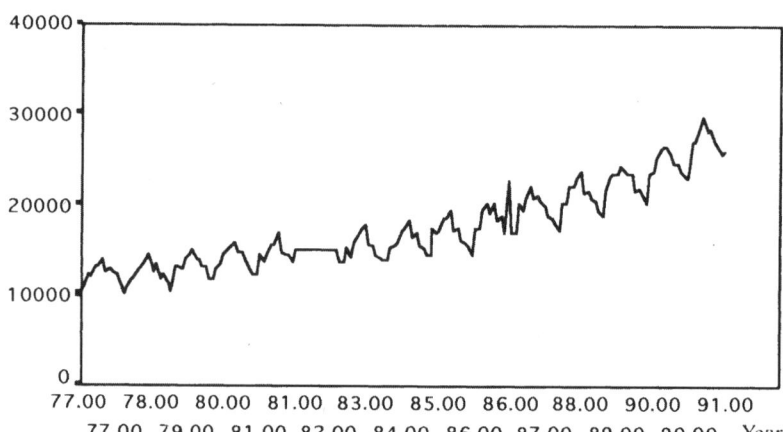

4 Policy Formulation: Do Networks Matter? Linking Policy Network Structure to Policy Outcomes: Evidence from Four Canadian Policy Sectors 1990–2000

Introduction: Metaphors and Models in Policy Network Analysis

Policy network theory has become a major approach to the study of public policymaking in Canada and elsewhere (Sabatier 1992; Lindquist 1996; Thatcher 1998). Thinking about policymaking as involving more or less fluid sets of state and societal actors linked together by specific interest and resource relationships has emerged as a powerful tool in policy analysis, both from a theoretical and a practical perspective. Conceptually, it has helped to address several important questions relating to the role of actors, ideas, and interests in policymaking processes. Organizing actors and institutions into identifiable sets of policy-relevant interactions has facilitated policy analysis by helping to transcend the limitations of purely behavioural or institutional modes of analysis which focus exclusively on structure or agency in their presuppositions and methodologies (Knoke 1993; Klijn and Koppenjan 2000). Practically, it has provided a model of the structure and operation of policy processes which governments and other policy actors can use to better design and affect outcomes (de Bruijn and ten Heuvelhof 1995; Bressers and O'Toole 1998).

However, several key aspects and assumptions of network theory have come under increasing scrutiny. Most important from a policy studies perspective, the assumption underlying all network-based studies, that the characteristics of network structure affect policy processes and outcomes, has been challenged (Kassim 1994; Mills and Saward 1994; Dowding 1995). This challenge has raised the question whether networks matter in the sense of being a significant variable helping to understand, explain, and predict policy outcomes, as adherents of this approach attest, or if the characterization of policy actors and processes in network terms is simply a heuristic, useful for descriptive purposes but lacking analytical power.

There is some disagreement as to the actual content of the criticisms made, and whether or not they point to fundamental and insurmountable weaknesses in the network approach.[1] However, there is general agreement that the relationship between network structure and policy outcomes should be the subject of much more systematic investigation than was often the case in past studies (Bressers, O'Toole, and Richardson 1994; Rhodes 1997).

This chapter discusses the manner in which structures of interest networks and discourse communities, or policy subsystems, affect the articulation of ideas and interests in public policymaking. It proposes a model setting out how different subsystem configurations relate to particular paradigmatic and intra-paradigmatic processes of policy change, and suggests that specific configurations of subsystem membership and modes of interaction are directly linked to propensities for specific types of policy change. This hypothesis is tested against evidence accumulated from several case studies of policy change and the evolution of policy subsystems in four prominent Canadian federal policy sectors over the decade 1990–2000.

The Link between Subsystem Structure and Policy Change in Policy Network Analysis

The concept of a "policy subsystem" was developed in the United States on the basis of the observation that American federal interest groups, congressional committees, and government agencies had developed systems of mutual support in the course of constant interaction over legislative and regulatory matters. The rigid, three-sided relationships or "subgovernments" originally observed in areas such as agriculture, transportation, and education were often dubbed "iron triangles" to capture the essence of their ironclad control over many aspects of the policy process. They were often condemned for having "captured" the policy process, subverting the principles of popular democracy by ensuring that the self-interests of triangle members prevailed over those of the general public (Cater 1964; Lowi 1969). Regardless of the merits of these arguments about the democratic nature of policy processes, however, an important aspect of these first studies was to highlight a significant relationship existing between subsystem structure and policy change. That is, rigid closed subsystems were closely associated with stable, routine policymaking in which outputs tended to incrementally advance the interests of subsystem members (Huntington 1952; Bernstein 1955).

This link between subsystem structure, policy process, and, ultimately, policy outcomes was further bolstered by subsequent studies in the 1960s and 1970s which uncovered an alternative form of subsystem and associated it with a different set of policy dynamics. Research by Hugh Heclo and others revealed that iron triangle-type subgovernments were not omnipresent and that policy subsystems varied across issues and over time. In particular, a more flexible and less rigid type of subsystem, the "issue network," was identified and, it was argued, was becoming much more common in Washington (Hayes 1978; Heclo 1978; Ripley and Franklin 1980; Gais, Peterson, and Walker 1984). This type of subsystem was associated with a different, more open, characteristic policy process and a propensity for the adoption of more innovative policies than was typically found in sectors dominated by iron triangles.

Both the American and European studies which followed upon this work in the 1980s and 1990s used this basic spectrum of subsystem types and its association of different types of subsystems with different policy dynamics.[2] While the different origins of and terminologies employed in these studies caused some confusion and misunderstanding (Jordon 1981; Borzel 1998), all suggested the utility for policy analysis of conceiving of the range of actors and institutions involved in policymaking in network terms. Subsystems were seen to range from "open" to "closed," or highly to poorly "cohesive," in terms of their membership and institutional linkages and boundaries, with open subsystems associated with dynamic and innovative policy outcomes and closed subsystems with an incremental or status quo orientation (Rhodes and Marsh 1992; Smith 1993; Daugbjerg 1997). The network approach came with a ready toolbox of analytical tools and methods borrowed from sociologically inspired social network analysis (Wolfe 1978; Rice and Richards 1985; Wellman 1988), and after 1980 many political scientists and sociologists in Canada and elsewhere turned to studying policy actors and institutions using these methods.[3]

Many students of policymaking found the subsystem approach useful in overcoming problems with earlier approaches – such as Marxism, pluralism, or corporatism – which unnecessarily reified social relations or ignored institutional and structural variables in their analyses.

However, the network approach was not without conceptual and methodological problems of its own, and by the mid-1990s some of its central tenets and hypotheses began to be called into question. Specifically, critics such as Keith Dowding argued that network studies tended to be overly descriptive and somewhat tautological in their reasoning and analysis. Although not denying that the network perspective could provide a useful heuristic for students of policymaking, it was asserted, among other things, that the links alleged to exist between subsystem structure and policy outcomes were not proven. Without better empirical evaluation, it was argued, contemporary debates over terminology promised to yield little in the way of additional explanatory power or conceptual integration. If the network approach was to move beyond metaphor, it was posited, network studies had to move beyond thick description and classification and demonstrate that structural aspects of political life actually had a predictable effect on policy outcomes (Dowding 1995).

Testing the Impact of Subsystem Structure on Policy Outcomes: The Elements of an Operational Model of Policy

Subsystem Configurations and Policy Change

If subsystem structure affects policy outcomes, then, at minimum, in inspecting specific policy sectors over some fairly long period of time, one would expect to find some correlation between changes in policy outcomes and changes in subsystem structure. As Sabatier and Jenkins-Smith suggested, conducting such a demonstration involves measuring policy change and subsystem change in specific sectors over at least a decade and comparing the record or pattern of changes in policy subsystems with the record of changes in policy outcomes (Sabatier 1993). While this sounds simple enough, conducting such a test first requires clarifying several outstanding definitional questions pertaining to the nature of differences in network structures and the description of policy change; and the development of an operational model or theory hypothesizing specific linkages between specific types of policy change and specific types of policy subsystems.

Operationalizing Policy Change

Constructing an operational model of policy change begins with the observation that most policies made by governments are, for the most

Table 16. A Basic Taxonomy of Policy Change by Mode and Speed of Change

	Speed of Change	
Mode of Change	Fast	Slow
Paradigmatic	*Rapid Paradigmatic*	*Gradual Paradigmatic*
Normal	*Rapid Incremental*	*Gradual Incremental*

Source: Adapted from Durant and Diehl (1989).

part and most of the time, in some way a continuation of past policies and practices. Even what are often portrayed as "new" policy initiatives are often simply variations on existing practices (Polsby 1984). That is, in normal circumstances, a policy problem or issue will be dealt with by reference to an existing practice, or in what has been described by many as a marginal or "incremental" fashion (Lindblom 1959; Hayes 1992). This pattern of piecemeal policy change is the stuff of "normal" policymaking.

Similarly, it has also been observed that a second, less frequent, pattern of policy change involves the more dramatic reconceptualization and restructuring of policy. This type of policy change is usually described in the literature as "paradigmatic" (Baumgartner and Jones 1993).[4] Overall, paradigmatic change is seen as involving periods of stability and incremental adaptations interspersed by periods of revolutionary upheaval, resulting in what has often been referred to as a "punctuated equilibrium" pattern of policy dynamics (Eldredge and Gould 1972; Gersick 1991).

A useful way to look at these different basic types of policy change has been suggested by Durant and Diehl (1989). Analogizing from work on patterns and processes of evolutionary change in paleobiology, they have argued that policy change has two components. Policies can vary not only in terms of the mode of change – between the normal pattern of piecemeal incremental change and the pattern of paradigmatic change mentioned above – but also in terms of the tempo or speed of change. This model suggests (see Table 16) that paradigmatic change, although infrequent, can be either rapid[5] or slow.[6] The same is true for incremental change, which can occur at either tempo.

The predominance of a "normal" pattern of relatively gradual incremental policy change has usually been explained by reference to the fact that the same set of actors and ideas is involved in the policy process over a long period of time.[7] Observers have often noted how, in the course of interaction among themselves and in their day-to-day dealings with a public problem, policymakers tend to develop a common episteme (Sabatier 1988; Kenis 1991; Haas 1992), or way of looking at and dealing with, a problem. Slight adaptation and adjustment of views on the basis of experience and new information is endemic to the policy process, but most studies have found that understandings of the nature of public problems and the acceptable or feasible solutions to them are often remarkably durable and, once in place, are difficult to change (Sabatier 1987; Pierson 2000). This common understanding obtaining in a policy subsystem, however, can at times break down, setting the stage for the emergence of new and different policy discourses, consideration of new policy options, and, ultimately, innovative policy outcomes. The reasons behind the infrequency of such paradigmatic policy change – whether rapid or gradual – are not well understood. However, a strong trend in the policy literature has been to discuss paradigmatic policy change as occurring as a result of the activities of specialized policy actors reacting to discordances or discrepancies between events on the ground and their theorization within the dominant paradigm. That is, much as was argued by Thomas Kuhn and others in the case of the advance of scientific knowledge (Kuhn 1962 and 1974), the discovery of "anomalies," or events and activities not expected or understandable in terms of prevalent theories, allows innovative actors – "policy entrepreneurs" – to respond to changing circumstances and their own ambitions by introducing new ideas into the policy milieu.[8] These new actors are often seen as engaged in a struggle with established ones, who usually resist the introduction of non-paradigmatic ideas and defend the status quo, or at least attempt to limit changes to those compatible with existing arrangements (Jenkins-Smith, St. Clair, and Woods 1991; Howlett and Rayner 1995; Nunan 1999).

Thus explanations of observed patterns of policy change highlight the role played by both ideas and interests in this process. That is, a change in the episteme or knowledge base of policy ideas, for example, can result in either rapid or slow paradigmatic policy change depending on whether the second condition – a change in key actors/interests – is also present. Without a change in ideas, policy change will be incremental, but its tempo will also be determined by whether or not new actors or interests have been introduced into policy processes (Hoberg 1996; Braun 1999; Daguerre 2000; Pemberton 2000; Schmidt 2001). This means that the expected types of change featured in Table 16 can be rewritten substituting the entrance of new ideas for "mode of change" and the entrance of new actors for "speed of change."

This initial step helps to operationalize part of a basic model of policy change. However, it still does not provide any indication of how policy change should be assessed. What constitutes "paradigmatic" and incremental change? What differentiates "gradual" from rapid paradigmatic, or gradual from rapid incremental, change? And how can these be measured? In answering these questions, it is helpful to consider the popular threefold conception of policy change put forward by Peter Hall (1993) in his work on economic policy change in Britain. Hall identified three different types of change: first-order change, in which only the settings of policy instruments vary; second-order change, in which change occurs in the basic types or categories of instruments used to effect policy; and third-order change, in which the goals of policy are altered.[9] While useful, some of this terminology is confusing and should be changed, while the logic of the model also suggests that there should be four basic types of change, not three. With respect to terminology, the use of the term "settings" to describe first-order change can be confusing, since most uses of the term would lead one to consider the location of a policy instrument within a policy environment, when Hall means to describe the calibration or fine-tuning of an instrument's content or component parts. More significant, Hall's model is based on distinguishing between the means and ends of policymaking and between abstract and concrete aspects of policy outputs (Campbell 1998). Given these two dimensions, four distinct categories of policy change are possible, not three.[10] These can be described as changes related to abstract policy goals or more concrete program specifications, referring to the ends of policymaking; and to basic policy instrument type or genus, as opposed to alterations of existing instrument components, when discussing changes in policy means.

Combining the discussion of actors and ideas above with the four basic types of potential policy change identified above allows the creation of a fully operational model of policy change. That is, rapid paradigmatic change can be thought of as featuring changes in policy goals and gradual paradigmatic change as featuring changes in program specifications. Changes in instrument type would be characteristic of rapid incremental change, while gradual incremental change would feature changes in instrument components or "settings." Rewriting Table 16 in this vein generates the model set out in Table 17.

Table 17. An Operationalized Model of Policy Change

	Entrance of New Actors	
Entrance of new ideas	Yes	No
Yes	*Policy Goals*	*Program Specifications*
No	*Policy Instrument Types*	*Instrument Components*

4. Operationalizing Policy Subsystems

The second requirement of the analysis of the impact of subsystem structure on policy change, of course, is a similarly operational model of significant differences in subsystem structures which can be linked to the former through the specification of clear, testable propositions or hypotheses concerning the impact of structure on outcomes. Unfortunately, there is no generally accepted model of subsystem structure, as there has been a distinct penchant in the literature for incompatible ad hoc categorizations to be developed inductively from the results of empirical case studies (Van Waarden 1992; Borzel 1998). Critics such as Dowding and Borzel, and also adherents like Evert Lindquist, R.A.W. Rhodes, and David Marsh, have all criticized the needless proliferation of concepts attempting to capture different kinds of communities, networks and associations that often intersect, overlap or operate at different levels of analysis (Marsh and Rhodes 1992; Lindquist 1996; Marsh 1998).

It is important to note, however, that this concern is not with taxonomy construction, per se, but with the construction of taxonomies whose purposes are unclear and whose categories are neither exhaustive nor mutually exclusive. With respect to developing a test of the effect of policy subsystems on policy change, it is possible to utilize a relatively simple model which relates basic subsystem types to the two central variables thought to lie behind fundamental policy dynamics: the presence or absence of new ideas and new actors in policy deliberations. Doing so generates the simple taxonomy found in Table 18. Relating these basic types to propensities for specific types of policy change

Table 18. Basic Policy Subsystem Configurations

	Receptive to New Actors	
Receptive to New Ideas	No	Yes
No	*Closed Subsystem*	*Resistant Subsystem*
Yes	*Contested Subsystem*	*Open Subsystem*

Source: Adapted from Howlett and Ramesh (1998).

requires operationalizing the four basic subsystem variants in terms of their different structural characteristics.

In this regard, an important insight generated by numerous empirical studies is that subsystems tend to have two types of members: those involved on a day-to-day basis in policy deliberations and actions, and those whose activities are generally less prominent within the network and whose links to other network members are less frequent or "dense" (Schneider 1992; Stokman and Zeggelink 1997; Daugbjerg and Marsh 1998). Thus a major element of the conception of the structure of policy subsystems involves viewing them as composed of two interrelated subsets of all the actors potentially present in the policy "universe" (Pross 1992). The larger set of actors is composed of those who have some knowledge of the policy issue in question and who collectively construct a policy discourse within a *discourse community* (Singer 1990; Bulkeley 2000; Chadwick 2000). A subset within this larger, knowledge-based grouping is composed of those participants who participate in exchange relationships with each other, an *interest network* (Pappi and Knoke 1991; Pappi and Henning 1999).

There are several advantages to distinguishing in this manner among levels or groupings of actors in policy subsystems. At the conceptual level, this distinction allows the integration in network analysis of knowledge and interests as two unevenly distributed sets of motivations guiding the actions of policy actors and subsystem members. By associating a discourse community with actors grouped around a specific knowledge base and an interest network with actors interacting in the pursuit of their interests, the impact of these two different aspects of subsystem membership and activity come into sharper focus. Moreover, at a more practical level, a workable taxonomy of policy subsystems can be built upon this distinction, one which can be directly linked to specific hypotheses about the propensities of different subsystems for specific types of policy change. That is, an important aspect of the "cohesiveness" or "closedness" of policy subsystems, identified in earlier studies as a key dimension of subsystem structure related to policy change, is the nature of the relationship existing between the discourse community and the interest network (Schaap and Van Twist 1997; Bulkeley 2000). Subsystems which feature closely integrated communities and networks will be more cohesive and better able to resist the entrance of new ideas and actors into policy processes than will those which feature sizable distances between the two subsets of actors.

Although this insight is similar to that used in earlier studies to generate a simple spectrum or continuum of subsystem types – ranging from "integrated" to "unintegrated" and usually related to a single variable such as subsystem size – these did not fully capture the complexity of subsystem structure (Marsh and Rhodes 1992).[11] Rather, there are two important dimensions of subsystem structure and issue network – discourse community configurations which affect "cohesiveness." First, in an absolute sense, the potential for new actors to move from the community to the network is dependent on the degree of "symmetry," or the extent of overlap between the network and the community, existing in the subsystem. Subsystems which feature a relatively small interest network within a much larger discourse community will, all other things being equal, be more susceptible to new actors than will those featuring very little distance between the two component parts. Second, regardless of the overall size of the subsystem and its components, the extent to which an interest network is insulated from its associated discourse community will also be a significant factor in understanding the extent to which new ideas can move between the community and network or, for that matter, between the policy universe and the community.

Examining the degree of symmetry and the extent of insulation between network and community allows an operational model of subsystem structure to be developed which can be linked to propensities for the different types of policy change. Table 19 rewrites the four main subsystem configurations listed in Table 18, focusing on these two dimensions of community-network structure.

Table 19. Preliminary Operationalizing of Policy Subsystem Configurations

Extent of symmetry between community and network	Network's degree of insulation from community	
	High	Low
High	*Closed Subsystem*	*Resistant Subsystem*
Low	*Contested Subsystem*	*Open Subsystem*

Linking Subsystem Configurations to Policy Change

In the case of "closed" subsystems, the distinction between community and network almost disappears, as the network is virtually synonymous with those actors involved in exchange relationships and the boundary between the two is at its greatest. This represents the classic, highly stable, "cohesive" subsystem described in the early network literature. Given the limitations this places on the flow of actors and ideas into policy processes, one would expect this kind of subsystem to be the most stable, and therefore to tend towards a propensity to develop only limited forms of changes in policy outputs, such as changes in policy instrument components or "settings." At the opposite extreme, an "open" subsystem is one in which there is the greatest space between discourse community and interest network, and the boundaries between the two are the most easily penetrable. In this case, one would anticipate the possibility of all different kinds of changes in policy outputs occurring, including changes in policy goals.

In between are the two cases which exist when the gap between network and community is small but the boundary between the two groups is easily crossed – the "resistant" subsystem – and that where there is a large difference between the two units but the boundary between them is thick – the "contested" subsystem. In the former, one would expect changes to be restricted largely to instrument components, but with some experimentation involving program specifications, as some new ideas about policy goals could penetrate across subsystem boundaries but would be dealt with largely by existing actors. In the latter, thick boundaries would prevent the consideration of

Table 20. Hypothesized Relationship Existing between Policy Subsystem Configurations and Propensity for Specific Types of Changes in Policy Outputs

Extent of symmetry between community and network	Degree of insulation of network from community	
	High	Low
High	Closed Subsystem tends towards change only in Instrument Components	Resistant Subsystem tends towards change only in Instrument Components and Program Specifications
Low	Contested Subsystem tends towards change only in Policy Instrument Types and Instrument Components	Open Subsystem tends towards change in Instrument Components, Program Specifications, Policy Instrument Types, and Policy Goals

new goals but contestation might lead to some experimentation with new policy instrument types.

Table 20 illustrates how the four main subsystem configurations set out in Table 19 would be expected to be related to the specific types of policy change outlined in Table 17.

Given this analysis of policy change, subsystem structure, and their interrelationships, therefore, the following hypotheses can be formulated with respect to the impact of subsystem structure on policy change:

Hypothesis Hl: As has been argued in the past, subsystems that are asymmetrical and have thin boundaries between their component parts will be open to new actors, hospitable to fresh ideas, and, hence, more likely to develop changes in policy goals than are those which are highly symmetrical and well insulated. These latter subsystems will be closed and inhospitable to new actors and ideas, and will tend to exhibit only changes in policy instrument components or "settings."

Hypothesis H2: Subsystems which have symmetrical issue networks and discourse communities but whose boundaries are fluid will be open to new ideas but dominated by the same actors; thus they will tend to feature changes in instrument components and program specifications.

Hypothesis H3: Subsystems which have asymmetrical issue networks and discourse communities but whose boundaries are fixed will be open to new actors but will tend to be dominated by the same set of ideas, hence they will tend to feature change in instrument types and components.

Testing the Model: Empirical Evidence from Four Canadian Cases 1990–2000

Methodology

Although a complete analysis of these effects would require extensive longitudinal analysis of subsystem membership and interactions based on primary interview data, it is possible to construct a simple preliminary test of the viability of this model from existing secondary data sources.[12]

The first step in this preliminary test, selecting cases for analysis, was determined by a number of criteria. First, existing analyses of associational behaviour suggested factors such as the extent of state involvement play a large role, affecting the range of social actors found in a subsystem and its level of organizational development. In order to control for this variable, a range of domains should be examined with different levels of state involvement and institutionalization (Schmitter and Streeck 1999). Second, given the potential for comparative research, case selection included examples of cases already examined in other countries using similar methodologies. A third criterion was the ease of availability of current and historical data on subsystem composition and membership. Taking these criteria into account, the subsystems chosen for examination in this project at the federal level in Canada were transport, trade, education, and banking. These sectors provide a basis for comparison of older, highly institutionalized sectors – transportation, banking – and newer or less well institutionalized sectors – trade, education – and a basis for comparison with studies completed in other countries – trade, banking.

To avoid overgeneralizing a sector or policy domain and predetermining vague subsystem boundaries,[13] a two-stage strategy was followed in which a large multi-issue sector was examined and then a specific, significant issue selected upon which to focus the analysis. These investigations led to a focus on four specific subsystems centred upon airline deregulation (transport), continental free trade (trade), post-secondary funding (education), and bank deregulation (banking).

Events and occurrences in these areas were examined for the period 1990–2000 and chronologies of policy change were prepared. Policy changes revealed in these chronologies were then classified according to the fourfold taxonomy set out above. The highlights of these chronologies are contained in the appendix.

In order to identify subsystem changes, each issue area was examined in order to assess subsystem membership at the start and end points of the period under investigation. Following the insights and methodologies set out by Grace Skogstad (1985) and Leslie Pal (1993) in earlier investigations, instances where groups and individuals were encouraged and funded to present briefs to parliamentary committees and to relevant commissions and enquiries in the domains under examination were selected for this purpose. "Bookend" situations, which could reasonably be expected to reveal a large percentage of subsystem members, were identified and analysed in terms of changes in membership and activities over the decade. The dimension of subsystem insulation was assessed by examining the number of repeat members of the subsystem present in the total membership at the end of the period; with a high percentage of continuing members indicative of a high degree of insulation. The dimension of symmetry was gauged simply in terms of the percentage increase in the number of subsystem members over time, with a large positive increase indicating a low level of symmetry. The sources on membership changes are also set out in the appendix. Summary figures are provided in Table 21 by membership category type.

The results from these analyses of policy and subsystem membership changes over the period 1990–2000 were then compared in order to establish the nature of the relationship existing between subsystem structure and policy change in each case.[14] The overall picture with respect to the frequency and nature of policy changes in each sector over the decade under investigation is contained in Table 22.

Analysis

Prima facie, the pattern of change found in Table 22 is in keeping with expectations concerning the (in)frequency of paradigmatic change involving shifts in policy goals and program specifications, relative to the frequency of incremental changes involving shifts in instrument types and components. That is, in the four sectors under investigation, only six instances of changes in policy ends occurred over the decade, while

Table 21. Subsystem Membership Change by Sector and Organization Type, 1999–2000

Organization Type	Transport		Trade		Education		Banking		Total
	Start	End	Start	End	Start	End	Start	End	
Government	17	6	3	8	5	17	3	15	74
Industry groups	21	13	19	14	4	18	6	33	128
NGO	1	6	18	6	6	15	1	12	65
Foreign governments	0	0	3	0	0	0	0	0	3
Consultants	0	0	4	1	0	1	0	1	2
Academic/Think tank	8	8	11	10	3	2	0	5	47
Corporate actors	20	22	8	1	3	5	1	51	111
Unions/Associations	0	0	14	2	1	10	0	0	27
Individuals	0	0	0	4	0	32	0	20	56
First Nations	0	0	0	0	0	2	0	0	2
Political parties	1	0	5	0	0	0	0	0	6
Totals	68	55	85	46	22	102	11	137	521

Table 22. Policy Change by Sector, 1990–2000

	Change Type				
	Policy Goals	Program Specifications	Instrument Types	Instrument Components	Total
Transport	0	0	8	7	15
Trade	0	0	5	0	5
Education	0	2	3	6	11
Banking	1	2	1	5	9
Total	1	4	17	18	40

fifty-six instances of changes in basic instrument type or instrument components were found.

Changes in policy subsystem structure over the same period are found in Table 23. Overall, these data reveal a common pattern of substantial fluctuations in subsystem membership. However, they also reveal different patterns of change by sector. Two of the sectors, postsecondary education and banking, had the most significant increases in membership and the lowest percentage of original 1990 members remaining in the 2000 subsystem. Transport and trade, on the other hand, decreased in size and had the highest percentage of original members.

From these results, two principal conclusions can be drawn. First, there was considerable subsystem membership change in each sector.

Table 23. Subsystem Change by Sector, 1990–2000

	Change Type				
	Original Size	End Size	Per cent Change from Original	Number of Original Members Remaining	Remaining Original Member as Percentage of Size	
Transport	68	55	−19	15	27	27
Trade	85	46	−46	9	20	20
Education	22	102	+363	8	8	8
Banking	11	137	+1145	6	4	4

Table 24. Actual Subsystem Change 1990–2000 and Predicted Policy Output Changes

	Actual Pattern of Subsystem Change				
	Expansion/ Contraction (Symmetry)	Membership Continuity (Insulation)	Changes in Subsystem Characteristics	Subsystem Change Type	Expected Type of Policy Change
Transport	−19	27	Increased symmetry, high insulation	Contested to Closed	Instrument Types and Components
Trade	−46	20	Increased symmetry, high insulation	Contested to Closed	Instrument Types and Components
Education	+363	8	Decreased symmetry, low insulation	Resistant to Open	Policy Goals and Program Specifications
Banking	+1145	4	Decreased symmetry, low insulation	Resistant to Open	Policy Goals and Program Specifications

However, the sectors differed in the direction of change, some growing substantially and others shrinking. Second, the membership of the sectors differed, with some retaining a solid core of members while others saw their original membership component shrink. This generates the overall pattern presented in Table 24.

As Table 24 indicates, given the nature of changes in subsystem structure over this decade, if the hypothesized relationships between structure and outputs hold, we would expect changes in transport and trade to be limited to instrument types and components, while the post-secondary education and banking sectors would also change in policy goals and program specifications. The key questions in the assessment of the relationship between subsystem structure and policy change are shown in Table 25.

The hypothesized expectation was for changes in the relationships between issue networks and their communities to be closely correlated with specific types of policy change, as new members and new ideas flowed into subsystem deliberations and altered exchange relationships within networks. The expected relationships between changes in subsystem structure and policy outputs were found to exist in all of the

Table 25. Predicted and Actual Policy Output Changes, 1990–2000

	Policy Changes		Expected vs. actual pattern of subsystem and policy change	
	Policy Goals and Program Specifications	Instrument Type and Components	Expected	Actual
Transport	0	15	Instrument Type and Components	As predicted
Trade	0	5	Instrument Type and Components	As predicted
Education	2	9	Policy Goals and Program Specifications in Addition to Instrument Types and Components	As predicted
Banking	3	6	Policy Goals and Program Specifications in Addition to Instrument Types and Components	As predicted

cases examined here, as changes in policy goals and program specifications occurred only in the two sectors which had substantial growth and had the smallest continuity among core subsystem membership. Sectors with decreases in subsystem size and a high percentage continuity in membership had only alterations in instruments types and components.

Conclusion

The notion of a policy subsystem is a flexible concept designed to capture the complex interplay between actors and institutions, and knowledge and interests, in the policymaking process. It is a critical component of many modern approaches to the study of policymaking such as discourse and network analysis, providing as it does the "glue" linking actors, ideas, and interests together in models of policy processes and choices (Knoke 1993). Network analyses are also becoming an increasingly significant aspect of governmental praxis as planning and policy design move further and further from coercive centralized methods towards the more flexible and complex public management strategies characteristic of the current era of governance (Howlett 2000; Milward and Provan 2000).

A challenge to any of the cornerstones of network analysis has both significant conceptual and practical implications. If network structure affects outcomes in predictable ways, as proponents of this approach attest, then, for example, government efforts at network management can be directed towards specific outcomes and such activities should be an important part of policy design considerations. However, if a network is merely a metaphor to describe actor interrelationships, without any predictable impact on policy outcomes, then network management efforts may not only be inefficient, but misplaced, and further theoretical and conceptual development in this area misguided.

Based on a preliminary analysis of secondary data sources of subsystem membership and output changes in four Canadian federal policy sectors, this chapter found evidence that, in contradiction to the assertions of some prominent critics, subsystem structure was correlated with specific types of policy change. The evidence presented above supports the assertion that subsystem structure is important because when the same core sets of policy actors are involved in defining policy options, the common understanding of a policy problem and the solutions they develop from shared experiences, combined with the durability of subsystem members' interests, promotes "incremental" change. Paradigmatic policy changes representing a significant, though not necessarily total, break from the past policy goals and program specifications, on the other hand, were found to have occurred only when new ideas and interests could penetrate policy subsystems. More precisely, this chapter provided evidence that these patterns of policy change are linked to two specific structural characteristics of policy subsystems, both related to the manner in which discourse communities and interest networks interact within a subsystem. These two dimensions of subsystem structure – the degree of insulation of the network from non-"interest-related" actors, and the extent of symmetry existing between communities and networks – proved to be significant inhibitors and facilitators of policy change.

This analysis, then, provides support for the arguments of adherents of the network approach to policy studies. It suggests that the presence of a specific kind of network in a given policy sector reveals a great deal about the propensity for it to experience intra- or inter-paradigmatic types of policy change. Hence the evidence from the four Canadian cases examined here suggests that "networks do matter," and that continued research in this vein can fruitfully contribute to addressing questions and issues raised in the study and practice of modern governance.

Appendix: Data Sources and Summaries

Federal Transport (Airline Deregulation) Policy Change

POLICY GOALS

Pre-1990: The federal government wants a new legislative framework for Canadian transportation that will minimize government control over shippers and carriers while ensuring that the public interest is met. Competition will be emphasized. Dispute resolution will be streamlined and made less cumbersome. A new regulatory agency will be smaller and more accessible. The emphasis will be on providing transportation services at the lowest possible cost, subject only to the overriding priority of a high level of safety. The thrust of these proposals, reliance on competition and market forces rather than regulations, is clearly the wave of the future.

PROGRAM SPECIFICATIONS

Pre-1990: Divesture and leasing of air operations, transforming the role of government from owner/subsidizer/operator to landlord/regulator; implementation of an aviation policy process that is transparent and accessible; economic restructuring, privatization, and commercialization of Canada's air navigation system; expansion in domestic and international air services and routes – globalization of airways; government deregulation in regards to domestic licensing criteria, domestic tariffs, and confidential private contracts in air industry.

INSTRUMENT TYPES

1992: National Airports Policy.
1994: Airport Transfer Act 1992 (Misc. Acts).
1995: International Air Policy Initiatives.
1995: Various "Open Skies Agreements" (most notably with the United States).
1995: Bilateral International Air Relations with various countries.
1996: Civil Air Navigation Services Commercialization Act.

1996: National Transportation Act/Canadian Transportation Act, 1996.

1988–2000: Privatization of Air Canada and its subsequent merger with Canadian Airlines.

INSTRUMENT COMPONENTS

1994–7: National Airport Policy plans to commercialize as many as 149 airports under the jurisdiction of Transport Canada; to ensure smooth implementation of the National Airports Policy, the federal government introduced measures in 1996 to allow greater flexibility in the negotiation of lease arrangements with Canadian Airport Authorities, such as payment plans for movable property and rent-free periods for smaller airports. In addition, the government announced that the Airports Capital Assistance Program would be made available to some subsidized airports – this was not previously the case – and would assist eligible airports in financing capital projects related not only to safety, but also to asset protection and operating cost reduction.

1994: Establishment of the Open Skies Agreement and the International Air Policy Initiatives (December 1994). Expansion of domestic and international air services.

1996: Creation of a new regulatory agency – the Canadian Transportation Agency (formerly known as the National Transportation Agency).

1997: The federal government put into place a four-year Aviation Fuel Excise Tax Rebate Program under which airline companies carrying on business in Canada would be able to obtain a rebate of up to $20 million a year on aviation fuel excise taxes. In exchange they would give up their entitlement to claim losses against income subject to tax, for up to ten dollars of their accumulated tax losses for every one dollar of rebate received. In addition, companies could later choose to repay the rebate received and fully reinstate the losses they had previously exchanged.

1998: NavCanada two-stage implementation of fee structure.

1998: More frequent use of code sharing with foreign alliance partners, which allows Canadian carriers a presence in a vastly increased number of markets without having to provide their own aircraft.

Sources: Donald Mazankowski, *Freedom to Move: A Framework for Regulatory Reform* (Ottawa: Supply and Services Canada, 1985); Mary R. Brooks,

Monitoring Transportation Regulatory Reform (Oceans Institute of Canada, 1988); *Transportation in Canada: Annual Review* (Ottawa: Public Works and Government Services Canada, various years); *Sustainable Transportation in Canada* (National Roundtable on the Environment and the Economy, 1996); Transport Canada, "Transport Canada's Planning Outlook to the Mid 1980s" (Strategic Planning Group, September 1981); John Christopher, "Background Paper: Transportation Issues In Canada" (Ottawa: Supply and Services Canada, 1992 and 1994); Transport Canada, Strategic Plan for Transportation Safety and Security, 1999 (http://www.tc.gc.ca/tcss/main_e.htm); and Transport Canada, Sustainable Development Strategy 1997 (http://www.tc.gc.ca/en/ap.htm).

NETWORK STRUCTURE
Sources: Canada, House of Commons, Special Committee on Canada-United States Air Transport Services, Minutes of Proceedings and Evidence, Ottawa: Queen's Printer 1990–1, 34 Parl. Session 2, 1990; and Canada, House of Commons, Report of the Standing Committee on Transport, Restructuring Canada's Airline Industry: Fostering Competition and Protecting the Public Interest, December 1999.

Federal Trade (Continental Free Trade) Policy Change

POLICY GOALS
Pre-1990: Trade liberalization.

PROGRAM SPECIFICATIONS
Pre-1990: Extension of trade liberalization through multilateral and bilateral agreements.

INSTRUMENT TYPES
1993: Signing of North American Free Trade Agreement.
1994: Revising the norms of the international economic regime through World Trade Organization.
1996: Signing of international treaties on extra-North American free trade – Israel.
1997: Signing of international treaties on extra-North American free trade – Chile.
1998: Signing of the Multilateral Agreement on Investment (MAI). Instrument Components
Pre-1990: Establishment of tariff reducing treaties with quasi-judicial dispute arbitration.

Sources: Department of Foreign Affairs and International Trade, "Trade Negotiations and Agreements" (http://www.dfait-maeci.ca/tna-nac/menu-e.asp); World Trade Organization, "Trade Policy Review. Canada" (Geneva: WTO, 1990, 1992, 1994, 1996, 1998, 2000).

NETWORK STRUCTURE

Sources: Canada, House of Commons, Minutes of Proceedings and Evidence of the Sub-Committee on International Trade of the Standing Committee on External Affairs and International Trade Respecting Business of the Sub-Committee Pursuant to Standing Order 108(2), Consideration of the Current GATT Negotiations, June and October 1991; Canada, Department of External Affairs and International Trade, Public Consultation on FTAA and WTO Negotiations, May 20, 1999.

Federal-Provincial Post-Secondary Education (Funding) Policy Change

POLICY GOALS

Pre-1990: Post-secondary education should be accessible and affordable for all Canadians.

PROGRAM SPECIFICATIONS

1995: Canada Financial Assistance Act introduced. The federal government entered into risk-share agreements with nine lending institutions for the financing and delivery of student assistance.

1996: Bankruptcy and Insolvency Act amended. Students are unable to include their Canada Student Loan in a bankruptcy proceeding within two years after completing studies.

INSTRUMENT TYPES

1993: Introduction of interest subsidy for full-time students with Canadian Student Loans.

1996: Federal government introduced the Canada Health and Social Transfer (CHST) to replace all existing transfer programs for post-secondary education, health care, and social assistance.

1996: Canada Millennium Scholarship Program introduced. The program aims to increase access by defraying (through a $2,000 scholarship) some of the costs of post-secondary education.

INSTRUMENT COMPONENTS

1990: Federal government announced that the amount of the Established Programs Financing per capita cash transfer would be frozen

for all provinces – to be frozen for a two-year period but later extended for three additional years.

1994: Federal loan limit for full-time students increased from $110 per
week to $165 per week.

1995: Interest Relief Plan amended. Interest relief benefits extended
from eighteen months to a maximum of thirty months for borrowers
with Canada Student Loans.

1998: CHST funding level increases during this period reflect commitment of federal government to address the severe challenges facing
the health care and provincial education systems.

1998: Interest Relief Plan amended by adjusting income thresholds in
the eligibility criteria, thus allowing more borrowers to benefit.

1998: Bankruptcy and Insolvency Act amended. Students are unable
to include their Canada Student Loan in a bankruptcy proceeding
within ten years after completing studies.

*Sources: Canadian Federation of Students, A Blueprint for Access: An Alter-
native for Accessible, High Quality Post Secondary Education* (Ottawa: CFS,
1997); Finance Canada, "Federal Transfers to the Provinces and Territories" (www.fin.gc.ca/FEDPROV/hise.html); David C. Smith, Programs
of the Canada Millennium Scholarship Foundation: Issues, Options
and Suggested Directions. December 1998; Statistics Canada, Education
Quarterly Review, 5, 4 (1999); Paul Boothe, "Finding a Balance: Renew-
ing Canadian Fiscal Federalism" (C.D. Howe Institute Benefactors Lecture, Toronto, 1998); and Canada Millennium Scholarship Foundation,
"Millennium Scholarships" (http://www.millenniumscholarships.ca).

NETWORK STRUCTURE
Sources: Canada, House of Commons, Report of the Standing Committee on National Finance, Federal Policy on Post-Secondary Education, March 1987; and Canada, Senate. Special Senate Committee
on Post-Secondary Education, A Senate Report on Post-Secondary
Education in Canada, 1997 (http://www.parl.gc.ca/36/1/parlbus/
commbuYte/com-e/post-e/rep-e/repfinaldec97-e.htm).

Federal Banking (Deregulation) Policy Change

POLICY GOALS
1995: While general market stability and consumer/liability protec-
tions were the crucial concerns in the past, in the 1990s competitive-
ness and efficiency emerged as the dominant goals.

PROGRAM SPECIFICATIONS

1992: Bank Act amended. The 1992 amendments, which involved a substantial rewrite of the Bank Act, continued the process of dissolving the traditional pillars of federal banking policy by erasing many of the limitations on financial service providers' right to offer services outside of their domain either through the purchase of subsidiaries already active in other sectors or in some cases directly through new "in-house" powers.

1998–9: The legislation of new rules which allow foreign banks to operate branches in Canada directly (which was announced in the 1997 changes to the Bank Act) were finally tabled and passed.

INSTRUMENT TYPES

1996: Two advisory bodies were formed to help direct future changes to the financial services sector: The Payments System Advisory Committee and the Payments System Advisory Committee (est. August 1996) which was co-chaired by the Department of Finance and the Bank of Canada.

INSTRUMENT COMPONENTS

1992: Banks could now own insurance companies.

1992: Widely held non-bank financial service providers (trust companies, schedule II banks without the required ten-year divestiture) were now allowed to "network" different financial services offered by subsidiary or parent companies.

1992: Trust, loan, and life insurance companies now had full consumer and commercial lending powers (which only banks had in the past). Reciprocally, a two-year phase-out was announced for the non-interest-bearing reserves that banks were required to hold but other financial service providers were not. Also banks could now offer portfolio management and investment advice directly.

1994: The non-interest-bearing reserve requirement for banks was eliminated as per the 1992 amendments to the Bank Act. Under the terms of the North American Free Trade Agreement, size restrictions on foreign bank operations were lifted for Mexican banks.

1997: Bank Act amended for a second time in the decade as required by the five-year sunset clause implemented in 1987. The changes intended to fine-tune and extend the changes made in 1992: several new provisions designed to protect consumer privacy. Banks not engaged in retail deposit taking were now allowed to opt out of membership in the deposit insurance agency.

Sources: Charles Freedman, "The Canadian Banking System," revised version of a paper delivered at the Conference on Developments in the Financial System: National and International Perspectives, The Jerome Levy Economics Institute of Bard College, New York, 1997; Charles Freedman, "Financial Structure in Canada: The Movement Towards Universal Banking," in *Universal Banking: Financial System Design Reconsidered*, ed. A. Saunders and I. Winter (Chicago: Irwin Professional Publishing, 1996), 724–36; Charles Freedman, "Universal Banking: The Canadian View," in *Financial Regulation; Changing the Rules of the Game*, ed. D. Vittas (Washington: World Bank, 1992), 369–90; and Charles Freedman and Charles Goodlet, "The Financial Services Sector: Past Changes and Future Prospects," background paper for the Ditchley Canada Conference, Toronto, 1997.

NETWORK STRUCTURE

Sources: Canada, House of Commons Sub-Committee on Financial Institutions Legislation of the Standing Committee on Finance, Minutes of Proceedings and Evidence of the Sub-Committee on Financial Institutions Legislation of the Standing Committee on Finance (Ottawa: Queen's Printer 1991–3); and Canada, Senate, Report of the Standing Senate Committee on Banking, Trade and Commerce, "A Blueprint for Change: Response to the Report of the Task Force on the Future of the Canadian Financial Sector" (http://www.parl.gc.ca/36/1/parlbus/commbus/senate/com-e/bank-e/rep-e/rep17dec98-e.htm)

5 Decision Making – Analysing Multi-Actor, Multi-Round Public Policy Decision-Making Processes in Government: Findings from Five Canadian Cases

Introduction

Some public policy decisions made by governments are fairly simple. The parameters and outcomes of a decision may be well known, the number of actors involved quite small and hence the uncertainty and risk associated with different possible courses of action easily calculated (Morgan and Henrion 1990; Payne, Bettman, and Johnson 1993). Unfortunately these conditions, which may be present in many private and public management situations, rarely hold in practice when it comes to public policymaking (Jones 1994, 2002). Instead, public policymakers typically face situations in which decisions are taken in complex administrative and legislative settings involving multiple actors and often involving multiple levels of institutions, either intra- or intergovernmental or both. In these situations, as Carol Weiss first noted, multiple actors interact in different "arenas" and decision making typically takes place in multiple "rounds" or phases in which individual decisions in each round accrete to generate a final result (Weiss 1980). These complex settings add a great deal of uncertainty to decision making and affect the nature and type of outcomes which result from such processes. Understanding how decision making in such complex structures occurs, and not mistaking them for simpler processes, is a prerequisite for understanding policymaking in modern societies.

Only very recently, however, have public policy researchers begun to grapple with these complex public policy decision-making processes (Richardson 1999; Teisman 2000; From 2002). Contemporary European, especially Dutch, analysts have begun to examine the nature of the impasses and breakout processes which characterize decision-making rounds in the effort to better prescribe the kinds of network management activities governments can use to navigate their way through such processes (de Bruijn and ten Heuvelhof 2000 and 2002; From 2002; Van Bueren, Klijn, and Koppenjan 2003; Van Merode et al. 2004).[15] In so doing, they have generated a body of concepts, hypotheses, and cases which can be compared against Canadian evidence to help shed light on the workings of this understudied decision-making style.[16]

These studies provide a set of initial hypotheses concerning accretion-type public policy decision-making processes which can be refined and tested in the Canadian case. From, in particular, concluded that in a successful decision accretion process:

1. Government actors are the main agenda setters responsible for initiatives and activities which drive decision processes towards their conclusion;
2. An initiating government actor takes on different roles at different stages of the decision-making process and behaves differently at each stage; and
3. The internal organizational characteristics of the initiating agency play a significant role in affecting the capacity of the agency to successfully undertake these roles and hence shape the final outcome in accordance with their preferences (adapted from From 2002).

Although From does not develop similar observations concerning the behaviour of non-governmental actors in these processes, others such as Koppenjan and Klijn (2004) have worked in this area (Billings and Hermann 1998; see also Agranoff and McGuire 2003). One of their findings is that while government behaviour may vary by stage of the policy process, it is relatively constant throughout successive rounds compared to non-governmental actor behaviour, which can be more volatile and change in different rounds in order to better influence outcomes. Non-governmental actor behaviour, they argue, is linked to the nature of the resources different non-governmental actors have at their disposal, their interest in an issue, and the stage at which deliberations on that issue are proceeding (Van Bueren, Klijn, and Koppenjan 2003).[17]

Combining elements of From's observations on the role played by government actors and those of Koppenjan and Klijn on non-governmental ones allows us to set out several testable hypotheses regarding expected patterns of policy actor behaviour in successful multi-actor, multi-round "decision accretion" public policy decision making:

H1: That (a) the number of governmental actors and their activity level will remain relatively constant throughout successive rounds while (b) non-governmental actors flow in and out of different rounds depending on their perception of their interests, their resource capacities, their estimations of likely policy outcomes, and their interpretations of the existing state of play of ongoing policy processes;

H2: That the participation of major non-governmental actors in successive rounds is inversely related to their congruence with government aims. Issue areas with significant discordance between government and non-governmental actors' aims and interests will witness higher levels of non-governmental participation;

H3: That the activities of non-governmental actors will change as rounds progress from a focus on influencing the context or environment of decision making (e.g. public opinion or media) in early rounds to one concerned with influencing decision makers in later rounds as discussions become more detailed, focused, technical, and legalistic.

In what follows below, these hypotheses are tested against evidence gleaned from online newspaper and media index services concerning actor interactions in five cases of multi-round decision making in Canada over the period 1995–2005: amendments to the Indian Act, the creation of species at risk legislation, alterations to the Bank Act, the extension of Freedom of Information legislation to the private sector, and efforts to develop a Free Trade Area of the Americas Agreement (FTAA). The reasons for choosing these cases and the methods followed in collecting the data are set out below.

The Concept of a Public Policy Decision-Making Style

In his early work on the subject of public policy decision making, John Forester argued that a limited set of contextual variables led to a distinct set of discrete decision-making "styles" with significant impact of the nature and type of decisions which emerged from each decision-making process. As he put it in a 1984 article:

> Depending upon the conditions at hand, a strategy may be practical or ridiculous. With time, expertise, data, and a well-defined problem, technical calculations may be in order; without time, data, definition, and expertise, attempting those calculations could well be a waste of time. In a complex organizational environment, intelligence networks will be as, or

more, important than documents when information is needed. In an environment of inter-organizational conflict, bargaining and compromise may be called for. Administrative strategies are sensible only in a political and organizational context. (Forester 1984: 25)

Forester suggested that, ultimately, decision-making styles varied according to six key contextual variables: first, the number of *agents* (decision makers); second, the organizational *setting*; third, the degree to which the organizational setting is *isolated* from other organizations; fourth, the degree to which the *problem* is well defined; fifth, the availability of complete, accessible, and comprehensible *information* on the problem and potential solutions; and, finally, the amount of *time available* to make a decision (Forester 1984). To the extent these six conditions define the context of a decision-making process, he argued, different styles of decision making, and different results, would prevail.

Forester's model generates too many possible permutations to be of much use in empirical studies. However, more recently, Howlett and Ramesh (2003) proposed a simplifying taxonomy of decision-making styles based on Forester's work which is more useful in this regard. Combining "agent" and "setting" into a single variable related to the *complexity of policy context*, and the notions of the "problem," "information," and "time" resources into a single variable relating to the *severity of the resource constraints* placed upon decision makers, this model provides a clearer portrayal of the impact of contextual variables on decision-making styles and outcomes. Table 26 outlines the four basic decision-making styles that emerge on the basis of this analysis.

In this model, traditional *rational decision making*, in which outcomes are expected to be optimal or maximizing, occurs only in a type I environment, where "bounded rationality" prevails and the policy context is simple and constraints are low (Simon 1991). Lindblom-style *incremental decision making*, where the outcome is likely to result only in a marginal shift from the status quo, is more likely to occur in a type II environment, where the policy context is still fairly simple but constraints on decision makers are higher. Both of these styles, of course, are well known and their parameters and consequences have been more or less fully explored (Lindblom 1959; Carley 1980; Berry 1990; Cahill and Overman 1990; Simon 1991; Hayes 1992; Weiss and Woodhouse 1992; Bendor 1995).

While these two types of decision making may be quite common in routine business and public administration, however, they are much

Table 26. Basic Decision-Making Styles after Howlett and Ramesh

	Complexity of the Policy Context	
Severity of Constraints on Decision Makers	Low (Single or limited actor, single setting)	High (Multi-actor, multi-setting)
Low (Clear problem definition, available information, available time)	TYPE I "Rational" decision making	TYPE III Multiple-round, "decision-accretion" decision making
High (Poor problem definition, limited information, limited time)	TYPE II "Incremental" decision making	TYPE IV Heuristic, bureaucratic politics or "garbage can" decision making

less common in public policy decision making, where decisions typically involve multiple actors in multiple settings (Howlett and Ramesh 2003). Decision making in more complex environments falls into types III and IV and is much less well studied and understood. When these complex multi-actor, multi-setting processes have been examined, it has often been in the case of heuristic-driven foreign policy decision making, especially decisions to go to war, which are often severely time constrained and hence fall into type IV (Mintz 1997; Mintz and Geva 1997). Allison's work on the Cuban Missile Crisis and the subsequent research it engendered on bureaucratic politics is an example of work which has dealt with decision making in this environment (Allison 1969, 1971; Allison and Halperin 1972; Bendor and Hammond 1992). Cohen, March, and Olsen's work on *garbage can decision making* is probably the best known in this area (Cohen, March, and Olsen 1979; March and Olsen 1979; see also Mucciaroni 1992; Bendor, Moe, and Shotts 2001; Olsen 2001). All of these analyses emphasize the contingent and somewhat unpredictable, or "irrational," nature of the decisions which emerge from these processes. However, again, while it is clear that type IV processes may characterize some public policy decision-making contexts, it is not clear that these are in any way typical of decision making in this area.

The fourth type of decision making, that of complex multi-actor, multi-setting *decision-accretion decision making* in a relatively unconstrained environment (type III) remains very much underinvestigated (Agranoff and McGuire 2003), despite its very common appearance in governments, especially multilevel ones featuring legislation-based policymaking (Weiss 1980; Steunenberg and Schmidtchen 2000). This is a significant lacuna in the public policy literature since this decision-making style, like the others, can be expected to carry its own consequences for the nature of the policy outcomes which emerge from such processes.

That is, each of these four styles carries with it important implications for the types of decisions likely to emerge from public policy decision-making deliberations. Type I, rational decision making, as discussed above, attempts to maximize or optimize resources and generate technically efficient solutions to public policy problems (Sanderson 2002a). Type II, incremental processes are biased towards conservatism or the marginal adjustment of the status quo (Hayes 1992). And type IV, garbage can processes, are, at best, satisfycing and also possibly chaotic and random (Mucciaroni 1992). But what of decision-accretion processes? While deliberative, they are inherently political, and hence can be expected to combine rational and irrational elements in final decisions, as does incrementalism, but with less consistently predictable results, allowing for large swings in decisions depending on the nature of the "vetopoints" and other characteristics of actor behaviours available and exercised in each round (Tsebelis 1990; Scharpf 1991). Unlike garbage can processes, however, these rounds are structured and formalized, and outcomes are neither random nor purely contingent, but rather the result of careful but complexly structured multi-actor deliberations. But is this all we can say about this very common public policy decision-making style and its likely impact on policy outcomes?

Public policymaking in Canada provides a good test case for advancing our understanding of these type III processes. With its complex, legislature-based federal system, multi-actor, multilevel, multi-round decision making is quite common (Scharpf 1994; Grande 1996; Howlett 1999; Peters and Pierre 2001). Analysing such processes in Canada can help us understand the factors which contribute to type III policy outcomes and the implications and impact such processes have on subsequent policy outcomes.

Method and Case Selection

The research program for this study is based upon that set out by European analysts, such as Van Bueren, Klijn, and Koppenjan (2003) and From (2002), in their studies of Dutch multi-round decision making. Using newspaper accounts of policy development "events," it traces the pattern of development of specific policy outcomes and decision processes at the federal level in Canada and assesses the accuracy of existing conclusions in the literature regarding the structuring and outcomes of multiple arena decision making.[18] It identifies common patterns of actor behaviour in each round in order to illuminate the variables and factors which facilitate or inhibit successful decision-accretion decision making and tests the extent to which the hypotheses derived from European cases can be transferred to different national contexts.

Methodology

The methodology followed in this investigation involved (1) identifying a number of cases to be investigated as examples of existing

Canadian multi-actor, multi-round policy decision-making processes; (2) constructing chronologies and descriptions of those processes over the past decade; (3) constructing databases of actors and actor activities in each selected case; and (4) analysing the results against the expectations derived from the existing literature on the subject.

The research program proceeded in two stages. In phase I, chronologies of selected public policy decision-making cases were constructed and inventories of the actors and activities involved in each decision-making round were established. In phase II, the main activity involved testing several of the observations generated from European cases against evidence from the Canadian cases. The similarities and discrepancies between the hypothesized and observed decision-making behaviour were then analysed.

Case Selection Criteria

The policy domains chosen for examination in this project were environment, aboriginal affairs, trade, banking, and privacy. Decision-making processes in these areas related to adoption of (1) species at risk legislation (SARA); (2) reforms to the Indian Act (DIA); (3) the development of the Free Trade Area of the Americas Agreement (FTAA); (4) reforms to the Bank Act; and (5) the extension of freedom of information (FOI) and privacy legislation to the private sector.

The choice of cases to be examined in this evaluation is, of course, critical (Eckstein 1975; George 1979). A number of criteria determined the selection of cases. First, all featured ongoing and active multi-actor, multi-round decision-making processes. Second, the selection of policy domains reflected processes for which at least one round was well under way rather than those still under consideration or just beginning. Third, given the need to compare Canadian cases with the results of similar studies in other countries, case selection included examples of cases examined in other countries using similar methodologies. Fourth, case selection was related to the ease of availability of current and historical data on activities in the area concerned.

Data

Chronologies of decision-making processes in each domain were gleaned from records of legislative activity in each of the five issue areas covering 1988–2005, the period for which electronic records of

Table 27. Key Dates of Legislative Activity for Five Canadian Cities

Issue Round	Bank 1	Bank 2	Bank 3		FOI 1	FOI 2	FOI 3
Legislation/proposal	Pre-1992 changes	C38/C8	2006		1993	c-6	c-201
Date	Pre-1992	1993–2001	Post-2001		Pre-1993	1994 – 2001	2002 – 2005
Issue Round	FTAA 1	FTAA 2	DIA 1	DIA 2	SARA 1	SARA 2	SARA 3
Legislation/proposal	Pre-1999	Post-1999	c-31	c-31, c-7, c-6	c-65	c-33	c-5
Date	Pre-1999	Post-1999	Pre-2002	Post-2002	Pre-1997	1998 – 2000	2001 – 2002

actor activity are available (see Appendix 1 for sources and keywords searched). Inventories of policy actors and actor activities in each round were established through the coding of newspaper reports and records of parliamentary, judicial, and administrative activity in the domain over the period. Subject searches of media indices generated lists of reports related to each topic. Reports which mentioned specific policy actors were retained. Each report was coded for, among other things, the number, nature, and type of actors involved in an event; the type of event; the target of policy-relevant activity; and other information related to policy activity and actor behaviour. Duplicate reports of the same event were combined to identify additional actors. In total, 2,654 discrete actor events were identified in the five subject areas (see Appendix 4).

Inspection of legislative policy chronologies constructed for each case identify several key rounds in each issue area in the discussion, and, ultimately, adoption, of legislation in these areas (see Table 27 and Appendix 2 for a description and characterization of these changes). Key points in rounds coincide with the introduction or withdrawal of legislative proposals which, ultimately, are the focus of actor activity in these spheres.[19]

Appendix 3 records the aggregate level of actor activity in each unique event or instance of actor policy-oriented behaviour coded in the database. Each of these cases is either left censored or right censored, or both, in the sense that the evaluation was driven by the availability of online data, so each record provides a snapshot of an ongoing policy process. However, in all cases, at least a ten-year record was available and evidence of round-type activity was observable in each case. As Figure 26 shows, prima facie, each case involves significant fluctuations in the level of actor activity over the time period examined, consistent with the basic rounds hypothesis and the number of rounds identified in Table 27. As expected, SARA shows three peaks, FTAA one, the Bank Act three, DIA one, and FOI three.

Analysis

Evaluating Hypothesis 1

Evaluating hypothesis 1 requires first establishing that decision rounds in the Canadian federal context are linked to different levels of governmental and non-governmental activity. The initial description provided

Figure 26: Actor Policy Activity for Five Canadian Cases – By Year

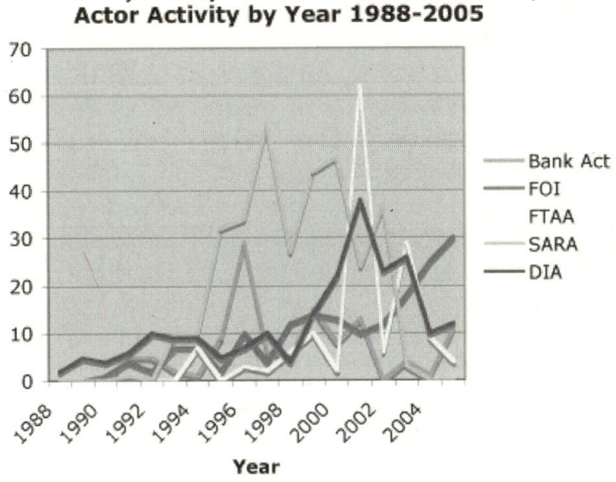

Actor Activity by Year 1988-2005

in Figure 26 and Table 28 show that there are definite patterns of increased and decreased activity in each issue area linked to legislative timetables. However, this does not in itself reveal the extent to which each cycle is affected by either or both of increased/decreased governmental or non-governmental actor activity. In order to answer this concern, it is necessary to disaggregate each case by actor and look at patterns of activity on the part of each category of actor in each year (see Appendix 3). Table 28 provides measures of dispersion and range of actor activity.

As Table 28 shows, the mean number of government actors in all but one case (FOI) is less than that of non-governmental actors. In some cases (SARA, FTAA, Bank Act), this volatility is quite pronounced, with NGO activity exceeding that of governments by a factor or two or more, while in one case (DIA), it is only slightly greater. The apparently anomalous FOI case can be explained by the primarily intra-governmental nature of this issue, meaning that, in this case, many of what would typically be outside interests affected by government actions are, in fact, governmental ones. This suggests that, rather than a consistent pattern, as From and others have suggested, the variation in

Table 28. Range and Variation of Government and NGO Actors 1988–2005

Field/Actor	N (Years)	Minimum # of actors per year	Maximum # of actors per year	Mean	Std. Deviation	Govt mean as a % NGO
SARAGOV	11	2.00	18.00	10.2	6.3	51.56
SARANGO	12	1.00	36.00	17.4	12.2	
FOIGOV	16	1.00	17.00	6.8	5.3	137.13
FOINGO	13	1.00	14.00	4.82	3.8	
FTAAGOV	10	1.00	20.00	6.5	6.8	52.33
FTAANGO	9	1.00	42.00	8.33	13.00	
DIAGOV	16	1.00	14.00	5.7	4.14	74.26
DIANGO	18	2.00	25.00	6.9	5.6	
BANKGOV	13	.00	6.00	2.5	1.8	28.33
BANKNGO	13	.00	23.00	6.3	6.4	
Total Govt					17.63	75.34
Total NGO					23.40	

Figure 27: Governmental and Non-Governmental Actor Activity by Issue Area and Year

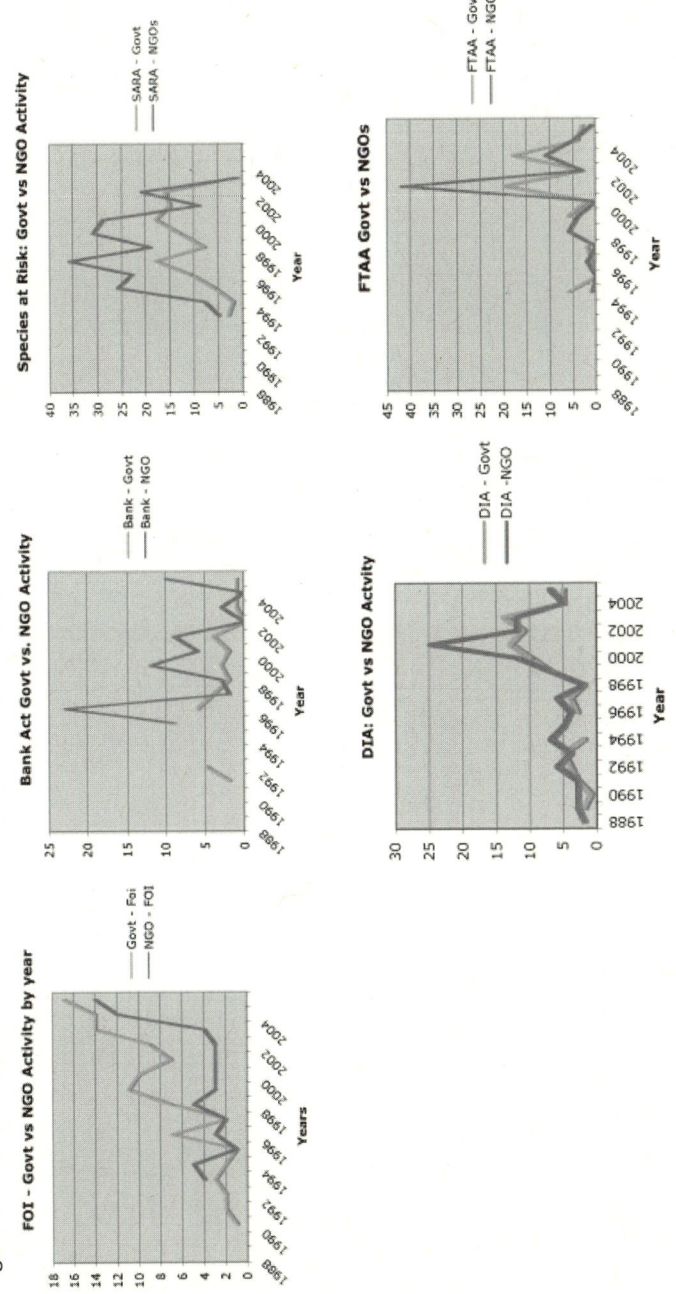

actor activity in different issue areas per round varies with the type of issue at stake and the interest actors have in it.[20]

Figure 27 sheds more light on these patterns of activity, breaking down government and NGO involvement in policy events on an annual basis. It reveals a more complex pattern of interactions in each issue area than is revealed by simply examining the range of overall level of actor behaviour over the entire period examined. With the exception of the Bank Act, it shows that in most cases – SARA, DIA, and FTAA – government and NGO activity closely parallel each other each year, with levels of NGO activity usually greater than government activity. Even in the FOI case, of course, governmental activity also moved cyclically, although remaining greater than NGO activity except for the earliest (pre-1996) phase of activity.

These patterns reveal the general ebb and flow of governmental and NGO activity anticipated in hypothesis 1, with governmental actors remaining generally less active than non-governmental ones in all issue areas except FOI.

Evaluating Hypothesis 2

Evaluating this hypothesis requires a comparison of the level of NGO support/opposition to a proposal vis-à-vis that of governments. The general situation is set out in Tables 29 and 30, first in absolute terms and then expressed as a percentage of each actor's activity.

The tables show, for each case, that:

1. SARA had the highest level of participation in rounds one and two, when both government and non-governmental actors opposed the bill being presented. However, in round three, the NGOs supported the bill and the number of actors dropped dramatically.
2. Banking had its highest level of participation in·round two, when both governments and NGOs supported the proposed bill.
3. FOI participation was highest in rounds two and three, when NGOs generally opposed proposed legislation.
4. DIA participation was highest in round one, when NGOs were completely opposed to the bill being put forward and governments overwhelmingly in favour.
5. FTAA activity was highest in round two, when governments were highly in favour of the bill and NGOs were overwhelmingly opposed.

Table 29. Actor Type and Issue Support by Round

Issue	SARA			Bank			FOI			DIA		FTAA	
Round	1	2	3	1	2	3*	1	2	3	1	2	1	2
Govt Pro	11	16	5	4	10	0	28	23	23	9	28	9	41
Govt Con	18	22	24	2	0	0	6	20	23	0	1	0	14
Total Govt	29	38	29	6	10	0	34	43	46	9	29	9	55
NGO Pro	9	5	15	3	14	0	7	16	19	5	13	5	13
NGO Con	78	73	10	1	8	0	64	7	10	5	19	5	51
Total NGO	87	78	25	4	22	0	71	23	29	10	32	10	64
Total N (Actors)	116	116	54	10	32	0	105	66	75	19	61	19	119

* Bank Act revisions round three samples very small and statements neutral or too vague to code.

Table 30. Actor Type and Issue Support by Round (per cent)

Issue	SARA			Bank			FOI			DIA		FTAA	
Round	1	2	3	1	2	3*	1	2	3	1	2	1	2
Govt Pro	38	42	17	43	100	0	67	53	50	82	97	100	75
Govt Con	62	58	83	57	0	0	33	47	50	18	3	0	25
Total Govt	100	100	100	100	100	0	100	100	100	100	100	100	100
NGO Pro	10	6	60	67	64	0	75	70	66	10	41	50	20
NGO Con	90	94	40	33	36	0	25	30	34	90	59	50	80
Total NGO	100	100	100	100	100	0	100	100	100	100	100	100	100

* Bank Act revisions round three samples very small and statements neutral or too vague to code.

This means that only two cases – DIA and FTAA – fit the expected relationship of governmental and non-governmental incongruence set out in the hypothesis derived from From's work. FOI also fits the pattern, but reversed, as would be expected given the findings related to hypothesis 1, with higher levels of activity when NGOs were in favour of the legislation and governments opposed. In the other two cases, banking and SARA, NGO opposition also resulted in high activity rates, but in conjunction with government opposition.

This provides only partial confirmation of hypothesis 2, that is, in all cases the most significant determinant of high levels of NGO activity was opposition to proposed legislation. However, this appeared to be a factor regardless of the level of government support or opposition; actor interests may be seen as an important determinant of activity levels, but in an absolute fashion rather than a relative one. The positions held by governmental actors did not appear to be a major determinant of NGO activity levels.

Evaluating Hypothesis 3

The final hypothesis to be tested concerns what kinds of resources actors bring to successive rounds in a decision-accretion decision-making situation. The general types of activities all actors engaged in are set out in absolute terms in Appendix 4 in terms of the type of actors targeted by these activities. The data show that most actors engaged in multiple activities and that the most frequently used appeals were directed towards the media, public, and directly at decision makers. Much less frequent were appeals to parliamentary committees, Parliament itself, and the judiciary. These last three areas in total involved little more than 15 per cent of all actor activity.

Table 31 aggregates activities directed at the public and the media and those more directly focused on decision makers, including those directed at committees, decision makers themselves, parliamentarians, and members of the judiciary, by issue area. The figures for these two remaining categories of activities are displayed as a percentage of total actor activity by round.

With the exception of the FTAA and SARA cases, the overall pattern that emerges shows little variation in the targets of activities by issue area, despite the very different overall levels of activity found in each round. On average, activities were directed almost evenly between the public at large and political elites, regardless of the stage of the decision

Table 31. Aggregated Types of Actor Activity by Rounds and Issue Areas (per cent)

Issue Area	Rounds	Public/Media	Comm/Dec./Parl.
DIA	1	46	54
	2	53	47
FOI	1	40	60
	2	40	60
	3	44	53
Bank	1	57	43
	2	55	45
	3	42	48
FTAA	1	17	83
	2	64	36
SARA	1	63	37
	2	60	40
	3	36	64

process. In the SARA case, more attention was paid in earlier rounds to the public and more towards elites in the last round, as might be expected if hypothesis 3 was correct. The FTAA case also shows some evidence of this occurring.

However, it is also necessary to examine these findings in terms of each major category of actor involved. This data is set out in Table 32.

These data show significant differences in the use of public and elite influencing resources on the part of the two major types of actors involved in these decisions. In all cases, there is no evidence of substantial changes in NGO strategy between earlier and later rounds. With the exception of the FOI case, the NGO focus was always on the public/media regardless of the issue area or round, ranging from a high of 75 per cent in round one of the Bank Act revisions in 1992 to a low of just under 60 per cent in several cases.

The FOI case remains anomalous, but still has NGO activity evenly divided between public and elite influencing during all three rounds of the decision process.

Table 32. Aggregated Types of Actor Activity by Rounds and Main Category of Actor (per cent)

			Print/Media Target	Comm/Dec./ Parl. Target
			(%)	(%)
SARA	C-65	Gov	54	46
		NGO	65	35
	C-33	Gov	56	44
		NGO	62	38
	C-5	Gov	39	61
		NGO	66	34
DIA	C-31	Gov	65	35
		NGO	53	47
	C-7, C-6	Gov	52	48
		NGO	58	42
FTAA	pre-1999	Gov	59	41
		NGO	60	40
	post-1999	Gov	49	51
		NGO	62	38
FOI	1993	Gov	30	70
		NGO	50	50
	2001	Gov	40	60
		NGO	43	57
	c-201	Gov	41	59
		NGO	53	47
BANK	1992	Gov	78	22
		NGO	75	25
	2001	Gov	51	49
		NGO	70	30
	2006	Gov	100	0
		NGO	58	42

Government activity shows more variation, ranging from a low of 30 per cent of efforts directed towards the public in the first round of the FOI case, to a high of 100 per cent in the final round of the Bank Act case. However, with the exception of the Bank Act case (and less so the FOI case), there does appear to be a trend in government activities away from the public in earlier rounds of decision making towards decision makers themselves in later rounds.

Hence this analysis, too, provides only partial confirmation for the suppositions contained in hypothesis 3.

Conclusion: Findings and Future Research Directions

Multiple decision-making styles exist in government, and it is important to understand their dynamics and modes of operation (Lustick 1980; Thomson, Stokman, and Torenvlied 2003; Heikkila and Isett 2004; Weirich 2004; Mintz 2005). Depending on the number and type of actors involved in a decision and the kinds of resources they possess, public policy decisions can proceed in one of several different styles or fashions. Rational decision making can proceed when, for example, the number of actors is small and the parameters well enough known to allow more or less unconstrained decision making. However, as these challenges accrue, different modes or styles are adopted.

This discussion suggests that, since the publication of Forester's groundbreaking work, at least three of the four basic public policy decision-making styles that can be identified on the basis of his analysis have been investigated, including the well-known incremental and rational models, as well as others, such as the highly contingent heuristic or garbage can models. Through a process of empirical and conceptual conjecture and refutation, the theory has now been developed to the point where it is possible to conclude with some certainty when a specific decision-making style is likely to prevail and, hence, in three of four cases, what the general character of outcomes from that process is likely to be (Lustick 1980; Mucciaroni 1992; Jones, True, and Baumgartner 1997; Bendor, Moe, and Shotts 2001). This understanding remains incomplete, however, as long as knowledge of a common type of public policy decision making – that of multi-actor, multi-round decision-accretion decision making – remains inadequate.

This chapter advanced analysis of public policy decision making in Canada through the replication and development of recently published European studies of government decision making in this third "ideal" multi-actor, multi-round type. It set out several key hypotheses derived from the emerging European literature on the subject and tested the generalizability of the findings of these studies outside the European context. It did so by tracing the behaviour of governments and non-governmental policy actors involved in five multi-actor, multi-round processes in Canada over the period 1988–2005.

Three specific hypotheses concerning expected actor behaviour in multi-round, multi-actor decision-making processes were examined:

H1: That (a) the number of governmental actors and their activity level will remain relatively constant throughout successive rounds while (b) non-governmental actors flow in and out of different rounds depending on their perception of their interests, their re-source capacities, their estimations of likely policy outcomes, and their interpretations of the existing state of play of ongoing policy processes;

H2: That the participation of major non-governmental actors in successive rounds is inversely related to their congruence with government aims. Issue areas with significant discordance between governmental and non-governmental actors' aims and interests will witness higher levels of non-governmental participation;

H3: That the activities of non-governmental actors will change as rounds progress from a focus on influencing the context or environment of decision making (e.g. public opinion or media) in early rounds to one concerned with influencing decision makers in later rounds as discussions become more detailed, focused, technical, and legalistic.

While it was found that different rounds could be identified in the five policy areas under consideration and that actor activity varied across rounds, the direction of these changes was not straightforward and the analysis found only limited support for these hypotheses.

With respect to hypothesis 1, it was found that both governmental and NGO activity fluctuated greatly over different rounds. The continual anomaly of the FOI case illustrates that different patterns of activities are present in different issue areas and suggests that this has to do with the nature of the "publicness" of the issue area in question. With respect to hypothesis 2, it was found that (in)congruence of government and NGO interests was only a secondary factor explaining variations in actor behaviour. NGO activity in particular was in all cases driven by opposition to proposed bills. And, with respect to hypothesis 3, virtually no evidence was uncovered of NGO actor behaviour changing in the expected direction of targets anticipated by Koppenjan and Klijn, but rather remained steadily focused on the media and public.

Taken together, these findings suggest the workings of multi-actor, multi-round decision making may be both more and less predictable than earlier works would suggest. A pattern in which governmental and non-governmental actors react to each other in an inverse way has been observed – in Europe, in particular – with government and NGO behaviour establishing predictable patterns by round, with controversy-laden early rounds leading to more focused interactions in later ones. In the five Canadian cases examined, however, non-governmental actors tend to remain in opposition to governments through successive rounds and both governments and non-governmental actors tend to always target their activity towards influencing the public (and media) rather than proximate decision makers inside Parliament or the judiciary, regardless of the stage of a multi-round process.

These results are consistent with the idea of European policymaking behaviour being more corporatist and less antagonistic than pluralist systems such as Canada's, and, indeed, perhaps it should be expected that lengthy, multi-actor policy processes should come to approximate overall policy styles in government (Howlett and Ramesh 2003). That is, round behaviour in each system suggests that some predictability of outcomes may exist in each case, linked to larger sociopolitical institutional arrangements.

More specifically, though, with respect to the Canadian case itself, the findings suggest rounds are more likely to succeed or proceed more quickly when their subject matter is largely internal to governments or where it has non-governmental support at the outset. Round behaviour does not seem especially propitious for removing or altering initial opposition to policy initiatives, which continues to manifest itself throughout each round in a multi-round process and features a highly politicized atmosphere in which there is a continual effort on the part of both governmental and non-governmental actors to appeal to the public to support their position(s). This suggests that events occurring in the pre-decisional stages of the policy cycle may be critical to the outcome of multi-round decision processes and understanding the manner in which rounds commence, especially, should be a focus of future research efforts investigating this decision-making style.

Appendix 1: Data Sources and Coding

FTAA Case

Document source: CBCA and Summit of the Americas Web site with FTAA documents.

Date range: 1 January 1994 – 1 October 2005. The last Summit of the Americas meeting in November 2005 was not included as database research ended 15 October 2005.

Keywords: FTAA, Free Trade Agreement of the Americas, free trade, Summit of the Americas.

Records examined: 155.

Records coded: 140.

DIA Case

Document source: "CBCA Complete" database.

Date range: The range of dates includes June 1988 – August 2005.

Keywords: "Indian act" and "Canada" and "federal" and not "land claims" and not "treaties" and not "rights."

Records examined: This combination extracted 231 records as of 15 October 2005 and generated 216 usable records of policy-relevant actor activity.

FOI Case

Document source: "CBCA Complete."

Date range: February 1990 – August 2005.

Keywords: "Canada" and "federal" and "freedom of information."

Records examined: This combination extracted 188 records on 17 June 2005 (date of first access), and 194 records in August 2005. Thus the total number of records examined is 194. Of these, 171 referred to policy-relevant actor activity.

Banking Case

Document source: "CBCA Complete."

Date range: The time range comprised 1991–2001.

Keywords: "Bank AND act AND Canada, citation and abstract" only.

Records examined: As the result, 1,696 documents (mainly Canadian national and local newspaper articles) were found and examined. Only 114 dealt with policy-relevant actor activity.

Species at Risk Case

Document source: "CBCA Complete."
    Date range: 1990–2005.
    Keywords: The parameters of the keyword search were "(species) AND (risk) AND (act) in citation and abstract" only and "(Canada) AND (endangered species) OR (extinct species) in citation and abstract."
    Records examined: Initially, 510 documents representing mainly articles from national and local Canadian newspapers were found and examined. Additional searches led to 1,163 results. Ultimately, 321 instances of policy-relevant actor activity were found to be relevant and coded.

Appendix 2: Description of Key Legislative Changes by Issue Area

Issue	Round	Key Points	Description	Substance of Change	Character of Changes
Bank Act	1992		Bank Act revisions	De-pillarization. Banks allowed to purchase securities firms and brokerages. Foreign ownership levels changed.	Major
	2001		C-38/C-8 Bills	Changes to cross-pillar ownership regulations.	Minor/ Housekeeping
	2006		Proposed Bank Act revisions	Complete de-pillarization of insurance companies. Allow bank mergers.	Major, if passed
FOI	1993		Parliamentary Committee review	First major (ten-year) review of Access to Information and Privacy Act. Recommends major extensions.	Major, but failed to pass
	2001		C-54/C-6	Extension of Access to Information to private sector through personal information protection and electronic documents act.	Major
	2005		C-201	Open Government/Government Accountability Act (2006) Extensions	Major, but failed to pass/if passed
FTAA	1999		Toronto Summit	FTAA ministerial meeting in Toronto following 1998 Santiago commitment to proceed with talks.	Major
DIA	2002		c-7/c-6	Reforms to 1985–6 c-31 altering band status and membership. Prescribes adoption of governance codes for Indian bands and other aspects.	Major, but failed to pass
SARA	1997		c-65	Consolidation of existing statutes and coverage on federal lands.	Major, but failed to pass
	2000		c-33	Similar to C-65 but with provincial coverage	Major, but failed to pass
	2001		c-5	Similar to c-33	Major

Appendix 3: Governmental and Non-governmental Actor Activity by Issue and Year

	SARA		Bank Act		FOI		FTAA		DIA		
	Govt	NGO	Govt	NGO	Govt	NGO	Govt	NGO	Govt	NGO	
1988										2	2
1989									2	3	5
1990					1				1	3	5
1991		1	2	3	2				3	3	14
1992		0	5	0	2				4	6	17
1993	3	5	0	2	3	4			5	4	26
1994	2	8	1	0	2	5	6	1	2	7	34
1995	6	26	0	9	1	1	0	0	0	5	48
1996	11	23	6	23	7	3	1	2	3	4	83
1997	18	36	4	2	2	2	2	0	4	6	76
1998	8	19	2	3	7	5	0	6	2	2	54
1999	13	31	3	12	11	3	6	4	7	7	97
2000	18	29	2	6	10	3	2	0	10	12	92
2001	15	9	4	9	7	3	20	42	13	25	147
2002	16	21	0	0	9	3	3	3	11	12	78
2003	2	1	1	3	14	4	18	11	14	12	80
2004			1	0	14	12	4	5	5	5	46
2005			1	10	17	14	3	1	5	7	58
Total N	112	209	32	82	109	62	65	75	91	125	962
	321		114		171		140		216		962

Appendix 4: Types of Actor Activity by Rounds

Issue Area	Rounds	Total	Public	Media	Comm.	Dec	Parl.	Jud
DIA	1	240	73	39	5	72	4	47
	2	162	39	47	11	43	8	14
FOI	1	20	4	4	2	6	2	2
	2	142	29	29	16	38	11	19
	3	150	33	36	15	38	14	14
Bank	1	37	8	13	3	8	3	2
	2	353	83	109	44	81	17	19
	3	220	64	50	29	49	14	14
FTAA	1	51	17	15	0	18	1	0
	2	333	95	117	0	114	6	1
SARA	1	385	110	129	19	120	7	0
	2	389	106	128	11	121	14	9
	3	172	36	58	17	50	10	1
TOTAL		2654	697	774	172	758	111	142
PER CENT		100	26.2	29.1	6.5	28.5	4.2	5.3

6 Policy Implementation: Managing the "Hollow State": Procedural Policy Instruments and Modern Governance

Contemporary governance takes place within a very different context from that of past decades. Government capacity in terms of human and organizational resources remains high by historical standards, but the autonomy or ability of governments to independently affect change has been eroded by such factors as the growth of powerful international actors and systems of exchange (Cerny 1996). Moreover, at the domestic level, modern societies have developed increasingly complex networks of interorganizational actors whose coordination and management are increasingly problematic. Many states have undergone a kind of "hollowing out," as various functions and activities traditionally undertaken by governments – from highway maintenance to psychiatric care – have been contracted out or otherwise devolved to non- or quasi-governmental organizations, further deepening the network structure and character of contemporary life (Lehmbruch 1991; Mayntz 1993; Milward, Provan, and Else 1993; Milward and Provan 2000).

These processes and paradoxes challenge public administrators in the new millennium (Peters 1996; Peters and Pierre 1998). In coming to terms with these challenges, many governments, including Canada's, have developed a renewed interest in understanding the techniques of policy implementation. They have turned away from an exclusive reliance on a relatively limited number of traditional, more or less command-and-control-oriented, "substantive" policy tools such as public enterprises, regulatory agencies, subsidies, and exhortation that directly affect policy outcomes.[1] Instead, they have increasingly come to rely on the use of a different set of "procedural" tools designed to indirectly affect outcomes through the manipulation of policy processes.[2] Canadian public administration moved quite far down this road in the

1990s, as administrators experimented with stakeholder participation, a multitude of different types of private-public partnerships, and various other forms of "collaborative government" (Kernaghan 1993; Graham and Phillips 1997; Armstrong and Lenihan 1999; Gross Stein et al. 1999; Delacourt and Lenihan 2000).

Conceptual work on procedural policy instruments, however, lags behind administrative practice. This chapter endeavours to advance this emerging area of study by drawing on the methods and findings of studies of substantive instruments to develop a taxonomy categorizing procedural instruments; propose a spectrum that sets out the general nature of the relationship between basic categories of tools; and outline the elements of a theoretical model concerning the hypothesized rationale for governments choosing between instrument categories.

Studying Policy Instruments

The policy sciences have always been interested in policy processes and in the manner in which governments manipulate these processes in order to achieve their ends. In his path-breaking early works on public policymaking, for example, Harold Lasswell conceived the main instruments of politics as involving, among other things, the manipulation of symbols, signs, and icons. Lasswell (1954 and 1971) noted the extent to which governments could affect each stage of the policy process through such manipulations and argued that a principal task of the policy sciences must be to understand the nuances of these actions and their effects.[3]

This orientation was retained by many early students of policymaking, who tended to have a very flexible notion of the multiple means by which governments could affect or give effect to policy (Dahl and Lindblom 1953; Kirschen et al. 1964; Lowi 1966). In these early works, "policy instruments" were defined broadly so as to include a wide range of tools and techniques of governance, including both those instruments used to actually deliver goods and services and those directed at affecting policy development. By the early 1980s, however, under the urgings of Lester Salamon (1981) and others, attention began to be focused on more precisely categorizing policy instruments in order to better analyse the reasons for their use. Careful examination of instruments and instrument choices, it was argued, would not only lead to considerable insight into the factors driving the policy process and the characterization of long-term patterns of public policymaking, but would also

Table 36. A Taxonomy of Substantive Policy Instruments
(Cells provide examples of instruments in each category)

Principal Use	Governing Resource			
	Nodality	Authority	Treasure	Organization
Effectors	*advice training*	*licences user charges regulation certification*	*grants loans tax expenditures*	*bureaucratic administration public enterprises*
Detectors	*reporting registration*	*census-taking consultants*	*polling, policing*	*record-keeping surveys*

Source: Adapted from Hood 1986: 124–5.

allow practitioners to more readily draw lessons from the experiences of others with the use of particular techniques in specific circumstances (Woodside 1986).

This new emphasis on the systematic study of policy instruments quickly generated a large academic literature and resulted in immediate application in the design of new policy initiatives in areas such as pollution prevention and professional regulation (Trebilcock 1983; Huppes 1988). Studies in Canada and elsewhere generated useful taxonomies (Tupper and Doern 1981; Hood 1986; Howlett 1991; Vedung 1997) and shed light on significant subjects such as the reasons behind shifts in patterns of instrument choices associated with the waves of privatization and deregulation that characterized the period.[4]

Most of these studies, however, focused exclusively on substantive instruments that directly affected the production and delivery of goods and services in society. These included the construction and establishment of regulatory and other political and administrative agencies and enterprises, traditional financial inducements, and the "command-and-control" measures adopted by administrative agencies. Much less attention was paid to the systematic analysis of their procedural counterparts. Nevertheless, as shall be argued below, the model-building

methods used in substantive instrument studies can be applied analo-
gously to advance the study and understanding of "procedural" policy
tools.

a. Substantive Policy Instruments

In the case of substantive policy instruments, or those instruments intended to directly affect the nature, types, quantities, and distribution
of the goods and services provided in society, a great deal of conceptual progress has occurred over the past two decades. Taxonomies, for
example, have been provided by many authors, one of the most well
known developed by Christopher Hood (1986).[5] In this scheme, instruments are grouped together according to 1) whether they rely on the
use of "nodality" (or information), authority, treasure, or the organizational resources of government for their effectiveness; and 2) whether
the instrument is designed to effect a change in a policy environment
or detect changes in it. A taxonomy of substantive policy instruments
based on Hood's schema is presented in Table 36 above.

These taxonomies were elevated from the level of pure description
and classification to a more theoretical or conceptual one through the
construction of models that specified the relationship between general
categories of instruments.[6] Howlett and Ramesh (1995), for example,
developed a spectrum of substantive instruments based on Hood's taxonomy. They focused on the level of direct state involvement in the
provision of goods and services as the chief criterion for distinguishing
between categories of "effector" instruments.[7] This placed "voluntary"
instruments that require minimal state involvement at one end of a continuum, with state-based instruments such as public enterprises placed
at the opposite end. Between the two poles lies a wide range of "mixed"
instruments involving varying levels of state and private provision of
goods and services (see Figure 28).

It is only a start, however, to say that a variety of substantive instrument choices exists that can alter patterns of goods and services available in society and that these choices differ in terms of the extent of
state involvement in their production and delivery to the public. In
order for the instrument choice perspective to say anything meaning-
ful about policymaking, univariate spectra had to be elevated further
to the theoretical level, by linking specific instrument choices to specific
sets of choice-influencing variables.

Figure 28: A Spectrum of Substantive Policy Instruments

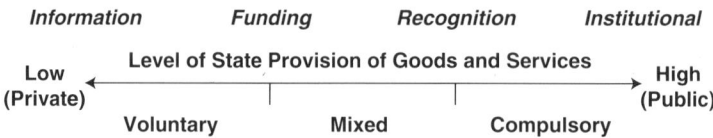

Source: Howlett and Ramesh 1995.

In this regard, most students of substantive policy instruments have focused on two interlinked sets of independent variables: 1) the organizational ability or capacity of states to affect societal actors; and 2) policy subsystem complexity, or the number and types of actors governments must affect in designing and implementing their programs and policies (Linder and Peters 1989; Schneider and Ingram 1990; Bressers and O'Toole 1998). That is, it is hypothesized that the type of instrument chosen by governments to affect the production or delivery of goods and services in society in specific empirical circumstances will depend on the intersection of state capacity and the complexity of the networks of social actors states wish to influence.

Howlett and Ramesh, again, provide an example of how these two variables, and their expected relationship to each other, can be used to generate a simple model containing a set of hypotheses regarding substantive instrument choices (see Table 37). In this model, for example, it is argued that subsidy or market instruments should only be used, or can only be used effectively, when a high level of state capacity and a complex policy subsystem exist – as is the case, for example, with most competitive economic situations faced by modern states. If a state faces a complex network or subsystem but has only limited capacity, on the other hand, it is expected that it will tend to utilize regulatory or information-based instruments. Direct provision and public enterprises would be expected to be used only when a state has high capacity but faces a relatively simple social or policy environment characterized by few actors and a small number of significant interorganizational relationships. Finally, when state capacity is low and the policy environment is not very complex, reliance on voluntary instruments can be effective, as was the case historically in many areas of social and health policy (Tupper 1979; Laux and Molot 1988; Eisner 1994; Vogel 1996; Hall and Banting 2000).

Table 37. A Model of Substantive Instrument Choice
(Cells indicate likely instrument choice)

| Principal Use | Governing Resource | | | |
	Nodality	Authority	Treasure	Organization
Positive	education exhortation advertising training	agreements treaties advisory group creation	interest group fundings research and intervenor funding	hearings evaluations institutional-bureaucratic reform
Negative	misleading information propaganda	banning groups and associations	eliminating funding	administrative delay information suppression

Source: Adapted from Howlett and Ramesh 1995.

These kinds of models do not delve into the detail of fine gradations of instrument use within each general category, nor the specific contexts of individual decisions that can result in errors being made in instrument choices. However, they suggest that, although substantive instrument choices are complex, general patterns of such choices can nevertheless be discerned and explained. The development of instrument taxonomies and spectra and the formulation of bivariate conceptual models helped to identify these patterns and the limited number of variables responsible for them. As shall be argued below, these same methods of model building and theory construction can also be applied to the study of procedural policy instruments, aiding the understanding of the nature of such instruments and illuminating the factors that lie behind their use.

Analysing Procedural Policy Instruments

Existing analyses of recent administrative developments provide some clues as to where to begin the study of procedural instruments.[8] As suggested above, examination of the techniques and results generated in the study of substantive instruments indicates that the general methodological approach to procedural instrument study involves 1) the construction of a taxonomy that classifies such instruments based on the governing "resources" they utilize; 2) construction of a "spectrum" of procedural instruments identifying a single criterion that highlights the similarities and differences between instrument categories; and 3) the generation of a theory or model of instrument choice based on these earlier steps, in which the reasons for using any of the instruments listed in the taxonomy are hypothesized.[9]

A Partial Inventory of Procedural Policy Instruments

Fortunately, the current generation of instrument theorists did not completely neglect procedural instruments. Several works dealing with aspects of the subject give us a broad sense of which direction to pursue in attempting to elevate this area of instrument studies to the level attained by substantive instrument research.

In their 1988 work, for example, Hans Bressers and Pieter-Jan Klok noted the ways in which "subjective rational actors" can be influenced by manipulation of the alternatives placed before them. They observed that different instruments can affect the number of policy options developed in the policy process, or the calculations of costs and benefits of alternative courses of action made by policy actors. While some of the instruments they examined were "substantive" (for example, the use of licences to affect the cost of certain activities), most of the instruments captured by their scheme were procedural – especially those dealing with the selective creation, provision, and diffusion of information to policy actors.

Similarly, in their 1990 study, Anne Schneider and Helen Ingram also focused on government's ability to alter the underlying behaviour of policy actors. In proposing their own scheme for categorizing policy instruments, they argued that policymaking "almost always attempts to get people to do things that they might not otherwise do." They noted:

> [I]f people are not taking actions needed to ameliorate social, economic or political problems, there are five reasons that can be addressed by policy: they may believe that law does not direct them or authorize them to take action; they may lack incentives or capacity to take the actions needed; they may disagree with the values implicit in the means or ends; or the situation may involve such high levels of uncertainty that the nature of the problem is not known, and it is unclear what people should do or how they might be motivated. (Schneider and Ingram 1990, p. 514)

These they called "authority," "incentives," "capacity building," "symbolic and hortatory," and "learning" instruments.[10] As was the case with Bressers and Klok, this scheme included both "procedural" and "substantive" tools. While the discussion virtually ignores pure public provision of goods and services by government agencies and corporations, the "authority" and "incentive" examples cited are typical substantive instruments involving mixed provision of goods and services by a combination of private and public actors. "Capacity," "symbolic," and "learning" tools, however, are much more procedurally oriented, affecting the policy institutions and processes within which policy decisions are taken.

Taken together, the works of Bressers and Klok, Schneider and Ingram, and others identified a large number of typical procedural policy instruments. These include education, training, institution creation, the selective provision of information, formal evaluations, hearings, and institutional reform (Wraith and Lamb 1971; Chapman 1973; Kernaghan 1985; Peters 1992; Weiss and Tschirhart 1994; Bellehumeur 1997). Research into the tools and mechanisms used in intergovernmental regulatory design by Canadian analysts and others has also identified several other such instruments, including "treaties" and a variety of "political agreements" that can affect target group recognition of government intentions and vice versa (Bulmer 1993; Doern and Wilks 1998; Harrison 1999). Other research, again much of it Canadian, into interest group behaviour and activities has highlighted the existence of tools related to group creation and manipulation, including the role played by private or public sector patrons in aiding the formation and activities of such groups (Burt 1990; Phillips 1991; Pal 1993; Finkle et al. 1994; Nownes and Neeley 1996; Lowry 1999). Still other specialized research into aspects of contemporary policymaking has highlighted the use of techniques such as provision of research funding for and access to investigative hearings and tribunals (Salter and Slaco 1981; Gormley 1989; Cairns 1990; Jenson 1994).

A Taxonomy of Procedural Instruments

In order to make sense of this disparate (and partial) inventory, it is necessary to identify some means by which instruments can be categorized into general classes. As was the case with Hood's taxonomy of substantive policy instruments, classifying procedural instruments in accordance with the type of "governing resource" they rely on generates a useful preliminary taxonomy (see Table 38).[11] While most researchers have focused on the manner in which these instruments have been used

Table 38. A Resource-Based Taxonomy of Procedural Policy Instruments
(Cells provide examples of instruments in each category)

	Principal governing resource used			
	Nodality	Authority	Treasure	Organization
General purpose of instrument use				
Positive	EducationInformation provisionFocus groups	LabellingTreaties and political agreementsAdvisory group creation	Interest group creationIntervenor and research funding	Institutional reformJudicial reviewConferences
Negative	PropagandaInformation suppressionDenial of access	Banning groups and associations	Eliminating funding	Administrative delay and obfuscation

to enhance participation and policy-relevant knowledge, it should also be emphasized that procedural tools can also be used to negatively affect interest groups and other actor behaviour. That is, for example, information-based procedural instruments include both the provision of information as well as its suppression and the release of misleading as well as accurate information. Deception, obfuscation, and other forms of administrative delay, similarly, are all forms of authority-based procedural instruments (Mueller 1973). Hence, drawing a distinction between "positive" and "negative" uses of governing resources in terms of whether they encourage or discourage actor participation in policy processes is a useful aspect of the preliminary classification of such instruments.

As was the case with substantive instruments, this taxonomy is useful insofar as it highlights the different basic resources used by different types of instruments and therefore allows a virtually unlimited number of instruments to be placed in a limited number of general categories. However, as was the case with substantive instruments, this taxonomy is only the first step in the construction of a testable model of procedural instrument choice.

A Spectrum of Procedural Instruments

The second step in the development of such a model is the identification of a single dimension along which the categories of an instrument taxonomy vary. Here it should be recalled that the fundamental purpose of procedural policy instruments is to alter or manipulate the policy process. As Dutch scholars such as Erik-Hans Klijn (1996), W.J.M. Kickert, J.F.M. Koppenjan, and especially J.A. de Bruijn and E.F. ten Heuvelhof (1995 and 1997; see also Leik 1992) have argued, this primarily involves manipulating the links and nodes of the networks of actors involved in policymaking. That is, procedural instruments are used to manipulate the number or nature of actors arrayed in the policy subsystems that policymakers face. Each category of instrument uses a specific resource in order to manipulate aspects of a policy subsystem or network.

As de Bruijn and ten Heuvelhof (1995 and 1991; see also Klijn and Teisman 1991; Peters 1998) have pointed out, a wide range of activities is possible in network manipulation, ranging from limited "network management" to more fundamental "subsystem restructuring." Incorporating this distinction allows the procedural policy instruments found in Table 38 to be arrayed in a single spectrum according to the

Figure 29: A Spectrum of Procedural Policy Instruments

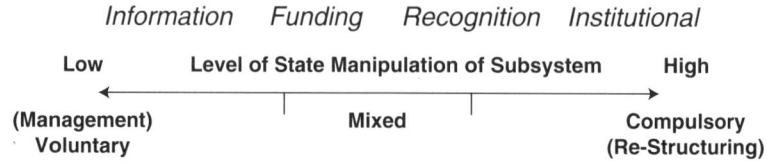

level of state manipulation of subsystem membership and activities (see Figure 29).

In this spectrum, procedural policy instruments can be seen to range from limited information suppression or release designed to mildly affect subsystem behaviour through "voluntaristic" responses from targeted actors, to group or institutional reforms designed to completely restructure existing subsystems by compulsory means (Smith, Marsh, and Richards 1993; Savoie 1999).

The Rationale for Procedural Instrument Choice

Establishing a taxonomy and a spectrum of procedural policy instruments is the first step towards enhancing understanding of these elements of contemporary public policymaking and administration. To construct a model of procedural instrument choice, however, the question of the rationale for tool selection also must be broached; that is, why would or why should a government utilize one type of procedural instrument rather than another? While more empirical research is required to test and construct such a theory, the evidence that does exist suggests that a government's desire to alter a policy process is intimately tied to the extent to which existing processes and procedures are considered credible by policy actors. As Peter May (1993 and 1996; May and Handmer 1992) and his colleagues have noted in the case of intergovernmental program design, for example, governments have attempted to build cooperation and commitment among the multiple actors involved in areas such as environmental regulation in Australia and the United States rather than prescribe penalties or utilize incentives, primarily because of the risk to future activities that conflict could bring. And, as Bridget Hutter (1989) has noted in the case of European Union program design, the question of precision and accuracy of targeting appears to have been more significant to policymakers than, for example, cost or administrative simplicity.

This suggests that a key feature to be modelled in understanding procedural instrument choice is the extent to which existing subsystems need to be manipulated in order to retain the political trust or legitimacy required for governments to govern. This raises to the forefront of the analysis of procedural policy instruments the relationship existing between legitimacy and governance (Stillman 1974; Weatherford 1989; Beetham 1991; Suchman 1995; Peters and Pierre 2000).

As is well known, democratic states require the attainment of a minimum level of societal consensus supporting their actions. When a serious loss of legitimacy or trust occurs, the subject of political conflict often shifts from the actual substantive content of government actions towards a critique of the processes by which those actions are determined (Habermas 1975; Mayntz 1975; Howlett 1990; Coleman 1991; Rajan 1992; Simmons and Keohane 1992; Jentoft 2000). This can occur at either the macro, or system-wide, level or at the meso, or sectoral, level, but, in either case, in order to construct or regain legitimacy, governments resort to the use of procedural instruments to alter network configurations.

This discussion suggests that two key variables that can capture important aspects of procedural policy instrument choice are the extent of existing sectoral delegitimization, which directly affects the extent of subsystem manipulation appropriate for the task of relegitimization, and the extent of systemic delegitimization, which affects the capacity of governments to use existing networks to continue policy deliberations (Merelman 1966; McWilliams 1971; Habermas 1973; Schaar 1981). On this basis, a model of procedural instrument choice, analogous to that previously developed for substantive instruments, can be set out (see Table 39).

In this model, one would expect governments faced with both sectoral and trans-sectoral systemic legitimization problems to utilize "compulsory" procedural instruments such as government reorganization in order to restructure policy networks and essentially reconstruct legitimacy and trust de novo (Suchman 1995; Heritier 1997 and 1999). Governments facing low levels of both sectoral and systemic delegitimization would be expected to favour the use of more modest "voluntary" instruments such as information manipulation through the release or withholding of documents, since only minor network manipulation is required to legitimate existing policy processes (Saward 1992; Rhodes 1997). In between would be found cases where sectoral distrust and discontent is high but systemic delegitimization low,

Table 39. A Model of Procedural Instrument Choice
(Cells indicate instrument choice)

Level of sectoral delegitimization	Level of systemic delegitimization	
	High	Low
High	*Institutional manipulation*	*Funding manipulation*
Low	*Recognition manipulation*	*Information manipulation*

meaning government funds can be used to re-legitimate policy processes through, for example, the infusion of cash to create or selectively support specific interest groups (Burt 1990; Browne 1991; King and Walker 1991; Pal 1993). Finally, where systemic delegitimization is high but sectoral delegitimacy is low, governments can recognize new actors or reorganize old ones through authoritative means such as the establishment of, for example, specialized quasi-independent advisory committees and enquiries that serve to distance sectoral policy processes from overall systemic legitimization concerns (Brown 1972; Dion 1973; Smith 1977; Hood 1986 and 1988).

Conclusion: Policy Instruments for Modern Governance

The study of policy instruments over the past twenty years has generated many insights into instrument use; insights that have helped academics to better understand policy processes and have helped practitioners in Canada and elsewhere design better policies.[12] However, in the process of developing the taxonomies and models of instrument choice, many investigators have focused almost exclusively on the specific set of instruments governments use to alter the distribution of goods and services in society. In focusing so intently on "substantive" policy instruments, sight has been lost of the need, identified by early students of public policy, to take both the substance and process of policymaking into account when conducting instrument analyses.

This has become a major problem in attempting to find solutions to the paradoxes of modern governance and to find the appropriate methods and tools to steer the "hollow state" (Kooiman; Peters and Pierre; Klijn and Koppenjan 2000; Walters, Aydelotte, and Miller 2000). While procedural policy instruments have been used on an ad hoc basis in the past, they have become an essential component of modern governance. Because of this shift in instrument use, developing more systematic assessments, inventories, categories, and models of procedural policy tools is increasingly a prerequisite both for contemporary public administration and public policy analysis. As Evert Lindquist (1992) argued, managing the hollow state requires:

> new analytical tools that will help [officials] to diagnose and map the external environments of public agencies, to recognize the inherent tensions and dynamics in these environments as they pertain to policy development and consensus-building, and to develop new strategies for "working" these environments in the interests both of their political masters and those of the broader communities they serve … If public servants are to learn from the experience of colleagues working in other sectors and levels of government, they will need a vocabulary to facilitate the dialogue (p. 159)

In pursuing this effort, policy analysts have developed a renewed appreciation for the multiple different types of policy instruments available to governments in policy design and have begun to identify a distinct set of procedural instruments, such as government-NGO partnerships, public advisory commissions, roundtables, interest group funding, and information dissemination, which all act to guide or steer policy processes in the direction government wishes through the manipulation of policy actors and their interrelationships (Goggin et al. 1990; Pal 1997; O'Toole 2000; Peters 2000).

This chapter has adapted techniques used in the classification and analysis of substantive policy instruments to the study of their procedural counterparts. It developed a taxonomy based on the nature of the governing resources used by such instruments, and, focusing on the level of network manipulation involved in instrument use, established a continuum highlighting the significant similarities and differences found in each general category of instrument. Finally, emphasizing the manner in which instrument choices are affected by the generalizability of the legitimization problems a government faces, a model of procedural instrument choice was developed that set out several hypotheses pertaining to likely situations where use of particular instruments would occur.

Developing improved models of procedural instrument choice is of use to both analysts and practitioners in Canada and elsewhere who are interested in policy implementation and policy design in the contemporary era. Like the models of substantive tools developed in the 1970s and 1980s, this effort promises to illuminate the range of options available to public administrators and decision makers in their efforts to meet the challenges of modern governance.

For both practitioners and theorists, more precise definition, classification, conceptualization, and modelling helps to generate a fruitful future research agenda. Among other things, such research might well examine questions related to the manner in which political institutions gain and lose "political capital" and legitimacy in the course of their day-to-day activities and how this affects their ability to innovate (Mondak 1992; O'Toole 1997) or those involving the description and improved understanding of the precise requisites for sectoral policy relegitimization (Suchman 1995). For those interested in the conceptual aspects of instrument choice, it begins the process of understanding the "dialectic of legitimacy" or the manner in which not only state actors but also societal ones must inspire trust and loyalty if policymaking processes and outcomes are to remain effective (Tyler 1990; Stryker 1994; Lindquist 1996).

For practitioners, an improved understanding of procedural policy instruments helps to better outline the options available to governments in specific circumstances. More significant, it provides guidelines indicating which procedural choice is appropriate in which circumstance, such as when to hold multi-stakeholder consultations and when not to, or when to release or withhold information. If the management of the hollow state is to be more than simply an ad hoc process, developing such models is an essential part of modern governance.

7 Policy Evaluation – Policy Advice in Multilevel Governance Systems: Sub-National Policy Analysts and Analysis

Introduction: The Supply and Demand for Policy Analysis in Government

Policy analysis is a subject that has not suffered from a dearth of attention. Many journals and specialized publications exist on the subject and specialized graduate schools operate in many countries, states, and provinces (Jann 1991; Geva-May and Maslove 2007). Studies have examined many hundreds of case studies of policymaking in numerous countries, and many texts describe in detail both the various analytical techniques expected to be used in public policy analysis (Weimer and Vining 2004) and the nuances of the policymaking processes(Howlett, Perl, and Ramesh 2009).

However, works examining the supply and demand for policy analysis in government are much rarer (Nutley, Walter, and Davies 2007). And where these exist they almost always focus on the demand side of the policy advice market, examining the strengths, weaknesses, and other characteristics of the knowledge utilization process in government (Weiss and Bucuvalas 1980; Beyer and Trice 1982; Pollard 1987; Weiss 1992; Rich 1997; Innvaer et al. 2002). Work on the behaviour and behavioural characteristics of in-house policy analysts in supplying advice to government, let alone those working outside it, is exceedingly rare (Aberbach and Rothman 1989; Nelson 1989; Wollmann 1989; Bushnell 1991; Radin 1992; Thompson and Yessian 1992; Boston 1994; Binz-Scharf, Lazer, and Mergel 2008).[1]

Given the significance of public sector analysts in the policy advice system of government, studies of their activities, behaviour, and impact should be a staple of the study and evaluation of policy analysis.

Nevertheless, while there is certainly no lack of studies that urge certain techniques or practices on professional bureaucratic policy analysts (see, for example, Patton and Sawicki [1993]; MacRae and Whittington [1997]; Dunn [2004] and many others), in most countries, empirical data on just about every aspect of policy analysis in government are lacking.[2]

This situation has led many observers both inside and outside government to decry the lack of even such basic data as how many policy analysts there are in government, working on what subjects, and with what techniques (State Services Commission 1991 and 1999; Waller 1992 and 1996; Hunn 1994; Uhr and Mackay 1996; Bakvis 1997; Weller and Stevens 1998; Behm, Bennington, and Cummane 2000).[3]

As Colebatch and Radin concluded in their 2006 survey of international practices:

(1) "We need more empirical research on the nature of policy work in specific contexts: how policy workers (and which sort) get a place at the table, how the question is framed, what discourse is accepted as valid, and how this work relates to the outcome at any point in time; (and)
(2) What sort of activity do practitioners see as policy work, and what sort of policy workers do they recognize?" (p. 225)

The Sub-National Case: Provincial Policy Analysts in Canada

This general situation is true of most countries. However, even where some little work has been done on the subject, serious gaps remain in our knowledge of bureaucratic policy analysts. If information on national or central governments is weak, the number of studies that focus on sub-national units in countries with multilevel governance systems can be counted on one hand (Larsen 1980; Hird 2005).

This latter point is a substantial issue for the study of policy advice systems and professional policy analysis in many federal countries, such as Brazil, Mexico, Australia, and the United States, where as many as 50 per cent of traditional bureaucratic policy analysts may work for sub-national state or provincial governments. In these multilevel systems, sub-national governments control many important areas of policymaking, including health, education, social services, local government and land, resources and the environment, and exercise controlling interest over policy development and implementation in these areas (Hooghe and Marks 2001, 2003; Bache and Flinders 2004).

Both these situations are true in Canada, where studies of policy analysts have traditionally focused almost exclusively at the federal level (Prince 1979; Prince and Chenier 1980; Hollander and Prince 1993; Voyer 2007) despite the fact that the provinces control many important areas of social, economic, and political life. This situation only began to change in 2006–7 when studies of non-governmental policy analysts (Dobuzinskis, Howlett, and Laycock 2007) and of regional and central policy analysts employed in the federal civil service appeared (Wellstead et al. 2007).

These studies have revealed a very different set of policy supply practices than those suggested by studies in other jurisdictions, highlighting, for example, significant differences in the attitudes and activities of federal analysts in Ottawa versus those in the regions, and the generally poorer policy capacity of regional organizations (Howlett 2009). Regionally based policy analysts working for the federal government, for example, were found to be more commonly engaged in "street-level" advice oriented towards day-to-day firefighting, while the analysts in Ottawa engaged in more "high-level" and long-term strategic planning. The kinds of skills and information sources required for each set of analysts were thus found to vary substantially. Such findings have refined and called into question many of the assumptions that went into policy capacity enhancement activities undertaken in the country since the publication of the Fellegi Report in 1996 (Anderson 1996; Fellegi 1996; Bakvis 2000; Aucoin and Bakvis 2005; Riddell 1998).

However, while these are important insights, given Canada's very decentralized federal system of government, approximately half of the more than ten thousand bureaucratic policy analysts employed in the country are working at the sub-national level in the civil services of the ten provinces and three territories. Information on analytical activities and the supply of policy advice at this level remains extremely rudimentary, generated exclusively from personal reflections and anecdotes of former analysts and managers or from a small number of single-province interviews or surveys (Rasmussen 1999; Singleton 2001; Hicks and Watson 2007; McArthur 2007; Policy Excellence Initiative 2007).

In order to correct these problems, in 2008–9, a survey similar to Wellstead et al.'s (2007) was made of policy analysts at the provincial level. This survey was designed specifically to examine the background and training of provincial policy analysts, the types of techniques they employed in their jobs, and what they did in their work on a day-by-day basis. It was intended to assess the extent to which, following Wellstead et al., provincial civil servants, too, fell into the categories of troubleshooters versus planners in terms of their day-to-day activities and orientations.

The results of the survey are presented below in the form of a profile of provincial policy analysts, following a brief discussion of the methodology employed in the survey work.

Methods

The personal and professional components of the policy advice supply system, along with their internal and external sourcing, are combined in different ratios in different countries. However, as Halligan has noted:

> The conventional wisdom appears to be that a good advice system should consist of at least three basic elements within government: a stable and reliable in-house advisory service provided by professional public servants; political advice for the minister from a specialized political unit [generally the minister's office]; and the availability of at least one third-opinion option from a specialized or central policy unit, which might be one of the main central agencies. (Halligan 1995: 162)

As Halligan also notes, however, "the emphasis on elements such as the role of political operatives ... depends very much on whether [they] are accorded seniority within the system of government," a practice that is a feature of the U.S. system but "less so in other countries" (Halligan 1995: 162). In other words, the primary component of the policy advice supply system in many countries is comprised of what Meltsner (1975) first identified as "bureaucratic policy analysts."[4] It is these professional policy advisors in the civil service who were the target of this study.

A survey of policy analysts employed by provincial civil services was carried out in November and December 2008 using an online commercial software service. It involved the completion of a sixty-four-item questionnaire by more than twelve hundred provincial and territorial civil servants situated in seven jurisdictions.

Mailing lists for the survey were compiled wherever possible from publicly available sources such as online government telephone directories, using keyword searches for terms such as "policy analyst" appearing in job titles or descriptions. In some cases, additional names were added to lists from hard copy sources such as government organization manuals. In other cases, lists or additional names were provided by provincial public service commissions, who also checked initial lists for completeness and accuracy.[5]

Lists were compiled for as many provinces and territories as possible, with the aim of obtaining comprehensive lists for at least one major Canadian province, at least one mid-sized jurisdiction, at least one smaller jurisdiction, and at least one territory. From 2,846 valid email addresses in seven jurisdictions, 1,258 valid survey completions were gathered for a total response rate of 44.2 per cent.

The Profile of Provincial Policy Analysts

The data collected from the survey allowed a profile of provincial public servants to be constructed for the first time. Data were divided into four topic areas: Demographic Characteristics and Job Experience; Education and Training; Day-to-Day Duties; and Techniques and Data Employed. Combined, these provide the basis for the first large-scale empirical analysis of the background and activities of sub-national government policy analysts.

Demographics and Job Experience

Basic demographic data were collected on provincial policy analysts in terms of characteristics such as gender and age. The responses revealed that provincial analysts are predominantly (60 per cent) female, and fairly young in that almost 70 per cent are under fifty years of age and over 40 per cent under forty years of age. Additional questions revealed that provincial analysts also tend to have come to their present career path and positions fairly recently. Over 40 per cent of provincial analysts had been involved in professional policy analytical activities for five years or less (Table 40).

Almost 60 per cent had also been in their present organizations for less than five years, including 15 per cent for less than one year. This contrasts sharply with the federal situation described by Wellstead et al. (2007), where a majority of analysts are male and a sizable number have been in their positions for over twenty years.

Finally, these analysts also do not expect to stay very long in their current positions, with two-thirds expecting to stay less than five additional years. This pattern accords closely with Meltsner's (1975)

Table 40. Length of Time

	... Employed as a Professional Policy Analyst		... Employed in Present Organization		... Expected to Remain in Present Position	
	Frequency	Per cent	Frequency	Per cent	Frequency	Per cent
	11	.9	6	.5	21	1.7
00–01 years	62	4.9	184	14.6	154	12.2
01–05 years	457	36.3	537	42.7	675	53.7
06–09 years	250	19.9	196	15.6	134	10.7
10–14 years	158	12.6	92	7.3	174	13.8
15–20 years	153	122	112	8.9	58	4.6
20 or more	167	13.3	131	10.4	42	3.3
Total	1,258	100.0	1,258	100.0	1,258	100.0

observation that the typical policy analyst believes he or she is upwardly mobile and "believes he [*sic*] is a short-timer, so he does not worry about maintaining the agency or conserving its jurisdiction" (Meltsner 1975: 117) and instead is able to be more "problem-focused" in orientation and approach.

Education and Training

A second set of questions examined the background education and training of provincial analysts. Table 41 highlights the generally very high level of formal education attained by this group of civil servants, with 57 per cent having at least some graduate or professional education and fully 95 per cent attaining university-level credentials.

Provincial analysts' study areas of expertise are quite varied, but heavily oriented (over 80 per cent) towards the social sciences (see Table 42).

The five leading degree fields were political science with 16.5 per cent, followed by business management with 13.2 per cent, economics with 11.5 per cent, public administration with 9.6 per cent, and sociology with 8.4 per cent. These five fields accounted for 48 per cent of degrees (allowing for multiple degrees) held by analysts, while a wide range of other social science, law, and humanities credentials accounted for another 40 per cent. Health sciences, computer science, engineering, and natural science degrees made up only 12 per cent of analysts' credentials. Both of these findings resemble the patterns found by Wellstead et al. at the federal level.

Table 41. Education

	Frequency	Per cent
Valid	93	7.4
		1.9
	24	
High School		
College or Technical	58	4.6
University	371	29.5
Graduate or Professional	712	56.6
Total	1,258	100.0

Table 42. Degree Subject Area

		Per cent
Business Management	166	132%
Education	56	45%
Engineering	30	2.4%
Humanities or Fine Arts	66	52%
Law	86	6.8%
Natural Sciences	85	6.8%
Planning	58	4.6%
Public Administration	121	9.6%
Political Science	208	165%
Economics	145	115%
Sociology	106	8.4%
Geography	85	6.8%
Other Social Sciences	126	10.0%
History	74	5.9%
English	57	45%
Other Arts or Humanities	31	25%
Public Policy	87	6.9%
Medicine	6	.5%
Other Health Sciences	37	2.9%
Computing Science	20	1.6%
Languages or Linguistics	28	22%
Communications or Journalism	25	2.0%
Environmental Studies	85	6.8%
Natural Resource Management	42	3.3%
Total	1,258	100.0%

Table 43. Previous Work Experience

	N	Per cent
Academia	278	22.1%
Municipal government department or agency	143	11.4%
Not-for-profit sector	316	25.1%
Private sector	211	16.8%
Other provincial government department or agency in your current province	549	43.6%
Department or agency in another provincial government	111	8.8%
Federal government	157	12.5%
Department or agency in another country	73	5.8%
Total	1,258	100.0%

As for previous work experience, provincial analysts have varied backgrounds, but tend to be recruited from academic institutions (22 per cent) or to have come up through their own provincial government, with 44 per cent citing previous work experience in this area. Less than 13 per cent claim experience in the federal government and 9 per cent in another provincial government (see Table 43).

Another 11 per cent cite experience at the municipal level and 6 per cent experience in another country. Just over 55 per cent cite any experience outside government, 17 per cent in the not-for-profit sector, and 22 per cent in academia. Only 17 per cent cite private sector experience. This is a much lower figure for private sector experience than is found at the federal level, and a much higher figure for not for profits.

Regardless of their work experience and academic background, however, provincial analysts tend to have had little training in formal policy analysis, either in their post-secondary educational career or in post-employment training.

As Table 44 shows, 41 per cent of analysts never took a single policy-specific course at the post-secondary level, and 60 per cent have taken two or fewer policy-related courses. Moreover, as Table 45 shows, close to 60 per cent of analysts have never completed a post-secondary course specifically dealing with formal policy analysis or evaluation.

Table 44. Number of Post-Secondary Policy Courses Completed

	Frequency	Per cent	Cumulative Per cent
Valid	124	9.9	9.9
0	519	41.3	51.1
1	113	9.0	60.1
2	118	9.4	69.5
3+	384	305	100.0
Total	1,258	100.0	

Table 45. Completion of Post-Secondary Policy Analysis Courses

	Frequency	Per cent
Valid	86	6.8
No	723	57.5
Yes	449	35.7
Total	1,258	100.0

Table 46. Completion of Formal Internal Training Courses

	Frequency	Per cent
Valid	104	8.3
No	697	55.4
Yes	457	36.3
Total	1,258	100.0

Table 47. Sources of Post-Employment Training

	N	Per cent
Attended policy-related conferences	805	64.0%
Attended policy workshops or forums	940	74.7%
Completed public administration, political science, economics, or other policy-relevant courses at a university or college	246	19.6%
Completed policy courses with the Canada School of Public Service or any other government-run or government-sponsored training institute	123	9.8%
Total	1,258	100.0%

Another possible source of training, of course, is internal, government-provided training. However, as Table 46 shows, about the same proportion of provincial analysts (55 per cent) have also never completed any formal internal governmental training on these subjects. Also, as Table 47 reveals, by far the most common form of post-employment "training" is attendance at policy-related conferences, workshops, or forums. Only 10 per cent of provincial analysts cited completion of policy courses with government-run or sponsored training institutes, while another 20 per cent cited completion of policy-relevant courses at a university or college. The former figure, in particular, is much lower than at the federal level.

Day-to-Day Duties

What do these sub-national analysts do in their day-to-day jobs? First, they tend to work in small groups, as almost 90 per cent work in formal policy units. This is in keeping with the recommendations of many government reports that analysts should be clustered rather than separated or isolated in departments (State Services Commission 1991; Hawke 1993; Fellegi 1996). These units are located overwhelmingly in the provincial capital, with 78 per cent of respondents indicating a very high frequency of daily activities in the capital (see Table 48).

As for the activities carried out in these units, most analysts are still quite isolated in that they work almost exclusively within their own

Table 48. Work

	... in Provincial Capital		... Within own government	
	Frequency	Per cent	Frequency	Per cent
Valid				
Never	52	4.1	68	5.4
Annually	51	4.1	67	5.3
Quarterly	71	5.6	138	11.0
Monthly	58	4.6	267	212
Weekly	36	2.9	446	35.5
Daily	983	78.1	261	20.7
Total	1,251	99A	1,247	99.1
Missing	7	.6	11	.9
Total	1,258	100.0	1,258	100

government. Eighty per cent of analysts report no daily interactions on issues related to international government, 65 per cent few or infrequent interactions with local governments, and 50 per cent infrequent interactions with the federal or other provincial or territorial governments. Fifty-six per cent, however, report very frequent, daily, or weekly interactions with other ministries within their own government (see Table 48).

These units are also small. As Table 49 shows, 60 per cent of analysts work in units of fewer than ten employees and about 30 per cent in units of fewer than five full-time equivalent employees. And, as Table 49 also shows, 50 per cent of these units have fewer than five people actually working on policy issues.

As for the nature of the issues upon which they work, about 40 per cent of analysts report fairly frequently working on issues ongoing for more than a year, about the same proportion as report frequently working on issues ongoing for between six and twelve months and between one and six months. Fifty per cent, however, report frequently working on issues that can be resolved in less than a month, while about 60 per cent report working on issues and problems that demand immediate attention (i.e. "firefighting") on either a daily or weekly basis (see Table 50).

Table 49. Number of FTEs

	... Working in Policy Unit		... Working in Unit on Policy Issues	
	Frequency	Per cent	Frequency	Per cent
Valid	15	1.2	14	1.1
01–05	344	27.3	619	492
06–10	426	33.9	399	31.7
11–20	304	242	164	13.0
21–50	138	11.0	47	3.7
50 plus	31	2.5	15	1.2
Total	1,258	100.0	1,258	100.0

Table 50. Frequency of Work on Short-Term Issues

	Frequency	Per cent
Valid n/a	33	2.6
Never	40	3.2
Annually	45	3.6
Quarterly	89	7.1
Monthly	182	14.5
Weekly	432	34.3
Daily	299	23.8
Total	1,120	89.0
Missing	138	11.0
Total	1,258	100.0

This finding about the prevalence of short-term work at this level of government is often decried in the existing literature on the subject (Gregory and Lonti 2008), but can also be considered a primary raison d'être of the policy bureaucracy. As Hawke put it:

Fire-fighting is part of the job of any manager and is especially promi-nent in the public service because of the pressures on ministers. *It is worth remembering that a key reason for having departmental policy advice agencies rather than distinct contracts for each piece of policy development is the desirability of immediate and unplanned access to informed advice.* (Hawke 1993: 64) (italics added)

Techniques and Data Employed

What analytical techniques do provincial policy analysts employ and with what information sources? First, it is important to note that provincial policy analysts think of their jobs as involving the development of analytical services in order to provide advice (analysis) to governments. As Table 51 shows, 82 per cent of analysts describe their role as either "analysis" or "advice provision." Only 46 per cent think of themselves as "researchers," slightly more than the percentage who think of themselves as "co-ordinators."

Table 51. Description of Policy Role(s)

	Included	
	N	Per cent
Advisor	969	77.0%
Analyst	1,025	81.5%
Communications Officer	193	15.3%
Coordinator	551	43.8%
Director	118	9.4%
Evaluator	269	21.4%
Liaison Officer	191	15.2%
Manager	224	17.8%
Planner	318	25.3%
Researcher	581	46.2%
Public Participation Expert	90	7.2%
Program Analyst	332	26.4%
Program Manager	127	10.1%

Table 52. General Policy Tasks Undertaken

	N	Per cent
Department or agency planning	550	43.7%
Environmental scans/Issue tracking	860	68.4%
Legal analysis	332	26.4%
Preparing Budget/Treasury Board submissions	481	38.2%
	896	71.2%
Networking	825	65.6%
Preparing briefing notes or position papers	1,095	87.0%
Providing options on issues	1,064	84.6%
Undertaking research and analysis	1,089	86.6%
Providing advice	1,081	85.9%
Total	1,258	100.0%

These findings are very similar to those reported by Radin (1992) in her study of role descriptions found in the U.S. Department of Health and Human Services, and highlight the existence of several general types of analysts working at this level: researcher/analysts, evaluators, co-ordinators, and managers; with the former three groups each equal to about half the size of the cohort of researcher/analysts.

This structure is borne out by the general kinds of tasks conducted at this level, with less formal duties such as environmental scans and issue tracking outweighing more technical financial or legal tasks, and with all analysts involved in the development of ministerial briefing notes that outline options and provide advice to governments (see Table 52).

The primary analytical techniques used in these activities are also generally more informal than formal. Eighty-four per cent of respondents (Table 53) claim to be involved in "brainstorming," followed by about 70 per cent in "consultation" and 60 per cent in using "checklists." Cost-benefit analysis is the only formal technique to attain use by over 50 per cent of respondents, only slightly higher than other less formal techniques such as expert elicitation (48 per cent) and scenario analysis (50 per cent). While this pattern goes against the instructions and admonitions of many textbooks, it is in keeping with the findings of many utilization studies which have found a distinct preference for

Table 53. Specific Analytical Technique(s) Used

	N	Per cent
Brainstorming	1,054	83.8%
Consultation exercises	859	68.3%
Focus groups	468	37.2%
Free-form gaming or other policy exercises	82	6.5%
Problem mapping	393	31.2%
Checklists	744	59.1%
Decision/probability trees	300	23.8%
Expert judgments and elicitation	603	47.9%
Development of sophisticated modelling tools	150	11.9%
Markov chain modelling	10	.8%
Monte Carlo techniques	20	1.6%
Process influence or social network diagrams	101	8.0%
Scenario analysis	633	50.3%
Cost-effectiveness analysis	538	42.8%
Cost-benefit analysis	686	54.5%
Environmental impact assessment	348	27.7%
Financial impact analysis	91	7.2%
Preference scaling	765	60.8%
Risk analysis	200	15.9%
Robustness or sensitivity analysis	0	.0%
Total	1,258	100.0%

the use of "simple" tools versus complex ones on the part of both the producers and consumers of policy analysis (Sabatier 1978; Nilsson et al. 2008). It also suggests, again, that analysts fall into several distinct types which favour the use of specific analytical techniques.

Conclusion

Empirical research into the sub-national level in the Canadian case presented here reveals that many more analysts fall into the category of short-term, project-oriented "troubleshooters" than the long-term strategic "planners" many have thought them to be, based on incorrect inferences drawn from studies of national officials. Provincial analysts, like their federal counterparts, are highly educated, relatively young, and mobile. But they do not tend to have a great deal of formal training in policy analysis and mainly work in small units deeply embedded in provincial ministries. They tend to work on a relatively small number of issue areas, often on a "firefighting" basis, and, like their federal counterparts in the regions, a large percentage of analysts can be thought of as a kind of cadre of internal experts who can be brought into problem areas – a free-floating "brain trust" of internal "consultants" available to work on pressing and troubling policy issues.

In terms of the six styles of policy analysis identified by Mayer, Bots, and Van Daalen (2004) in their comparative study of policy analytical styles, the predominant sets of analysts identified in the sub-national analysis reported above can be thought of as providing strategic advice as well as design and recommendation, or as working in a "client-advice" style somewhat removed from both the traditional "rational" style promoted by textbook and policy schools, and in the more "interactive" or "participatory" styles identified by more recent national studies (Banfield 1977; Lindblom and Cohen 1979; Baehr 1981; Shulock 1999; Adams 2004). Their short-term orientation, relative inexperience, high levels of job mobility, and lack of training in formal policy analytical techniques also set them apart from their national counterparts and have significant implications for policy design and efficacy in multilevel states.

These findings are important not only to critics and theorists outside of government institutions who wish to better understand the operation and functioning of policy advice systems, and especially these systems' professional bureaucratic component, but also to those inside the system who wish to better assess and evaluate such activities in order to improve training and recruitment practices, enhance analysis, and, ultimately, improve policy outcomes (Di Francesco 1999 and 2000; State Services Commission 1999; ANAO 2001; Mintrom 2003). New sets of studies based on large-scale surveys at both the national and sub-national levels, such as the one reported here, are needed to bring more light to this topic. More accurate assessments of policy analytical activities in government, especially those governments operating within multilevel governance frameworks, are needed to inform any moves in this direction.

PART THREE

Conclusion

8 Conclusion – Policy Analytical Capacity and Evidence-Based Policy-Making: Lessons from Canada

Policy analysis is a relatively recent movement, dating back to the 1960s and the U.S. experience with large-scale planning processes in areas such as defence, urban redevelopment, and budgeting (Lindblom 1958; Wildavsky 1969; Behn 1981; MacRae and Wilde 1985; Garson 1986). Seen as a social movement, it represents the efforts of actors inside and outside formal political decision-making processes to improve policy outcomes by applying systematic evaluative rationality to public problems and concerns (Aberbach and Rockman 1989; Mintrom 2007). There have been debates about whether policy analysis has improved on the outcomes associated with processes such as bargaining, compromise, negotiation, and log rolling that are less instrumental (Majone 1989; Uhr 1996; Colebatch 2006). However, from within the policy analytical community, there has been no fundamental challenge to the primary raison d'être of policy analysis: to improve policy outcomes by applying systematic analytic methodologies to policy appraisal, assessment, and evaluation (MacRae 1991; Radin 2000; Nilsson et al. 2008).

Evidence-based or "evidence-informed" policymaking represents a recent effort to again reform or restructure policy processes by prioritizing evidentiary decision-making criteria (Pawson 2006; Sanderson 2006; Nutley, Walter, and Davies 2007). This is being done in an effort to avoid or minimize policy failures caused by a mismatch between government expectations and actual, on-the-ground conditions. The evidence-based policy movement is thus the latest in a series of efforts undertaken by reformers in governments over the past half-century to enhance the efficiency and effectiveness of public policymaking. In all of these efforts, it is expected that through a process of theoretically informed empirical analysis, governments can better learn from experience and avoid repeating the errors of the past as well as better apply new techniques to the resolution of old and new problems (May 1992; Sanderson 2002a).

Exactly what constitutes "evidence-based policymaking" and whether analytical efforts in this regard actually result in better or improved policies, however, are topics that remain contentious in the literature on the subject (Packwood 2002; Pawson 2002; Jackson 2007; Boaz et al. 2008). A spate of studies, for example, has questioned the value of a renewed emphasis on the collection and analysis of large amounts of data in policymaking circumstances (Tenbensel 2004). Among the concerns raised about an increased emphasis on evidence in contemporary policymaking are the following:

1. Evidence is only one factor involved in policymaking and is not necessarily able to overcome other factors such as constitutional divisions of powers or jurisdictions, which can arbitrarily assign locations and responsibilities for particular issue areas to specific levels or institutions of government and diminish the rationality level of policymaking by so doing (Radin and Boase 2000; Young et al. 2002; Davies 2004).
2. Data collection and analytical techniques employed in its gathering and analysis by specially trained policy technicians may not be necessarily superior to the experiential judgments of politicians and other key policy decision makers (Majone 1989; Jackson 2007).
3. The kinds of "high-quality" and universally acknowledged evidence initially proposed when "evidence-based policymaking" first entered the lexicon of policy analysts in the health care field – especially the "systematic review" of clinical findings – often has no analogue in many policy sectors, where generating evidence using the "gold standard" of random clinical trial methodologies may not be possible (Innvaer et al. 2002; Pawson et al. 2005).
4. An increased emphasis on evidence-based policymaking can stretch the analytical resources of participating organizations, be they governmental or non-governmental, to the breaking point (Hammersley 2005). That is, government efforts in this area may have adverse consequences for themselves in terms of requiring greater expenditures on analytical activities at the expense of operational ones. This is also true for many non-governmental policy actors, such as small-scale NGOs, whose analytical resources may be non-existent and who may also be forced to divert financial, personnel, and other scarce resources from implementation activities to policymaking in order

to meet increased governments' requests for more and better data on the merits and demerits of their proposed policy solutions and programs (Laforest and Orsini 2005).

Some of these concerns are misplaced or easily refuted and can be seen to result from an overly rationalistic view of policymaking (Howlett, Ramesh, and Perl 2009). For example, with respect to the first concern about the adverse effects of constitutional and institutional orders on policymaking, this can almost always be taken as a meta-contextual "given" within which any form of analysis, evidence based or otherwise, must take place. Concerns in this area then apply to all kinds of policy analysis and are not a function of any increased emphasis on knowledge utilization. With respect to the second concern – that the evidence-based movement represents a return to early ideas about technocratic, expert-driven policymaking and that such forms of policy analysis are not necessarily superior to political judgments based on experience – it should be noted that, unlike many earlier efforts at improving policy through analysis that did rely on an underlying apolitical, technocratic view of optimal policymaking, evidence-based policymaking represents a compromise between political and technocratic views of policymaking. That is, it relies on the notion of policymaking not as a purely rational affair but as an exercise in pragmatic judgment, whereby political, ideological, or other forms of "non-evidence-based" policymaking are tempered by an effort on the part of policy specialists to "speak truth to power" – to present evidence to policymakers that supports or refutes specific policy measures as appropriate to resolve identified policy problems (Wildavsky 1979; Sanderson 2002b), but does not attempt to replace their judgment with their own (Tenbensel 2004; Head 2008). The same is true with respect to the third concern – that systematic reviews do not exist in many sectors and issue areas. This should be seen more as a criticism of the lack of effort expended to date in collecting more and better data in many policy sectors than as a critique of the idea of the enhanced utilization of systematically complied and assessed evidence in public policy formulation and decision making (Young et al. 2002; Qureshi 2004; Warburton and Warburton 2004; Shaxson 2005).

The fourth concern – that many policy actors may not have the ability or resources required to carry out evidence-based policymaking – is much more serious. An increased emphasis on the use of evidence in policymaking requires that policy actors, especially governmental ones, have the analytical capability required to collect appropriate data and utilize it effectively in the course of policymaking activities. As such, it highlights the fact that a significant factor affecting the ability of policymakers to engage at all in evidence-based policymaking pertains to the level of both governmental and non-governmental actors' "policy analytical capacity."

Overall, Norman Riddell summarized the requisites of policy analytical capacity as lying in "a recognized requirement or demand for research; a supply of qualified researchers; ready availability of quality data; policies and procedures to facilitate productive interactions with other researchers; and a culture in which openness is encouraged and risk taking is acceptable" (Riddell 1998: 7). If evidence-based policymaking is to be achieved, policy actors require the ability to collect and aggregate information in order to effectively develop medium- and long-term projections, proposals for, and evaluations of future government activities. Organizations both inside and outside of governments require a level of human, financial, network, and knowledge resources enabling them to perform the tasks associated with managing and implementing an evidence-based policy process. Without this they might only marshal these resources in particular areas, resulting in a "lumpy" set of departmental or agency competences in which some agencies are able to plan and prioritize over the long term while others focus on shorter-term issues or, if evenly distributed, may only be able to react to short- or medium-term political, economic, or other challenges and imperatives occurring in their policy environments (Voyer 2007).

The evidence-based policy movement, thus, must confront the fact that many recent studies suggest that the level of policy analytical capacity found in many government and non-governmental organizations is low, a fact that may contribute significantly to the failure of efforts to enhance evidence-based policymaking and its ancillary goal of improving policymaking processes and policymaking outcomes. The theory, concepts, and evidence lying behind the idea of policy analytical capacity and its relationship to evidence-based policymaking are set out below.

Evidence-Based Policymaking as an Effort to Avoid Policy Failures and Enhance the Potential for Policy Success through Policy Learning

Evidence-based policymaking represents an attempt to enhance the possibility of policy success by improving the amount and type of information processed in public policy decision making as well as the methods used in its assessment (Morgan and Henrion 1990; Nilsson et al. 2008). Based on the idea that better decisions are those that incorporate the most available information, it is expected that enhancing the information basis of policy decisions will improve the results flowing from their implementation, while iterative monitoring and evaluation of results in the field will allow errors to be caught and corrected. Through improved information processing and utilization, it is expected that policy learning will be enhanced and result, at minimum, in the avoidance of policy failures or a reduction in the chances of their occurrence, with, accordingly, an increase in the potential for additional or greater success in attaining policy goals and anticipated or expected policy outcomes (March 1981, 1994; Bennett and Howlett 1992).

Evaluating these claims is difficult, of course, not least due to the fact that policies can succeed or fail in numerous ways, with significant variations at different levels of severity and aggregation. Sometimes an entire policy regime can fail, for example, while more often specific programs within a policy field may be designated as successful or unsuccessful. The most egregious cases are when an entire policy regime substantively fails, a failure that is typically very public and obvious to voters and the public at large. In such cases, policymakers may acknowledge that mistakes were made and attempt to gather information in order to clarify the reasons why the failure occurred and suggest alternative routes that would avoid repeating the same or similar errors in the future. This can involve the use of commissions and other types of enquiries linked to an evidence-based perspective (Bulmer 1981; Aucoin 1990), but can also often result in a strictly partisan critique based more on ideological and electoral considerations than on gathering and processing information (Schmidt 1996; Hird 2005). More often, however, it is specific programs within a policy field that are designated as unsuccessful. Such failures are often much less visible to non-experts and do not entail the threat of a general legitimization crisis requiring public intervention in the form of a commission or enquiry (Schudson 2006). Efforts to deal with such failures typically would include specialized legitimization-building exercises within the relevant policy community, such as specialized consultations with experts as part of efforts designed to correct such failures (Peters and Barker 1993). These latter failures are typically more amenable to the knowledge generation and utilization activities associated with evidence-based policymaking than are the more generalized and highly publicized regime failures.

Similarly, policies and programs can also succeed or fail either in substantive terms – that is, as objectively or perceived to be delivering or failing to deliver expected material outcomes – or, in procedural terms, as being legitimate or illegitimate, fair or unfair, just or unjust in their formulation, implementation, or results. Such judgments are often themselves highly unsystematic and partisan in nature. In fact, such judgments involve most of the key actors arrayed in policy subsystems in a variety of formal and informal venues for assessing and critiquing policy outcomes and processes. They almost always involve officials and politicians within government dealing with the policy in question, but may also involve members of the public, who often will have the ultimate say on a government's policy record when they vote at elections, and members of relevant interest groups, political parties, think tanks, the media, and other policy actors (Bovens, t'Hart, and Peters 2001; Brandstrom and Kuipers 2003). The political nature of judgments about policy success and failure also implies that such assessments will rarely be unanimous. This is in part due to the fact that political evaluations depend on the imputation of notions of intentionality to government actors made by policy evaluators – so that the results of policymaking can be assessed against expectations. This is often a highly partisan, controversial, and much less than neutral or objective task because 1) government intentions themselves can be, intentionally or otherwise, very vague and ambiguous, secret, or even potentially contradictory or mutually exclusive; 2) labels such as "success" and "failure" are inherently relative and will be interpreted differently by different policy actors; and 3) government policies take time to put into place and circumstances may change in such a way as to render moot initial government assessments of policy contexts and judgments of the severity of policy problems and the appropriateness of particular policy tools for their solution. Designations of policy success and failure are semantic tools themselves used in public debate and policy contestation in order to seek political advantage (Weaver 1986; Hood 2002; Sulitzeanu-Kenan and Hood 2005). Policy evaluations affect considerations and consequences related to assessing blame and taking credit for government activities at all stages of the policy process, all of which can have electoral, administrative, and other consequences for policy actors and affect the susceptibility of the evaluations to evidence-based criteria. Thus the sites of judgments of policy success and failure are broader than often suggested, and the resulting cacophony of judgments and evaluations can make the analysis of success and failure quite difficult.

Despite these ontological and epistemological issues, however, as proponents of enhanced evidence-based or evidence-informed policymaking have observed, it is possible to make some headway in assessing policy success and failure by examining the role evidence and knowledge play in the specific types of policy failures identified in the different stages of the policymaking process by the more systematic academic literature on the subject.

Types of Policy Failures and the Role Played by Evidence Therein

Unlike popular commentators who more often than not tend to blame policy failures on the personality quirks and psychological limitations (such as stupidity, venality, or corrupt behaviour on the part of politicians and administrators) of participants or on associated innate organizational failings (the "bureaucratic mentality"), the academic literature on policy failures has found that clearly identifiable policy failures have tended to occur only in very specific circumstances and have little to do with the psychological propensities of policy participants. They include the following situations:

1. an overreaching government has attempted to address "unaddressable" or "wicked" problems, where neither the cause of a problem nor the solution to it is well known (Churchman 1967; Pressman and Wildavsky 1973);
2. governments have failed to properly anticipate the consequences of their proposed courses of action or the general susceptibility of their policy or administrative systems to catastrophic and other kinds of collapse (Perrow 1984; Bovens and t'Hart 1996, 1995; Roots 2004);
3. a variety of "implementation failures" has occurred in which the aims of decision makers have failed to be properly or accurately translated into practice (Kerr 1976; Ingram and Mann 1980), often where there has been a lack of effective oversight over implementers on the part of decision makers (McCubbins and Schwartz 1984; McCubbins and Lupia 1994; Ellig and Lavoie 1995); and
4. governments and policymakers have failed to effectively evaluate policy processes and outcomes and/or have failed to learn the appropriate lessons from their own and other governments' previous experiences (Scharpf 1986; May 1992).

Each of these sources of failure originates in a different stage of the policy cycle (see Table 54 below). Each source of failure is also amenable,

Table 54. Stages of the Policy Process and Associated Policy Failures

Agenda setting	Overreaching governments establishing or agreeing to establish overburdened or unattainable policy agendas
Policy formulation	Attempting to deal with wicked problems without appropriately investigating or researching problem causes or the probable effects of policy alternatives
Decision making	Failing to anticipate adverse and other policy consequences or risk of system failures
Policy implementation	Failing to deal with implementation problems including lack of funding, legitimacy issues, principal-agent problems, oversight failures, and others
Policy evaluation	Lack of learning due to lack of, ineffective, or inappropriate policy monitoring and/or feedback processes and structures

at least in theory, to improvement through better information management in policymaking, as proposed by proponents of evidence-based policymaking. Solutions for overreaching governments, for example, lie in better information being provided to policymakers on their capabilities; better research and information on problem causes and policy effects can turn some apparently wicked problems into more manageable ones; better risk analysis can hedge against future consequences; better information systems can be implemented to aid implementation and enhance oversight; and more attention paid to policy monitoring and feedback processes can help ensure better evaluation of program and policy results and more effective policy learning (see Table 55). Policymakers and managers interested in avoiding these common sources of policy failure and enhancing the potential for greater policy success can address some of these causes of failure by insisting that government intentions be clarified and made consistent with resource endowments and can, at the same time, insist that criteria for measuring policy goals and their rationales be clearly specified. And they can continually monitor changing circumstances and alter some aspects of policies as these circumstances unfold (Waller 1992; Hawke 1993; Anderson 1996; Uhr and Mackay 1996).

Inspection of Table 55 shows that a significant factor affecting policy failures and their management through enhanced evidence-based

Table 55. Policy Failures and Management Strategies by Stage of the Policy Cycle

Stage of policy cycle	Problem	Solution
Agenda setting	Overreaching governments	Better clarification and precise articulation of government goals and resource capabilities
Policy formulation	Attempting to deal with wicked problems	Provision of better data and research on policy problem causation and alternative solutions
Decision making	Failing to anticipate policy consequences or risk of system structure failure	Better risk analysis and assessment and its integration into decision-making processes
Policy implementation	Principal-agent problems, oversight failures, etc.	More careful matching of administrative resources to policy goals and better design of monitoring and inspection systems
Policy evaluation	Lack of learning	Development of improved benchmarking and performance measurement systems and integration of this information into future policy deliberations

policymaking is closely related to governmental and non-governmental "policy analytical capacity." That is, each of the managerial strategies set out in Table 55 involves improvement of some aspect of information management for policy analysis. Enhancing policy analytical capacity is, in fact, an essential precondition for the adoption of evidence-based policymaking and the improvement of policy outcomes through its application, an essential precondition that is often ignored or downplayed in the literature.

Defining Policy Analytical Capacity

Policy capacity can be defined as a loose concept which covers the whole gamut of issues associated with the government's arrangements to review, formulate, and implement policies within its jurisdiction. It obviously includes the nature and quality of the resources available for these purposes – whether in the public service or beyond – and the practices and procedures by which these resources are mobilized and used (Fellegi 1996: 6).

While *policy capacity* can be thought of as extending beyond analysis to include the actual administrative capacity of a government to undertake the day-to-day activities involved in policy implementation (Peters 1996; Painter and Pierre 2005), *policy analytical capacity* is a more focused concept related to knowledge acquisition and utilization in policy processes (Lynn 1978; Leeuw 1991; MacRae 1991; Radaelli 1995; Adams 2004). It refers to the amount of basic research a government can conduct or access, its ability to apply statistical methods, applied research methods, and advanced modelling techniques to this data and to employ analytical techniques such as environmental scanning, trends analysis, and forecasting methods in order to gauge broad public opinion and attitudes, as well as those of interest groups and other major policy players, and to anticipate future policy impacts (O'Connor, Roos, and Vickers-Willis 2007; Preskill and Boyle 2008). It also involves the ability to communicate policy-related messages to interested parties and stakeholders and includes "a department's capacity to articulate its medium- and long-term priorities" (Fellegi 1996: 19) and to integrate information into the decision-making stage of the policy process.[1] These fundamental elements or components of policy analytical capacity are set out in Figure 30 below.

The policy functions outlined above require either a highly trained, and hence expensive, workforce that has far-seeing and future-oriented management and excellent information collection and data-processing capacities, as well as the opportunity for employees to strengthen their skills and expertise (O'Connor, Roos, and Vickers-Willis 2007) or the ability to outsource policy research to similarly qualified personnel in private or semi-public organizations such as universities, think tanks, research institutes, and consultancies (Boston 1994). It also requires sufficient vertical and horizontal coordination between participating organizations to ensure that the research undertaken is relevant and timely. "Boundary-spanning" links between governmental and nongovernmental organizations are also critical (Weible 2008). As George Anderson has noted, "a healthy policy-research community outside government can play a vital role in enriching public understanding and debate of policy issues, and it serves as a natural complement to policy capacity within government" (Anderson 1996: 486).

Figure 30: Aspects of Political Analytical Capacity

Components

Environmental scanning, trends analysis and forecasting methods

Theoretical research

Statistics, applied research and modeling

Evaluation of the means of meeting targets/goals

Consultation and managing relations

Program design, implementation monitoring and evaluation

Department's capacity to articulate its medium- and long-term priorities

Policy analytical resources — quantity and quality of employees; budgets; access to external sources of expertise

Source: Riddell 1998.

Assessing Policy Analytical Capacity in Practice

Whether or not, and to what degree, government and non-governmental policy actors in a policy analytical community have the capacity to actually fulfil these tasks remains an important and largely unanswered empirical question in the study of evidence-based policymaking (Wollmann 1989; Turnpenny et al. 2008).

Studies of the actual behaviour and job performance of policy analysts, for example, have constantly challenged the view often put forward in academic texts that policy analysis is all about the neutral, competent, and objective performance of tasks associated with the application and use of a small suite of technical policy analytical tools on the part of governmental or non-governmentally based analysts (Patton and Sawicki 1993; Boston 1994; Durning and Osama 1994; Boardman et al. 2001). This raises to the fore the question: "What do policy analysts actually do in contemporary governmental and non-governmental organizations?" And, related to this, "Are their training and resources appropriate to allow them to meet the requisites of evidence-based policy-making?" (Weller and Stevens 1998; New Zealand, State Services Commission 1999).

At present, only very weak and partial, usually anecdotal, information exists on the situations found in different countries. Over thirty years ago, Arnold Meltsner (1976) observed in the case of the United States that analysts undertook a number of roles in the policymaking process, most of which did not involve neutral information processing and analysis. Later observers, such as Beryl Radin (2000), Nancy Shulock (1999), and Sean Gailmard and John Patty (2007), observed much the same situation, along with a propensity for politicians to continually re-enact the same failed policies in many problem areas (Schultz 2007). In the United Kingdom and Germany, for example, contrary to the picture of carefully recruited analysts trained in policy schools to undertake specific types of microeconomic-inspired policy analysis (Weimer and Vining 1999), investigators such as Edward Page and Bill Jenkins (2005) and Julia Fleischer (2009) have provided some empirical evidence that British and German policymaking typically features a group of "policy process generalists" who rarely, if ever, deal with policy matters in the substantive areas in which they were trained and who have, in fact, very little training in formal policy analysis techniques such as cost-benefit analysis or risk assessment. As Page and Jenkins concluded:

> The broad features of our characterization of UK policy bureaucracy are that policy officials at relatively junior levels are given substantial responsibility for developing and maintaining policy and servicing other, formally superior officials or bodies, often by offering technical advice and guidance. These people are not technical specialists in the sense that they develop high levels of technical expertise in one subject or stay in the same job for a long time. They are often left with apparently substantial discretion to develop policy because they often receive vague instructions about how to do their jobs, are not closely supervised, and work in an environment that is in most cases not overtly hierarchical. (Page and Jenkins 2005: 168)

Similar findings have been made in the cases of the Netherlands, Australia, and New Zealand, by Robert Hoppe and Margarita Jeliazkova (2006), Patrick Weller and Bronwyn Stevens (1998), and Jonathan Boston and his colleagues (1996), respectively.

Policy Analytical Capacity in Canada

How does Canada shape up with regard to this important indicator (and predictor) of the successful application of enhanced evidence-based policymaking and, ultimately, improved policy success through the avoidance of policy failures? Little is known about the supply and demand for policy analysis in Canada, although recent critiques of the pedagogy of public administration and public policy programs suggest there is good reason to suspect that a significant gap between pedagogy and practice may exist in this country (Gow and Sutherland 2004).

Current evidence suggests that, with the possible exception of some major Canadian business associations and corporations (Stritch 2007), capacity in the non-governmental sector is very limited. This is true of a majority of actors involved in the Canadian labour movement (Jackson and Baldwin 2007), the voluntary sector (Laforest and Orsini 2005; Phillips 2007), as well as the media (Murray 2007), think tanks (Abelson 2002, 2007), and political parties (Cross 2007), most of which have very few if any permanent employees employed to conduct policy analysis of any kind. In many cases, analysis is carried out by consultants rather than paid staff, contributing to the transitory nature of much program design and policy analysis in Canada. However, even less is known about the training and activities of this "invisible public service" (Saint-Martin 1998; Bakvis 2000; Perl and White 2002; Speers 2007).

This portrayal of a generally impoverished and low-capacity policy analytical community pushes the emphasis for the prospects of enhanced evidence-based policymaking back onto Canadian governments, which, in theory at least, have access to the kinds of personnel, treasure, and organizational resources that would allow them to construct substantial policy analytical capacity. What little is known about the actual work of policy analysts in contemporary Canadian governments, however, reveals a picture of a very "lumpy" or uneven distribution of policy analytical capacity, varying by level of government and by department or agency involved.

Early works in the late 1970s and early 1980s on the emerging policy analysis professions provided little empirical evidence of what analysts actually did in practice (Prince 1979; Prince and Chenier 1980), but rather often simply assumed they would contribute to the increased rationality of policymaking through the application of systematic analytical techniques such as cost-benefit analysis to the evaluation of policies and policy alternatives. Studies undertaken by federal government analysts, however, raised doubts about this picture (Hartle 1978; French 1980). Later studies in the 1990s also noted the growth and subsequent decline of employment of policy analysts in government and their limited capacity for developing long-term strategic advice for governments (Bennett and McPhail 1992; Hollander and Prince 1993). Work since the early 1990s has suggested that tasks of policy analysts may be shifting, as in the United Kingdom and the other countries cited above, towards an increased emphasis on policy process design and network management activities and away from "formal" types of policy analysis (Lindquist 1992; Howlett and Lindquist 2004).

Governments and, increasingly, non-governmental actors in Canada and elsewhere are being asked to design effective long-term policy measures to deal with such problems without necessarily having the kinds of resources they require to successfully avoid common policy failures through the use of enhanced evidence-based analytical techniques.

This general pattern, however, varies greatly by level of government and, within each level, by the agency or department involved (Dobuzinskis, Howlett, and Laycock 2007). The current policy analytical capacity of the Canadian federal government, for example, although highly varied in terms of its distribution among departments and between departments and central agencies (Bakvis 1997, 2000; Voyer 2007), is reasonably high by historical and comparative standards (Prince 2007). Resources were cut during the budgetary crises of the 1980s and 1990s, setting back analytical capacity to levels not seen since the 1970s (Hollander and Prince 1993; Bakvis 2000). However, the federal government and several provinces eliminated their deficits in the late 1990s and began to revitalize their civil services in their new-found surplus positions. Federal government policy capacity needed re-energizing after the cuts of the 1980s and 1990s, particularly in key departments tasked to assist in identifying new priorities and strategies (Lindquist and Desveaux 1998), and efforts specifically directed at enhancing policy capacity were undertaken, beginning with Ivan Fellegi's 1996 Task Force on Strengthening Our Policy Capacity (Bourgon 1996). In the late 1990s, the Policy Research Initiative (PRI) promoted collaboration with an ever-expanding array of university institutes and think tanks (Bakvis 2000; Voyer 2007) as a way to rebuild federal policy analytical capacity in the new era of participatory governance. This is significant since the number and range of players in policy areas such as climate change – governments, interest groups, think tanks, aboriginal communities, NGOs, international organizations, and others – has expanded, along with the range of issues with which analysts must now be concerned (Lindquist 1992). Federal policy development processes now typically contain mandated criteria for consultations and political leaders and administrators typically access polling data and conduct focus groups as part of the standard process of policy development. This has created a far more complicated policymaking environment for governments, since different strategies for building arguments and cases for policy initiatives and far more consultation are required than in past eras (Howlett and Lindquist 2004). Ultimately, highly centralized and well-resourced decision-making systems eventually took shape in the hands of the prime minister and the minister of finance (Savoie 1999; Bernier, Brownsey, and Howlett 2005), with a focus on policy performance management (Saint-Martin 1998). This results orientation has led the federal government to increasingly promote horizontal and holistic analyses of policy problems, such as climate change adaptation, and to try to better align initiatives across governments and sectors, including recruitment and retention of policy analysts, in order to "even out" the uneven distribution of capacities across departments and units (Aucoin and Bakvis 2005).

Whether or not the policy analytical capacity of the federal government has grown sufficiently to deal with this increased scope, range, and complexity is uncertain, but there is little doubt that analytical capacity has improved since its nadir in the late 1980s (Wellstead, Stedman, and Lindquist 2007). However, evidence at the provincial, territorial, and local levels – although much less extensive than at the federal level – suggests that policy analytical capacity at these levels is much weaker (Rasmussen 1999; McArthur 2007; Stewart and Smith 2007) and leads to a short-term focus in many policies and programs adopted at these levels of government. However, efforts – such as the Policy Excellence Initiative in Nova Scotia, the Knowledge and Information Services initiative in British Columbia, the Policy Innovation and Leadership project in Ontario, as well as cabinet-level initiatives in Yukon, Manitoba, Newfoundland and Labrador, and Alberta – are under way in many jurisdictions to systematically grapple with this issue (Ontario, Executive Research Group 1999; Manitoba, Office of the Auditor General 2001; Hicks and Watson 2007; Nova Scotia, Policy Excellent Initiative 2007).

Conclusion

In their 2006 study of the policy analytical activities undertaken in the United States, the United Kingdom, and several other European countries, H.K. Colebatch and Beryl Radin concluded that there are currently three areas of priority for contemporary research work on policy analysis:

1. "How the question is framed, what discourse is accepted as valid, and how this work relates to the outcome at any point in time";
2. "What sort of activity do practitioners see as policy work, and what sort of policy workers do they recognize"; and

3. "There are questions for teaching and professional preparation" that will derive from these first two studies (Colebatch and Radin 2006: 225).

These are all important observations, both for the evaluation of the capacity of policy analytical communities to undertake high-level, long-term policy analysis and for the possibility of enhancing evidence-based policymaking processes and procedures in government. The set of jobs and duties actually performed by policy analysts in both government and non-governmental organizations is very closely tied to the resources they have at their disposal in terms of personnel and funding, the demand they face from clients and managers for high-quality results, and the availability of high-quality data and information on future trends.

In Canada, recent work provides some evidence of the activities of analysts in a wider range of situations, both inside and outside of government, than has usually been considered or investigated in the past. The basic "sociology" of policy analysis in Canada – who policy analysts are and what policy analysts actually do (and its pedagogy – how they are trained and how their training fits their job) – suggests the existence of a generally government-dominated policy analytical community, but also a very mixed pattern of policy analytical capacity by jurisdiction and administrative unit, with some central and departmental-level units in the federal government displaying the highest capacity and some provincial and local government agencies the lowest (Dobuzinskis, Howlett, and Laycock 2007).

The weak policy capacity found among most of the major actors involved in policy analysis, even in rich countries like Canada, is very problematic in the context of dealing with the challenges of improving policymaking through the adoption of evidence-based techniques for dealing with complex contemporary policy challenges. The short-term focus it often promotes, for example, is very ill suited for the development of the ongoing and long-term solutions required to deal with large multifaceted contemporary problems like climate change mitigation and adaptation (Adamowicz 2007).

Ultimately, both governments and, increasingly, non-governmental actors in Canada and elsewhere are being asked to design effective long-term policy measures to deal with such problems without necessarily having the kinds of resources they require to successfully avoid common policy failures through the use of enhanced evidence-based analytical techniques. Without prior or at least concurrent efforts to enhance policy analytical capacity, unfortunately, "failure may be the only option" available to governments in their efforts to deal with critical contemporary policy challenges.

Notes

3 Agenda Setting – Predictable and Unpredictable Policy Windows

1 Other authors, of course, argue that agenda setting is a much more random process. See Baumgartner and Jones 1993.
2 Much of Kingdon's analysis is based on earlier work undertaken by Jack Walker into the agenda-setting process followed in the U.S. Senate. Examining Walker's work, it becomes apparent that Kingdon's principal hypothesis related to the frequency of predictable and unpredictable windows was derived from the application of Walker's observation that U.S. Senate agenda items varied widely in their level of institutionalization or "routinization." Kingdon also made use of Walker's distinction between "discretionary" and "nondiscretionary" issues. See Walker 1977.
3 On these techniques see Chatfield 1989 and Gottman 1981. See also Priestley 1981 and Thrall and Engelman 1988.
4 Because the first order correlations are high for all series, ARIMA methods should be utilized rather than an ordinary least squares method (since the significant auto correlation in the series violate crucial assumptions in OLS analysis). See McCleary and Hay.
5 On this technique see McCleary and Hay, 240–3; Liu 1988, and Vandaele.
6 Coherency "measures the linear correlation between two series at each frequency and is analogous to the square of the ordinary product-moment correlation coefficient." See Chatfield, *The Analysis of Time Series*, 147.
7 Beecher et al. have argued that the key effect to watch for is "agenda-density," or how many issues are on the agenda at one time. See Beecher et al.
8 On this "traditional" behaviour of policy entrepreneurs, see Mintrom 1997 and Durant and Diehl 1989.

9 See especially Schneider and Frey 1988 for a review of the many empirical studies which have failed to reveal evidence of the existence of such cycles. For Canada see Johnston 1986 and Foot 1979.

10 Johnston found that "On balance, the now classic formulation of the political-business cycle finds little support in Canadian attitudinal data. Canadians are not systematically more averse to unemployment than to inflation; if anything the opposite is true. Over time, aversion shifts back and forth sharply, according to whichever of inflation or unemployment yields the worst reading" (Johnston 1986: 144). Foot argued that "generally, the cyclical economic and political factors at the national level examined in this chapter do not appear to have had a significant impact on the variation in the ratio of 'public' employment to total employment" (Foot 1979: 79).

4 Policy Formulation

1 Keith Dowding has argued that policy network theory may be more of a metaphor than a model, useful more for descriptive purposes than for predicting or explaining specific patterns or propensities for policy change. While this criticism began a significant debate in the field, much of the debate itself has been polemical and lacking in empirical referents. See Pappi and Henning 1998; Peters 1998; Keith Dowding 2001; and Marsh and Smith 2001.

2 Many works taken under the rubric of the "advocacy coalition framework," "neo-institutionalism," and "policy community" studies in the 1980s and 1990s utilized this basic typology of subsystem policy dynamics. Studies in Europe focused on the analysis of networks as a new empirical phenomenon, emerging out of the wreckage of national corporatist arrangements in the new Europe. Those in the United States concerned with advancing pluralist thought to incorporate long-term patterns of state-societal interactions did much the same thing, while similar concepts and terms arose out of studies of transnational patterns of policymaking and the interaction of elites at the international level. On U.S. studies see Laumann and Knoke 1987; Sabatier and Jenkins-Smith 1993; and Baumgartner and Jones 1993. For European examples, see Marin and Mayntz 1991; Rhodes; and Kickert, Klijn, and Koppenjan 1997. At the international level see Haas 1992.

3 In Canada, see, for example, Phillips 1991 and Coleman and Skogstad 1990. Prominent studies in the United States include Knoke 1990 and Heinz et al. 1993. Elsewhere, see Le Gales and Thatcher 1995.

4 Peter Hall defines a policy paradigm as establishing "the broad goals behind policy, the related problems or puzzles that policymakers have to solve to get there, and, in large measure, the kind of instruments that can be used to attain these goals" (Hall 1990: 59).

5 This is the usual way that paradigmatic policy change is thought to occur. See Hall 1993 and 1992.

6 Empirical evidence of such processes has been generated in diverse areas such as agricultural and aboriginal policy, among others. See Howlett 1994 and Coleman, Skogstad, and Atkinson 1996.

7 This is not a new insight, of course. The analysis of incremental decision making, for example, attributes a propensity for policy change to occur as a result of analysis of the marginal differences between existing and proposed policy options to the fact that the same sets of policymakers bargain among themselves to arrive at a decision, and are unlikely to overturn agreements based on past negotiations and compromises. Hayes 1991.

8 On the role of anomalies in policymaking, see Hall 1993. On the role of policy entrepreneurs, see Kingdon 1984; Mintrom 1997; Roberts and King 1991.

9 Examples of first-order changes in a health sector, for example, would include altering staffing levels in hospitals or altering physician fee schedules. Second-order changes would involve changing the type of instrument used to deliver health care such as moving from user fees to mandatory insurance arrangements. Third-order change would involve a shift in policy goals, such as moving away from a biomedical focus on the individual to a more holistic goal of collective, social, or community well-being. Hall, P. A. "Policy Paradigms, Social Learning and the State: The Case of Economic Policy Making in Britain." *Comparative Politics* 25, no. 3 (1993): 275–96.

10 For similar models based on a similar critique of Hall see Daugbjerg 2000.

11 While it is common to associate small subsystems with integration and large ones with incohesiveness, many studies have shown that small subsystems can exhibit unintegrated communities and networks, while being large, similarly, does not prevent subsystems from being unified and cohesive. See, for example, Zahariadis and Allen 1995; Giuliani 1999; and Kriesi and Jegen 2001.

12 This methodology does not allow for direct evaluation of all of the aspects of the models set out above, especially that related to the significance of the strengths of ties between subsystem members or the specific nature or content of the ideas held by specific actors. For examples of this kind of analysis see Zijlstra 1978; Gadde and Mattson 1987; and Laumann and Knoke 1987

13 This is, in itself, a somewhat contentious issue since there is no clear, accepted definition of a policy "domain" available in the policy literature. See Burstein 1991; Hosseus and Pal 1997. Problems with different domain definitions have been apparent in sociologically inspired network analyses and feature prominently, for example, in the debate surrounding the "hollow core" versus "inner circle" models found in this literature. See, for example, John P. Heinz et al., 1990 and Moore 1979.

14 Case studies which utilize a similar methodology include Sciarini 1986; Nunan; and Forrest 2000.

15 European observers, for example, have found it quite common for multiactor, multi-round decision-making processes to result in deadlock and never ultimately reach a final decision (Williams 2004). In groundbreaking case studies of complex multi-actor, multi-round decisions in Holland and Belgium, Van Bueren, Klijn, and Koppenjan (2001, 2003) and Verhoest et al. (2004), for example, suggested a number of hypotheses affecting the ability of such decision-making processes to arrive at some result, rather than simply degenerate into an impasse. These relate to the social, cognitive, and institutional causes of impasses and the (in)ability of network management efforts on the part of governments to overcome them. Hall and O'Toole (2004) in the United States, similarly, have highlighted the importance of the actual stage of the policy process involved in each round – (e.g. formulation of options, their assessment, or arrival at a final choice of instrument) – as a key factor affecting the number and type of actor present in each round.

16 In Canada, some work in this area exists, but most has tended to be somewhat partial or concerned with questions other than those related to explicating the relationships existing between policy environments and decision-making outcomes. For example, Michaud (2002) has worked on multi-round "white paper" policy processes, but within the context of a study of power relationships in Canadian defence policy formation. Salter (1981) and Pross, Christie, and Yogis (1990) have worked on various Royal commissions, which are also often a significant part of multi-round decision-making processes, but from the perspective of their organizational characteristics and investigative activities, rather than from that of decision making per se.

17 Other such hypotheses include Bueren, Klijn, and Koppenjan's finding that cohesive policy networks operating across multiple arenas overcome fragmentation and promote more rational outcomes, a finding consistent with other European studies, such as Teisman's (2000).

18 While these processes are more complex when they occur within a multilevel governance framework, these can be seen as either incrementally
   more sophisticated decision-making contexts or as two (or more) sepa-
   rate rounds processes temporarily separated from each other (Bache and
   Flinders 2004; Hooghe and Marks 2003). In either case, the analysis of
   single-level multi-actor, multi-round processes serves as an initial building block required for the analysis of even more complex decision-making
   situations.

19 As Klijn, Koppenjan, and others suggest, the start and end point of each
   round is somewhat arbitrary, but can be linked to what they term "crucial
   decisions," that is: "a round opens with an initiative or policy intention
   of one of the parties that serves as a 'trigger' to the others … Each round
   ends with a *crucial decision*, a decision that offers a solution for the question that is central in the particular policy round … A crucial decision her-
   alds a *new round* where it guides the subsequent policy game (Klijn and
   Koppenjan 2204: 60). In the policy case, a crucial decision is usually one in
   which the formalization of an issue in an established legal or authoritative
   decision-making body proceeds or does not proceed (Serdult and Hirschi
   2004). As Teisman (2000) has pointed out, this usually means deciding to
   proceed or not with the introduction or passage of legislation or regulatory changes in a formal decision-making body such as a parliament or
   legislature.

20 It is also suggestive that long-established sectors, such as banking, exhibit
   the greatest amount of government stability, while newer areas with a directly governmental focus, such as FOI legislation, engender the greatest amount of volatility among governmental actors vis-à-vis their NGO
   counterparts.

6 Policy Implementation: Managing the "Hollow State"

1 On "traditional" substantive tools see Salamon 1989; Bemelmans-Videc,
  Rist, and Vedung 1998; and Peters and Van Nispen 1998).

2 On recent European experiences see Hall and O'Toole 2000; Kohler-Koch
  1996; and Johansson and Borell 1999.

3 See also the discussion of 'symbolic" outputs in works such as Doern and
  Phidd 1988 and Doern and Wilson 1974.

4 For an overview of the application of this literature to privatization see
  Howlett and Ramesh 1993.

5 For an earlier, similar model see Anderson 1977.

6 A path-breaking effort in this process was found in the work of G. Bruce Doern and his colleagues in the 1970s and 1980s. See Doern and Aucoin 1971; Doern and Wilson 1974; Tupper and Doern 1981.

7 On the origin of the criterion of state-societal involvement see Nicolas Baxter-Moore, 1987.

8 While some links exist between this new emphasis in implementation studies and new public management ideas, NPM has not generated a useable model of instrument choice. Related work on "heresthetics" and "collibration" by William H. Riker and Andrew Dunsire provides only a very general introduction to the subject and neither author addresses instruments directly or moves in a systematic way towards theory construction. On problems with new public management theory see Hood 1995 and 1991; Dunleavy and Hood 1994. On heresthetics see Riker 1986 and 1983. On collibration see Dunsire 1993, 1986, and 1993.

9 On this methodology, generally, see McKelvey 1982.

10 Schneider and Ingram adopted much of their terminology from the work of Richard Elmore and his colleagues. Lorraine M. McDonnell and Richard F. Elmore (1987 and Elmore 1978 and 1987), for example, used a four-fold classification of instruments, although, unlike Hood, they classified instruments not according to the resources used, but according to the end desired. For these latter two authors, instruments could be categorized as "mandates," "inducements," "capacity building," and "system changing."

11 Michael Saward (1992: 27, 150, 153), for example, uses such a "resource-based" schema, although not explicitly.

12 For examples of some of the more sophisticated recent uses of substantive policy instruments, see Gibson 1999.

7 Policy Evaluation – Policy Advice in Multilevel Governance Systems

1 The policy advice system that supplies information to governments is, of course, very complex and includes many sources of information, from friends to spouses and close advisors (Meltsner 1990). However, alongside personal opinion and experience exists a more formal policy advice system which purports to deliver knowledge and expertise to governments. This supply network is composed of sources both within government, such as professional policy analysts employed in departments and agencies and political advisors attached to ministers' offices and central agencies, and external to government, such as experts in think tanks, universities, and political parties, ranging from private sector consultants and elsewhere (Boston 1994; Boston et al. 1996).

2 In many cases, observers have continued to rely on only one or two quite
    dated works in justifying their observations and conclusions, especially
    the early work of Meltsner (1975 and 1976) and Durning and Osama
    (1994). In Meltsner's case, his observations remain astute over thirty years
    later, but were based on 116 interviews he conducted in the United States
    in 1970–1 (Meltsner 1975: 14). While some data exist in these older stud-
    ies, they covered only a relatively small number of countries, mainly the
    United States (Meltsner 1976; Durning and Osama 1994; Radin 2000). More
    recent studies on "policy supply" have looked at the United Kingdom
    (Page and Jenkins 2005), Australia (Weller and Stevens 1998), New Zea-
    land (Boston et al. 1996), the Netherlands (Hoppe and Jeliazkova 2006),
    France (Rochet 2004), and Germany (Fleischer 2009), but in most jurisdic-
    tions the answers to basic questions, including how many people are in
    these positions or what they do, remain unknown.

3 And where they exist, these studies have tended to employ partial or un-
    systematic surveys (Page and Jenkins 2005), or anecdotal case studies and
    interview research (Radin 2000; Hoppe and Jeliazkova 2006). Comparative
    and synthetic studies of the supply and suppliers of policy advice are even
    rarer (Wagner and Wollmann 1986; Malloy 1989; Hawke 1993; Halligan
    1995; Thissen and Twaalfhoven 2001; Mayer, Bots, and Van Daalen 2004;
    Gregory and Lonti 2008; Weible 2008). The existing data are so poor that
    in most cases it is not clear even if the job classifications and titles typi-
    cally used by public service commissions to categorize professional policy
    analysts in government for staffing purposes are accurate or reflect a true
    sense of what policy analysts actually do on a day-to-day basis.

4 Very little is known about the nature of non-governmental policy analysis
    supplied through think tanks, political parties, and, especially, the growing
    legion of consultants who work for governments in the "invisible public
    service" (Speers 2007). On think tanks, business associations, political par-
    ties, and the press in Canada see Abelson 2007; Cross 2007; Murray 2007;
    Stritch 2007.

5 Provincial public service lists often included political appointees left off
    public lists. However, in most cases, public lists and internal lists were
    very close in size and coverage, with about an 80 per cent or higher over-
    lap rate. The lists revealed a roughly proportional per capita pattern of
    the size of the policy analytical community in Canadian provincial gov-
    ernments, with 1,800–2,000 individuals in Ontario, 400–500 in British Co-
    lumbia, and about 100 in the smallest jurisdictions. The total number of
    policy analysts at the provincial and territorial level therefore is probably
    about 5,300 (3,000 in Quebec and Ontario; 1,000 in BC and Alberta; 500 in

Saskatchewan and Manitoba; 400 in the Atlantic provinces, and 300 in the territories). It is expected that this number would be matched by the federal government (Wellstead having identified about 1,300 operating outside Ottawa, the remaining 4,000 located in the National Capital Region), bringing the total number of policy analysts actually employed in Canada to around 11,000. This is roughly the same per capita ratio as reported by Boston et al. in New Zealand, where of 35,000 core civil servants in a country of 3.6 million people at the time, 1,450 person-years were devoted to the provision of advice to departments and ministries in 1993 (Boston 1996: 124).

8 Conclusion – Policy Analytical Capacity and Evidence-Based Policy-Making

1 The willingness of policymakers to use the information generated in the way it was intended to be used is not always present. On the "strategic" and "argumentative" versus "evaluative" uses of research and analysis, see Whiteman (1985) and Landry, Lamari, and Amara (2003).

References

Abelson, D.E. "Any Ideas? Think Tanks and Policy Analysis in Canada."
In *Policy Analysis in Canada: The State of the Art*, ed. L. Dobuzinskis, M.
Howlett, and D. Laycock, 298–310. Toronto: University of Toronto Press,
2007.

Abelson, D.E. *Do Think Tanks Matter? Assessing the Impact of Public Policy Institutes*. Kingston, Montreal: McGill-Queen's University Press, 2002.

Aberbach, J.D., and B.A. Rockman. "On the Rise, Transformation, and Decline
of Analysis in the US Government." *Governance: An International Journal of
Policy, Administration and Institutions* 2, no. 3 (1989): 293–314. http://dx.doi.
org/10.1111/j.1468-0491.1989.tb00094.x.

Adamowicz, W. "Reflections on Environmental Policy in Canada." *Canadian Journal of Agricultural Economics* 55, no. 1 (2007): 1–13. http://dx.doi.
org/10.1111/j.1744-7976.2007.00076.x.

Adams, D. "Usable Knowledge in Public Policy." *Australian Journal of Public Administration* 63, no. 1 (2004): 29–42. http://dx.doi.
org/10.1111/j.1467-8500.2004.00357.x.

Adams, G.D. "Abortion: Evidence of an Issue Evolution." *American Journal of
Political Science* 41, no. 3 (1997): 718–37. http://dx.doi.org/10.2307/2111673.

Agranoff, R., and M. McGuire. "Inside the Matrix: Integrating the Paradigms
of Intergovernmental and Network Management." *International Journal of
Public Administration* 26, no. 12 (2003): 1401–22. http://dx.doi.org/10.1081/
PAD-120024403.

Allison, G. "Conceptual Models and the Cuban Missile Crisis." *American Political Science Review* 63, no. 3 (1969): 689–718. http://dx.doi.
org/10.2307/1954423.

Allison, G. *Essence of Decision: Explaining the Cuban Missile Crisis*. Boston: Little
Brown, 1971.

Allison, G.T., and M.H. Halperin. "Bureaucratic Politics: A Paradigm and Some Policy Implications." *World Politics* 24, no. S1, Supplement (1972): 40–79. http://dx.doi.org/10.2307/2010559.

ANAO. 2001. *Developing Policy Advice, Auditor-General Audit Report no. 21 2001–2002 Performance Audit.* Canberra, AFT: Australian National Audit Office.

Anderson, C.W. *Statecraft: An Introduction to Political Choice and Judgment.* New York: John Wiley and Sons, 1977.

Anderson, G. "The New Focus on the Policy Capacity of the Federal Government." *Canadian Public Administration* 39, no. 4 (1996): 469–88. http://dx.doi.org/10.1111/j.1754-7121.1996.tb00146.x.

Armstrong, J., and D.G. Lenihan. *From Controlling to Collaborating: When Governments Want to Be Partners: A Report on the Collaborative Partnerships Project. New Directions – Number 3.* Toronto: Institute of Public Administration of Canada, 1999.

Atkinson, M., and W. Coleman. "Strong States and Weak States: Sectoral Policy Networks in Advanced Capitalist Economies." *British Journal of Political Science* 19, no. 1 (1989): 47–67. http://dx.doi.org/10.1017/S0007123400005317.

Atkinson, M., and W. Coleman. *The State, Business, and Industrial Change in Canada.* Toronto: University of Toronto Press, 1989.

Aucoin, P. "Contribution of Commissions of Inquiry to Policy Analysis: An Evaluation." In *Commissions of Inquiry,* ed. A.P. Pross, I. Christie, and J.A. Yogis, 197–207. Toronto: Carswell, 1990.

Aucoin, P., and H. Bakvis. "Public Service Reform and Policy Capacity: Recruiting and Retaining the Best and the Brightest." In *Challenges to State Policy Capacity: Global Trends and Comparative Perspectives,* ed. M. Painter and J. Pierre, 185–204. London: Palgrave Macmillan, 2005.

Bache, I., and M. Flinders. *Multi-Level Governance.* New York: Oxford University Press, 2004. http://dx.doi.org/10.1093/0199259259.001.0001

Baehr, P.R. "Futures Studies and Policy Analysis in the Political Process: The Netherlands Scientific Council for Government Policy." In *Policy Analysis and Policy Innovation: Patterns, Problems and Potentials,* ed. P.R. Baehr and B. Wittrock, 93–118. Beverly Hills, CA: Sage Publications, 1981.

Bakvis, H. "Advising the Executive: Think Tanks, Consultants, Political Staff and Kitchen Cabinets." In *The Hollow Crown: Countervailing Trends in Core Executives,* ed. P. Weller, H. Bakvis, and R.A.W. Rhodes, 84–125. New York: St. Martin's Press, 1997.

Bakvis, H. "Rebuilding Policy Capacity in the Era of the Fiscal Dividend: A Report from Canada." *Governance: An International Journal of Policy,*

Administration and Institutions 13, no. 1 (2000): 71–103. http://dx.doi. org/10.1111/0952-1895.00124.

Banfield, E.C. "Policy Science as Metaphysical Madness." In *Statesmanship and Bureaucracy*, ed. R.A. Goldwin, 1–35. Washington, DC: American Enterprise Institute for Public Policy, 1977.

Baumgartner, F.R., and B.D. Jones. *Agendas and Instability in American Politics.* Chicago: University of Chicago Press, 1993.

Baumgartner, F.R., and B.D. Jones. "Agenda Dynamics and Policy Subsystems." *Journal of Politics* 53, no. 4 (1991): 1044–74. http://dx.doi. org/10.2307/2131866.

Baxter-Moore, N. "Policy Implementation and the Role of the State: A Revised Approach to the Study of Policy Instruments." In *Contemporary Canadian Politics: Readings and Notes*, ed. R.J. Jackson, D. Jackson, and N. Baxter-Moore, 336–55. Scarborough, ON: Prentice-Hall, 1987.

Beecher, J.A., R.L. Lineberry, and M.J. Rich. "Community Power, the Urban Agenda, and Crime Policy." *Social Science Quarterly* 62 (1981): 630–43.

Beetham, D. *The Legitimation of Power.* London: Macmillan, 1991.

Behm, A., L. Bennington, and J. Cummane. "A Value-Creating Model for Effective Policy Services." *Journal of Management Development* 19, no. 3 (2000): 162–78. http://dx.doi.org/10.1108/02621710010318756.

Behn, R.D. "Policy Analysis and Policy Politics." *Policy Analysis* 7, no. 2 (1981): 199–226.

Bellehumeur, R. "Review: An Instrument of Change." *Optimum (Paris)* 27, no. 1 (Summer 1997): 37–42.

Bemelmans-Videc, M-L, R.C. Rist, and E. Vedung, eds. *Carrots, Sticks and Sermons: Policy Instruments and Their Evaluation.* New Brunswick, NJ: Transaction Publishers, 1998.

Bendor, J. "A Model of Muddling Through." *American Political Science Review* 89, no. 4 (1995): 819–40. http://dx.doi.org/10.2307/2082511.

Bendor, J., and T.H. Hammond. "Re-Thinking Allison's Models." *American Political Science Review* 86, no. 2 (1992): 301–22. http://dx.doi. org/10.2307/1964222.

Bendor, J., T.M. Moe, and K.W. Shotts. "Recycling the Garbage Can: An Assessment of the Research Program." *American Political Science Review* 95, no. 1 (2001): 169–90.

Bennett, C.J., and M. Howlett. "The Lessons of Learning: Reconciling Theories of Policy Learning and Policy Change." *Policy Sciences* 25, no. 3 (1992): 275–94. http://dx.doi.org/10.1007/BF00138786.

Bennett, S., and M. McPhail. "Policy Process Perceptions of Senior Canadian Federal Civil Servants: A View of the State and its Environment."

Canadian Public Administration 35, no. 3 (1992): 299–316. http://dx.doi.
org/10.1111/j.1754-7121.1992.tb00696.x.

Bernier, L., K. Brownsey, and M. Howlett, eds. *Executive Styles in Canada: Cabinet Structures and Leadership Practices in Canadian Government.* Toronto: University of Toronto Press, 2005.

Bernstein, M.H. *Regulating Business by Independent Commission.* Princeton, NJ: Princeton University Press, 1955.

Berry, W.T. "The Confusing Case of Budgetary Incrementalism: Too Many Meanings for a Single Concept." *Journal of Politics* 52, no. 01 (1990): 167–96. http://dx.doi.org/10.2307/2131424.

Beyer, J.M., and H.M. Trice. "The Utilization Process: A Conceptual Framework and Synthesis of Empirical Findings." *Administrative Science Quarterly* 27, no. 4 (1982): 591–622. http://dx.doi.org/10.2307/2392533.

Billings, R.S., and C.F. Hermann. "Problem Identification in Sequential Policy Decision Making: The Re-representation of Problems." In *Problem Representation in Foreign Policy Decision Making*, ed. D.A. Sylvan and J.F. Voss, 53–79. Cambridge: Cambridge University Press, 1998.

Binz-Scharf, M.C., D. Lazer, and I. Mergel. 2008. Searching for Answers: Networks of Practice among Public Administrators. *Harvard Kennedy School Faculty Research Workshop Papers* RWP08–046.

Blom-Hansen, J. "A 'New Institutional' Perspective on Policy Networks." *Public Administration* 75, no. 4 (1997): 669–93. http://dx.doi.
org/10.1111/1467-9299.00080.

Boardman, A.E., D. Greenberg, A. Vining, and D. Weimer, eds. *Cost-Benefit Analysis: Concepts and Practice.* Upper Saddle River, NJ: Prentice Hall, 2001.

Boaz, A., G. Lesley, R. Levitt, and W. Solesbury. "Does Evidence-Based Policy Work? Learning from the UK Experience." *Evidence and Policy* 4, no. 2 (2008): 233–53. http://dx.doi.org/10.1332/174426408784614680.

Borzel, T.A. "Organizing Babylon – On the Different Conceptions of Policy Networks." *Public Administration* 76, no. 2 (1998): 253–73. http://dx.doi.
org/10.1111/1467-9299.00100.

Boston, J. "Purchasing Policy Advice: The Limits of Contracting Out." *Governance: An International Journal of Policy, Administration and Institutions* 7, no. 1 (1994): 1–30. http://dx.doi.org/10.1111/j.1468-0491.1994.tb00167.x.

Boston, J., J. Martin, J. Pallot, and P. Walsh. *Public Management: The New Zealand Model.* Auckland: Oxford University Press, 1996.

Bourgon, J. 1996. "Strengthening our Policy Capacity" In *Rethinking Policy: Strengthening Policy Capacity, Conference Proceedings*, 22–30. Canadian Centre for Management Development. Ottawa: Supply and Services Canada.

Bovens, M., and P. 't Hart. "Frame Multiplicity and Policy Fiascos: Limits to Explanation." *Knowledge and Policy* 8, no. 4 (1995): 61–82. http://dx.doi.org/10.1007/BF02832230.

Bovens, M., and P. 't Hart. *Understanding Policy Fiascos*. New Brunswick, NJ: Transaction Press, 1996.

Bovens, M., P. 't Hart, and B.G. Peters. "Analysing Governance Success and Failure in Six European States." In *Success and Failure in Public Governance: A Comparative Analysis*, ed. M. Bovens, P. 't Hart, and B.G. Peters, 12–32. Cheltenham, UK: Edward Elgar, 2001.

Brandstrom, A., and S. Kuipers. "From 'Normal Incidents' to 'Political Crises': Understanding the Selective Politicization of Policy Failures." *Government and Opposition* 38, no. 3 (2003): 279–305. http://dx.doi.org/10.1111/1477-7053.t01-1-00016.

Braun, D. "Interests or Ideas? An Overview of Ideational Concepts in Public Policy Research." In *Public Policy and Political Ideas*, ed. D. Braun and A. Busch, 11–29. Cheltenham: Edward Elgar, 1999.

Braybrooke, D., and C. Lindblom. *A Strategy of Decision: Policy Evaluation as a Social Process*. New York: Free Press of Glencoe, 1963.

Bressers, H., and P-J Klok. "Fundamentals for a Theory of Policy Instruments." *International Journal of Social Economics* 15, no. 3/4 (1988): 22–41. http://dx.doi.org/10.1108/eb014101.

Bressers, H. Th. A., and L.J. O'Toole, Jr. "The Selection of Policy Instruments: A Network-based Perspective." *Journal of Public Policy* 18, no. 3 (1998): 213–39. http://dx.doi.org/10.1017/S0143814X98000117.

Bressers, H. Th. A., L.J. O'Toole, Jr., and J. Richardson. "Networks as Models of Analysis: Water Policy in Comparative Perspective." *Environmental Politics* 3, no. 4 (1994): 1–23. http://dx.doi.org/10.1080/09644019408414165.

Brown, D.S. "The Management of Advisory Committees: An Assignment for the '70s." *Public Administration Review* 32, no. 4 (July–August 1972): 334–42. http://dx.doi.org/10.2307/974994.

Browne, W.P. "Issue Niches and the Limits of Interest Group Influence." In *Interest Group Politics*, ed. A.J. Cigler and B.A. Loomis, 345–70. Washington, DC: CQ Press, 1991.

Bulkeley, H. "Discourse Coalitions and the Australian Climate Change Policy Network." *Environment and Planning. C, Government & Policy* 18, no. 6 (2000): 727–48. http://dx.doi.org/10.1068/c9905j.

Bulmer, M. "Applied Social Research? The Use and Non-Use of Empirical Social Inquiry by British and American Governmental Commissions." *Journal of Public Policy* 1, no. 3 (1981): 353–80. http://dx.doi.org/10.1017/S0143814X00001665.

Bulmer, S.J. "The Governance of the European Union: A New Institutionalist Approach." *Journal of Public Policy* 13, no. 4 (September–December 1993): 351–80. http://dx.doi.org/10.1017/S0143814X0000115X.

Burstein, P. "Policy Domains·Organization, Culture and Policy Outcomes." *Annual Review of Sociology* 17, no. 1 (1991): 327–50. http://dx.doi.org/10.1146/annurev.so.17.080191.001551.

Burt, S. "Canadian Women's Groups in the 1980s: Organizational Development and Policy Influence." *Canadian Public Policy* 16, no. 1 (March 1990): 17–32. http://dx.doi.org/10.2307/3551256.

Bushnell, P. "Policy Advice: Planning for Performance." *Public Sector* 14, no. 1 (1991): 14–16.

Cahill, A.G., and E. Sam Overman. "The Evolution of Rationality in Policy Analysis." In *Policy Theory and Policy Evaluation: Concepts, Knowledge, Causes, and Norms*, ed. S.S. Nagel, 11–27. New York: Greenwood Press, 1990.

Cairns, A.C. "Reflections on Commission Research." In *Commissions of Inquiry*, ed. I. Christie, J.A. Yogis, and A. Paul Pross, 87–110. Toronto: Carswell, 1990.

Campbell, J.L. "Institutional Analysis and the Role of Ideas in Political Economy." *Theory and Society* 27, no. 3 (1998): 377–409. http://dx.doi.org/10.1023/A:1006871114987.

Carley, M. *Rational Techniques in Policy Analysis*. London: Heinemann, 1980.

Cater, D. *Power in Washington: A Critical Look at Today's Struggle in the Nation's Capital*. New York: Random House, 1964.

Cerny, P.G. "International Finance and the Erosion of State Policy Capacity." In *Globalization and Public Policy*, ed. P. Gummett, 83–104. Cheltenham: Edward Elgar, 1996.

Chadwick, A. "Studying Political Ideas: A Public Political Discourse Approach." *Political Studies* 48, no. 2 (2000): 283–301. http://dx.doi.org/10.1111/1467-9248.00260.

Chapman, R.A. "Commissions in Policy-Making." In *The Role of Commissions in Policy-Making*, ed. R.A. Chapman, 174–88. London: George Allen and Unwin, 1973.

Chatfield, C. *The Analysis of Time Series: An Introduction*. London: Chapman Hall, 1989.

Churchman, C.W. "Wicked Problems." *Management Science* 14, no. 4 (1967): B141–2.

Cobb, R.W., J.K. Ross, and M.H. Ross. "Agenda Building as a Comparative Political Process." *American Political Science Review* 70, no. 1 (1976): 126–36. http://dx.doi.org/10.2307/1960328.

Cobb, R.W., and C.D. Elder. *Participation in American Politics: The Dynamics of Agenda-Building*. Boston: Allyn and Bacon, 1972.

Cohen, M., J. March, and J. Olsen. "People, Problems, Solutions, and the Ambiguity of Relevance." In *Ambiguity and Choice in Organizations*, ed. J. March and J. Olsen, 24–37. Bergen: Universitetsforlaget, 1979.

Cohen, W.M., and D.A. Levinthal. "Absorptive Capacity: A New Perspective on Learning and Innovation." *Administrative Science Quarterly* 35, no. 1 (1990): 128–52. http://dx.doi.org/10.2307/2393553.

Colebatch, H.K. "Policy Analysis, Policy Practice and Political Science." *Australian Journal of Public Administration* 64, no. 3 (2005): 14–23. http://dx.doi.org/10.1111/j.1467-8500.2005.00448.x.

Colebatch, H.K., ed. *The Work of Policy: An International Survey*. Lanham, MD: Rowman & Littlefield, 2006.

Colebatch, H.K., and B.A. Radin. "Mapping the Work of Policy." In *The Work of Policy: An International Survey*, ed. H.K. Colebatch, 217–26. Lanham, MD: Rowman & Littlefield, 2006.

Coleman, W., and G. Skogstad, eds. *Policy Communities and Public Policies in Canada*. Toronto: Copp Clark, 1990.

Coleman, W.D. "Monetary Policy, Accountability and Legitimacy: A Review of the Issues in Canada." *Canadian Journal of Political Science* 24, no. 4 (December 1991): 711–34. http://dx.doi.org/10.1017/S0008423900005631.

Coleman, W.D. "Policy Convergence in Banking: A Comparative Study." *Political Studies* 42, no. 2 (1994): 274–92. http://dx.doi.org/10.1111/j.1467-9248.1994.tb01912.x.

Coleman, W.D., G.D. Skogstad, and M.M. Atkinson. "Paradigm Shifts and Policy Networks: Cumulative Change in Agriculture." *Journal of Public Policy* 16, no. 03 (1996): 273–302. http://dx.doi.org/10.1017/S0143814X00007777.

Cox, R.H. "Can Welfare States Grow in Leaps and Bounds? Non-Incremental Policymaking in the Netherlands." *Governance: An International Journal of Policy, Administration and Institutions* 5, no. 1 (1992): 68–87. http://dx.doi.org/10.1111/j.1468-0491.1992.tb00029.x.

Cross, W. "Policy Study and Development in Canada's Political Parties." In *Policy Analysis in Canada: The State of the Art*, ed. L. Dobuzinskis, M. Howlett, and D. Laycock, 233–42. Toronto: University of Toronto Press, 2007.

Daguerre, A. "Policy Networks in England and France: The Case of Child Care Policy 1980–1989." *Journal of European Public Policy* 7, no. 2 (2000): 244–60. http://dx.doi.org/10.1080/135017600343188.

Dahl, R.A., and C.E. Lindblom. *Politics, Economics and Welfare: Planning and Politico-economic Systems Resolved into Basic Social Processes*. New York: Harper and Row, 1953.

Daugbjerg, C. "Policy Networks and Agricultural Policy Reforms: Explaining Deregulation in Sweden and Re-regulation in the European Community." *Governance: An International Journal of Policy, Administration and Institutions* 10, no. 2 (1997): 123–41. http://dx.doi.org/10.1111/0952-1895.341997034.

Daugbjerg, C., and D. Marsh. "Explaining Policy Outcomes: Integrating the Policy Network Approach with Macro-Level and Micro-Level Analysis." In *Comparing Policy Networks*, ed. D. Marsh, 52–71. Buckingham: Open University Press.

Davies, P. "Is Evidence-Based Government Possible?" Jerry Lee Lecture presented to the 4th Annual Campbell Collaboration Colloquium, 19 February 2004, Washington, DC.

Dobuzinskis, L., M. Howlett, and D. Laycock, eds. *Policy Analysis in Canada: The State of the Art*. Toronto: University of Toronto Press, 2007.

de Bruijn, H., and E.F. ten Heuvelhof. "Conflicting Interests: Policy Analysis and Decision Making in a Network: How to Improve the Quality of Analysis and the Impact on Decision Making." *Impact Assessment and Project Appraisal* 20, no. 4 (2002): 232–42. http://dx.doi.org/10.3152/147154602781766627.

de Bruijn, H., and E.F. ten Heuvelhof. *Networks and Decision-Making*. Utrecht: Lemma Publishers, 2000.

de Bruijn, J.A., and E.F. ten Heuvelhof. "Instruments for Network Management." In *Managing Complex Networks: Strategies for the Public Sector*, ed. W.J.M. Kickert, E-H Klijn, and J.F.M. Koppenjan, 119–36. London: Sage Publications, 1997. http://dx.doi.org/10.4135/9781446217658.n7

de Bruijn, J.A., and E.F. ten Heuvelhof. "Policy Instruments for Steering Autopoietic Actors," In *Autopoiesis and Configuration Theory: New Approaches to Societal Steering*, ed. R. in't Veld, R.L. Schaap, C.J.A.M. Termeer, and M.J.W. Van Twist, 161–70. Dordrecht: Kluwer, 1991. http://dx.doi.org/10.1007/978-94-011-3522-1_14

de Bruijn, J.A., and E.F. ten Heuvelhof. "Policy Networks and Governance." In *Institutional Design*, ed. David L. Weimer, 161–79. Boston: Kluwer Academic Publishers, 1995. http://dx.doi.org/10.1007/978-94-011-0641-2_8

Delacourt, S., and D.G. Lenihan, eds. *Collaborative Government: Is There a Canadian Way? New Directions – Number 6*. Toronto: Institute of Public Administration of Canada, 2000.

Di Francesco, M. "An Evaluation Crucible: Evaluating Policy Advice in Australian Central Agencies." *Australian Journal of Public Administration* 59, no. 1 (2000): 36–48. http://dx.doi.org/10.1111/1467-8500.00138.

Di Francesco, M. "Measuring Performance in Policy Advice Output: Australian Developments." *International Journal of Public Sector Management* 12, no. 5 (1999): 420–31. http://dx.doi.org/10.1108/09513559910300181.

Dion, L. "The Politics of Consultation." *Government and Opposition* 8, no. 3 (Summer 1973): 332–63. http://dx.doi.org/10.1111/j.1477-7053.1973. tb00520.x.

Dobuzinskis, L., M. Howlett, and D. Laycock. *Policy Analysis in Canada: The State of the Art*. Toronto: University of Toronto Press, 2007.

Doern G.B., and P. Aucoin, eds. *The Structures of Policy-Making in Canada*. Toronto: Macmillan, 1971.

Doern, G.B., and R.W. Phidd. *Canadian Public Policy: Ideas, Structure, Process*. Toronto: Nelson, 1988.

Doern, G.B., and S. Wilks, eds. *Changing Regulatory Institutions in Britain and North America*. Toronto: University of Toronto Press, 1998.

Doern, G.B., and V.S. Wilson. "Conclusions and Observations." In *Issues in Canadian Public Policy*, ed. G.B. Doern and V.S. Wilson, 337–45. Toronto: Macmillan, 1974.

Dowding, K. "Model or Metaphor? A Critical Review of the Policy Network Approach." *Political Studies* 43, no. 1 (1995): 136–58. http://dx.doi. org/10.1111/j.1467-9248.1995.tb01705.x.

Dowding, K. "There Must Be End to Confusion: Policy Networks, Intellectual Fatigue, and the Need for Political Science Methods Courses in British Universities." *Political Studies* 49, no. 1 (2001): 89–105. http://dx.doi. org/10.1111/1467-9248.00304.

Downs, A. "Up and Down with Ecology – The 'Issue-Attention Cycle.'" *Public Interest* 28 (1972): 38–50.

Dror, Y. "Muddling Through – 'Science' or Inertia." *Public Administration Review* 24, no. 3 (1964): 153–7. http://dx.doi.org/10.2307/973640.

Dunleavy, P., and C. Hood. "From Old Public Administration to New Public Management." *Public Money and Management* 14, no. 3 (July–September 1994): 9–16.

Dunn, W. *Public Policy Analysis: An Introduction*. Upper Saddle River, NJ: Pearson/Prentice Hall, 2004.

Dunsire, A. "A Cybernetic View of Guidance, Control and Evaluation in the Public Sector." In *Guidance, Control, and Evaluation in the Public Sector*, ed. F-X Kaufman, G. Majone, and V. Ostrom, 327–46. Berlin: Walter de Gruyter, 1986.

Dunsire, A. *Manipulating Social Tensions: Collibration as an Alternative Mode of Government Intervention*. Discussion Paper 93/7. Koln: Max Plank Institut fur Gesellschaftsforschung, 1993.

Dunsire, A. "Modes of Governance." In *Modern Governance*, ed. J. Kooiman, 21–34. London: Sage Publications, 1993.

Durant, R.F., and P.E. Diehl. "Agendas, Alternatives and Public Policy: Lessons from the U.S. Foreign Policy Arena." *Journal of Public Policy* 9, no. 02 (1989): 179–205. http://dx.doi.org/10.1017/S0143814X00008114.

Durning, D., and W. Osuna. "Policy Analysts' Roles and Value Orientations: An Empirical Investigation Using Q Methodology." *Journal of Policy Analysis and Management* 13, no. 4 (1994): 629–57. http://dx.doi.org/10.2307/3325491.

Durr, R.H. "What Moves Policy Sentiment?" *American Political Science Review* 87, no. 1 (1993): 158–72. http://dx.doi.org/10.2307/2938963.

Eckstein, H. "Case Study and Theory in Political Science." In *Handbook of Political Science*, vol. VII, ed. F.I. Greenstein and N.W. Polsby, 79–138. Reading, MA: Addison-Wesley, 1975. http://dx.doi.org/10.4135/9780857024367.d11

Edelman, M. *The Symbolic Uses of Politics*. Chicago: University of Illinois Press, 1964.

Eden, C., F. Ackermami, J.M. Bryson, G.P. Richardson, D.F. Andersen, and C.B. Finn. "Integrating Modes of Policy Analysis and Strategic Management Practice: Requisite Elements and Dilemmas." *Journal of the Operational Research Society* 60, no. 1 (2009): 2–13. http://dx.doi.org/10.1057/palgrave.jors.2602575.

Edwards, W. "The Theory of Decision Making." *Psychological Bulletin* 51, no. 4 (July 1954): 380–417. http://dx.doi.org/10.1037/h0053870. Medline:13177802

Eisner, M.A. "Economic Regulatory Policies: Regulation and Deregulation in Historical Context." In *Handbook of Regulation and Administrative Law*, ed. D.H. Rosenbloom and R.D. Schwartz, 91–116. New York: Marcel Dekker, 1994.

Eldredge, N., and S.J. Gould. "Punctuated Equilibria: An Alternative to Phyletic Gradualism." In *Paleobiology*, ed. T.J.M. Schopf, 82–115. San Francisco, CA: Freeman, Cooper, 1972.

Ellig, J., and D. Lavoie. "The Principle-Agent Relationship in Organizations." In *Economic Approaches to Organizations and Institutions: An Introduction*, ed. P. Foss, 267–295. Aldershot: Dartmouth, 1995.

Elmore, R.F. "Instruments and Strategy in Public Policy." *Policy Studies Review* 7, no. 1 (Spring 1987): 174–86. http://dx.doi.org/10.1111/j.1541-1338.1987.tb00036.x.

Elmore, R.F. "Organizational Models of Social Program Implementation." *Public Policy* 26, no. 2 (Spring 1978): 185–228. Medline:10308533

Elster, J. "The Possibility of Rational Politics." In *Political Theory Today*, ed. D. Held, 115–142. Oxford: Polity, 1991.

Etzioni, A. "Mixed-Scanning: A 'Third' Approach to Decision-Making." *Public Administration Review* 27, no. 5 (1967): 385–92. http://dx.doi.org/10.2307/973394.

Fellegi, I. *Strengthening Our Policy Capacity*. Report of the Deputy Ministers Task Force Ottawa: Supply and Services Canada, 1996.

Finkle, P., et al. *Federal Government Relations with Interest Groups: A Reconsideration*. Ottawa: Privy Council Office, 1994.

Fleischer, J. "Power Resources of Parliamentary Executives: Policy Advice in the UK and Germany." *West European Politics* 32, no. 1 (2009): 196–214. http://dx.doi.org/10.1080/01402380802509941.

Foot, D.K. "Political Cycles, Economic Cycles and the Trend in Public Employment in Canada." In *Studies in Public Employment and Compensation in Canada*, ed. M.W. Bucovetsky, 65–80. Toronto: Institute for Research on Public Policy, 1979.

Forester, J. "Bounded Rationality and the Politics of Muddling Through." *Public Administration Review* 44, no. 1 (1984): 23–31. http://dx.doi.org/10.2307/975658.

Forester, J. *Planning in the Face of Power*. Berkeley: University of California Press, 1989.

Forrest, J.B. "The Drought Policy Bureaucracy, Decentralization, and Policy Networks in Post-Apartheid Namibia." *American Review of Public Administration* 30, no. 3 (2000): 307–33. http://dx.doi.org/10.1177/02750740022064696.

Freeman, G.P. "National Styles and Policy Sectors: Explaining Structured Variation." *Journal of Public Policy* 5, no. 04 (1985): 467–96. http://dx.doi.org/10.1017/S0143814X00003287.

Freeman, J.L. *The Political Process: Executive Bureau-Legislative Committee Relations*. New York: Random House, 1955.

French, R. *How Ottawa Decides: Planning and Industrial Policy-Making 1968–1980*. Toronto: Lorimer, 1980.

From, J. "Decision Making in a Complex Environment: A Sociological Institutionalist Analysis of Competition Policy Decision Making in the European Commission." *Journal of European Public Policy* 9, no. 2 (2002): 219–37. http://dx.doi.org/10.1080/13501760110120237.

Gadde, L-E, and L-G Mattsson. "Stability and Change in Network Relationships." *International Journal of Marketing* 4, no. 1 (1987): 29–41. http://dx.doi.org/10.1016/0167-8116(87)90012-7.

Gailmard, S., and J.W. Patty. "Slackers and Zealots: Civil Service, Policy Discretion, and Bureaucratic Expertise." *American Journal of Political Science* 51, no. 4 (2007): 873–89. http://dx.doi.org/10.1111/j.1540-5907.2007.00286.x.

Gais, T.L., M.A. Peterson, and J.L. Walker. "Interest Groups, Iron Triangles and Representative Institutions in American National Government."

British Journal of Political Science 14, no. 02 (1984): 161–85. http://dx.doi.org/10.1017/S0007123400003513.

Garson, G.D. "From Policy Science to Policy Analysis: A Quarter Century of Progress." In *Policy Analysis: Perspectives, Concepts, and Methods*, ed. W.N. Dunn, 3–22. Greenwich, CT: JAI Press, 1986. http://dx.doi.org/10.1111/j.1541-0072.1980.tb00964.x

Gawthrop, L. *Administrative Politics and Social Change.* New York: St. Martin's Press, 1971.

George, A.L. "Case Studies and Theory Development: The Method of Structured, Focused Comparison." In *Diplomacy: New Approaches in History, Theory and Policy*, ed. P.G. Lauren, 43–68. New York: Free Press, 1979.

Gersick, C.J.G. "Revolutionary Change Theories: A Multilevel Exploration of the Punctuated Equilibrium Paradigm." *Academy of Management Review* 16 (1991): 10–36.

Geva-May, I., and A.M. Maslove. "In between Trends: Developments of Public Policy Analysis and Policy Analysis Instruction in Canada, the United States and the European Union." In *Policy Analysis in Canada: The State of the Art*, ed. L. Dobuzinskis, M. Howlett, and D. Laycock, 186–216. Toronto: University of Toronto Press, 2007.

Gibson, R.B., ed. *Voluntary Initiatives: The New Politics of Corporate Greening.* Peterborough, ON: Broadview Press, 1999.

Giuliani, M. "'Soft' Institutions for Hard Problems: Instituting Air Pollution Policies in Three Italian Regions." In *The Politics of Improving Urban Air Quality*, ed. W. Grant, A. Perl, and P. Knoepfel, 31–51. Cheltenham: Edward Elgar, 1999.

Goggin, M.L., et al. *Implementation Theory and Practice: Toward A Third Generation.* Glenview: Scott, Foresman/Little, Brown, 1990.

Gormley, W.T. *Taming the Bureaucracy: Muscles, Prayers and Other Strategies.* Princeton, NJ: Princeton University Press, 1989.

Gortner, H., J. Mahler, and J. Bell Nicholson. *Organization Theory: A Public Perspective*, 257. Chicago: Dorsey Press, 1987.

Gottman, J.M. Time-Series Analysis: *A Comprehensive Introduction for Social Scientists.* Cambridge: Cambridge University Press, 1981.

Gow, J.L., and S.L. Sutherland. "Comparison of Canadian Masters Programs in Public Administration, Public Management and Public Policy." *Canadian Public Administration* 47, no. 3 (Autumn 2004): 379–405. http://dx.doi.org/10.1111/j.1754-7121.2004.tb01871.x.

Graham, K.A., and S.D. Phillips. "Citizen Engagement: Beyond the Customer Revolution." *Canadian Public Administration* 40, no. 2 (Summer 1997): 255–73. http://dx.doi.org/10.1111/j.1754-7121.1997.tb01509.x.

Grande, E. "The State and Interest Groups in a Framework of Multi-Level Decision Making: The Case of the European Union." *Journal of European Public Policy* 3, no. 3 (1996): 318–38. http://dx.doi.org/10.1080/13501769608407037.

Gregory, R., and Z. Lonti. "Chasing Shadows? Performance Measurement of Policy Advice in New Zealand Government Departments." *Public Administration* 86, no. 3 (2008): 837–56. http://dx.doi.org/10.1111/j.1467-9299.2008.00737.x.

Gross Stein, J. et al. "Citizen Engagement in Conflict Resolution: Lessons for Canada in International Experience." In *The Referendum Papers: Essays on Secession and National Unity*, ed. D. Cameron, 144–98. Toronto: University of Toronto Press, 1999.

Haas, P.M. "Introduction: Epistemic Communities and International Policy Coordination." *International Organization* 46, no. 1 (1992): 1–36. http://dx.doi.org/10.1017/S0020818300001442.

Habermas, J. *Legitimation Crisis*. Boston: Beacon Press, 1975.

Habermas, J. "What Does a Legitimation Crisis Mean Today? Legitimation Problems in Late Capitalism." *Social Research* 40, no. 4 (1973): 643–67.

Hall, M., and K. Banting. "The NonProfit Sector in Canada: An Introduction." In *The NonProfit Sector in Canada: Roles and Relationships*, ed. K. Banting, 1–28. Montreal, Kingston: McGill-Queen's University Press, 2000.

Hall, P. "Policy Paradigms, Social Learning and the State: The Case of Economic Policy-Making in Britain." *Comparative Politics* 25, no. 3 (1993): 275–96. http://dx.doi.org/10.2307/422246.

Hall, P.A. "The Change from Keynesianism to Monetarism: Institutional Analysis and British Economic Policy in the 1970s." In *Structuring Politics: Historical Institutionalism in Comparative Analysis*, ed. S. Steinmo, K. Thelen, and F. Longstreth, 90–113. Cambridge: Cambridge University Press, 1992. http://dx.doi.org/10.1017/CBO9780511528125.005

Hall, P.A. "Policy Paradigms, Experts, and the State: The Case of Macroeconomic Policy-Making in Britain." In *Social Scientists, Policy, and the State*, ed. S. Brooks and A-G Gagnon, 59. New York: Praeger, 1990.

Hall, T.E., and L.J. O'Toole, Jr. "Shaping Formal Networks through the Regulatory Process." *Administration & Society* 36, no. 2 (2004): 186–207. http://dx.doi.org/10.1177/0095399704263476.

Hall, T.E., and L.J. O'Toole, Jr. "Structures for Policy Implementation: An Analysis of National Legislation 1965–1966 and 1993–1994." *Administration & Society* 31, no. 6 (January 2000): 667–86. http://dx.doi.org/10.1177/00953990022019281.

Halligan, J. "Policy Advice and the Public Service." In *Governance in a Changing Environment*, ed. B. Guy Peters and T. Donald, 138–72. Montreal: McGill-Queens University Press, 1995.

Hammersley, M. "Is the Evidence-Based Practice Movement Doing More Good than Harm? Reflections on Iain Chalmers' Case for Research-Based Policy Making and Practice." *Evidence and Policy* 1, no. 1 (2005): 85–100. http://dx.doi.org/10.1332/1744264052703203.

Harrison, K. "Retreat from Regulation: The Evolution of the Canadian Environmental Regulatory Regime." In *Changing the Rules: Canadian Regulatory Regimes and Institutions*, ed. G. Bruce Doem, et al., 122–42. Toronto: University of Toronto Press, 1999.

Hartle, D.G. *The Expenditure Budget Process in the Government of Canada*. Toronto, Montreal: Canadian Tax Foundation, 1978.

Hawke, G.R. *Improving Policy Advice*. Wellington, NZ: Victoria University Institute of Policy Studies, 1993.

Hawkins, K., and J.M. Thomas. "Making Policy in Regulatory Bureaucracies." In *Making Regulatory Policy*, ed. K. Hawkins and J.M. Thomas, 3–30. Pittsburgh, PA: University of Pittsburgh Press, 1989.

Hayes, M.T. *Incrementalism and Public Policy*. New York: Longmans, 1992.

Hayes, M.T. "The Semi-Sovereign Pressure Groups: A Critique of Current Theory and an Alternative Typology." *Journal of Politics* 40, no. 01 (1978): 134–61. http://dx.doi.org/10.2307/2129979.

Heikkila, T., and K. Roussin Isett. "Modeling Operational Decision Making in Public Organizations: An Integration of Two Institutional Theories." *American Review of Public Administration* 34, no. 1 (2004): 3–19. http://dx.doi.org/10.1177/0275074003260911.

Head, B.W. "Three Lenses of Evidence-Based Policy." *Australian Journal of Public Administration* 67, no. 1 (2008): 1–11. http://dx.doi.org/10.1111/j.1467-8500.2007.00564.x.

Heclo, H. "Issue Networks and the Executive Establishment." In *The New American Political System*, ed. A. King, 87–124. Washington, DC: American Enterprise Institute for Public Policy Research, 1978.

Heinz, J.P., et al. *The Hollow Core: Private Interests in National Policy Making*. Cambridge, MA: Harvard University Press, 1993.

Heinz, J.P., E.O. Laumann, R.H. Salisbury, and R.L. Nelson. "Inner Circles or Hollow Cores? Elite Networks in National Policy Systems." *Journal of Politics* 52, no. 02 (1990): 356–90. http://dx.doi.org/10.2307/2131898.

Heritier, A. "Elements of Democratic Legitimation in Europe: An Alternative Perspective." *Journal of European Public Policy* 6, no. 2 (Summer 1999): 269–82. http://dx.doi.org/10.1080/135017699343711.

Heritier, A. "Policy-Making by Subterfuge: Interest Accommodation, Innovation and Substitute Democratic Legitimation in Europe – Perspectives from Distinctive Policy Areas." *Journal of European Public Policy* 4, no. 2 (Summer 1997): 171–89.

Hessing, M., and M. Howlett. *Canadian Natural Resource and Environmental Policy: Political Economy and Public Policy.* Vancouver: University of British Columbia Press, 1997.

Hibbs, D.A., Jr. *The Political Economy of Industrial Democracies.* Cambridge, MA: Harvard University Press, 1987.

Hibbs, D.A., Jr. "Political Parties and Macroeconomic Policy." *American Political Science Review* 71, no. 04 (1977): 1467–87. http://dx.doi.org/10.2307/1961490.

Hicks, R., and P. Watson. *Policy Capacity: Strengthening the Public Service's Support to Elected Officials.* Edmonton: Government of Alberta, 2007.

Hird, J.A. "Policy Analysis for What? The Effectiveness of Nonpartisan Policy Research Organizations." *Policy Studies Journal: The Journal of the Policy Studies Organization* 33, no. 1 (2005): 83–105. http://dx.doi.org/10.1111/j.1541-0072.2005.00093.x.

Hird, J.A. *Power, Knowledge and Politics: Policy Analysis in the States.* Washington, DC: Georgetown University Press, 2005.

Hoberg, G. "Putting Ideas in Their Place: A Response to 'Learning and Change in the British Columbia Forest Policy Sector.'" *Canadian Journal of Political Science* 29, no. 01 (1996): 135–44. http://dx.doi.org/10.1017/S0008423900007277.

Hogwood, B.W. Ups and Downs: Is There an Issue-Attention Cycle in Britain? No. 89. Glasgow: Strathclyde Papers in Government and Politics, 1992.

Hollander, M.J., and M.J. Prince. "Analytical Units in Federal and Provincial Governments: Origins, Functions and Suggestions for Effectiveness." *Canadian Public Administration* 36, no. 2 (1993): 190–224. http://dx.doi.org/10.1111/j.1754-7121.1993.tb00723.x.

Hood, C. "A Public Management for All Seasons?" *Public Administration* 69, no. 1 (Spring 1991): 3–19. http://dx.doi.org/10.1111/j.1467-9299.1991.tb00779.x.

Hood, C. "Contemporary Public Management: A New Global Paradigm?" *Public Policy and Administration* 10, no. 2 (Summer 1995): 104–17. http://dx.doi.org/10.1177/095207679501000208.

Hood, C. "The Hidden Public Sector: The 'Quangocratization' of the World?" In *Guidance, Control, and Evaluation in the Public Sector*, ed. F-X Kaufman, G. Majone, and V. Ostrom, 183–207. Berlin: Walter de Gruyter, 1986.

Hood, C. "Keeping the Centre Small: Explanation of Agency Type." *Political Studies* 36, no. 1 (March 1988): 30–46.

Hood, C. "The Risk Game and the Blame Game." *Government and Opposition* 37, no. 1 (2002): 15–37. http://dx.doi.org/10.1111/1477-7053.00085.

Hood, C. *The Tools of Government.* Chatham: Chatham House, 1986.

Hooghe, L. and G. Marks. 2001. "Types of Multi-Level Governance." *European Integration Online Papers* 5, no. 11.

Hooghe, L., and G. Marks. "Unraveling the Central State, but How? Types of Multi-Level Governance." *American Political Science Review* 97, no. 2 (2003): 233–43.

Hoppe, R., and M. Jeliazkova. "How Policy Workers Define Their Job: A Netherlands Case Study." In *The Work of Policy: An International Survey*, ed. H.K. Colebatch, 35–60. New York: Rowman and Littlefield, 2006.

Hosseus, D., and L.A. Pal. "Anatomy of a Policy Area: The Case of Shipping." *Canadian Public Policy* 23, no. 4 (1997): 399–416. http://dx.doi.org/10.2307/3552071.

Howlett, M.P. "Agenda-Setting in Canada: Evidence from Six Case Studies." Paper presented at the annual meeting of the British Columbia Political Studies Association, 1996a.

Howlett, M.P. "Do Networks Matter? Linking Policy Network Structure to Policy Outcomes: Evidence from Four Canadian Policy Sectors 1990–2000." *Canadian Journal of Political Science* 35, no. 2 (2002a): 235–68. http://dx.doi.org/10.1017/S0008423902778232.

Howlett, M.P. "Federalism and Public Policy." In *Canadian Politics*, 3rd ed., ed. J. Bickerton and A. Gagnon, 500–525. Peterborough, ON: Broadview Press, 1999.

Howlett, M.P. "Issue-Attention and Punctuated Equilibrium Models Reconsidered: An Empirical Examination of the Dynamics of Agenda-Setting in Canada." *Canadian Journal of Political Science* 30 (1997): 5–29. http://dx.doi.org/10.1017/S0008423900014918.

Howlett, M.P. *Legitimacy and Governance: Re-Discovering Procedural Policy Instruments.* Vancouver: Paper Presented to the Annual Meeting of the British Columbia Political Studies Association, 1996b.

Howlett, M.P. "Managing the 'Hollow State': Procedural Policy Instruments and Modern Governance." *Canadian Public Administration* 43, no. 4 (2000): 412–31. http://dx.doi.org/10.1111/j.1754-7121.2000.tb01152.x.

Howlett, M.P. "Policy Analytical Capacity and Evidence-Based Policy-Making: Lessons from Canada." *Canadian Public Administration* 52, no. 2 (2009): 153–175. http://dx.doi.org/10.1111/j.1754-7121.2009.00070_1.x.

Howlett, M.P. "Policy Development." In *The Oxford Handbook of Canadian Public Administration*, ed. C. Dunn. Toronto: Oxford University Press, 2002b.

Howlett, M.P. "Policy Instruments and Implementation Styles: The Evolution of Instrument Choice in Canadian Environmental Policy." In *Canadian Environmental Policy: Context and Cases*, ed. D.L. van Nijnatten and R. Boardman,. Toronto: Oxford University Press, 2002c. 25–45

Howlett, M.P. "Policy Paradigms and Policy Change: Lessons from the Old and New Canadian Policies Towards Aboriginal Peoples." *Policy Studies Journal: The Journal of the Policy Studies Organization* 22, no. 4 (1994): 631–49. http://dx.doi.org/10.1111/j.1541-0072.1994.tb01494.x.

Howlett, M.P. "Predictable and Unpredictable Policy Windows: Issue, Institutional and Exogenous Correlates of Canadian Federal Agenda-Setting." *Canadian Journal of Political Science* 31, no. 3 (1998): 495–524.

Howlett, M.P. "Policy Instruments, Policy Styles, and Policy Implementation: National Approaches to Theories of Instrument Choice." *Policy Studies Journal: The Journal of the Policy Studies Organization* 19, no. 2 (Winter 1991): 1–21. http://dx.doi.org/10.1111/j.1541-0072.1991.tb01878.x.

Howlett, M.P. "The Round Table Experience: Representation and Legitimacy in Canadian Environmental Policy Making." *Queen's Quarterly* 97, no. 4 (Winter 1990): 580–601.

Howlett, M.P., and E. Lindquist. "Policy Analysis and Governance: Analytical and Policy Styles in Canada." *Journal of Comparative Policy Analysis* 6, no. 3 (2004): 225–49. http://dx.doi.org/10.1080/1387698042000305194.

Howlett, M.P., and M. Ramesh. "Patterns of Policy Instrument Choice: Policy Styles, Policy Learning and the Privatization Experience." *Policy Studies Review* 12, no. 1–2 (Spring 1993): 3–24. http://dx.doi.org/10.1111/j.1541-1338.1993.tb00505.x.

Howlett, M.P., and M. Ramesh. "Policy Subsystem Configurations and Policy Change: Operationalizing the Postpositivist Analysis of the Politics of the Policy Process." *Policy Studies Journal: The Journal of the Policy Studies Organization* 26, no. 3 (1998): 466–81. http://dx.doi.org/10.1111/j.1541-0072.1998.tb01913.x.

Howlett, M.P., and M. Ramesh. *Studying Public Policy: Policy Cycles and Policy Subsystems*. Toronto: Oxford University Press, 1995.

Howlett, M.P., and M. Ramesh. *Studying Public Policy: Policy Cycles and Policy Subsystems*. Toronto: Oxford University Press, 2003.

Howlett, M.P., M. Ramesh, and A. Perl. *Studying Public Policy: Policy Cycles and Policy Subsystems*. Toronto: Oxford University Press, 2009.

Howlett, M.P., and J. Rayner. "Do Ideas Matter? Policy Network Configurations and Resistance to Policy Change in the Canadian Forest Sector."

Canadian Public Administration 38, no. 3 (1995): 382–410. http://dx.doi.
org/10.1111/j.1754-7121.1995.tb01055.x.

Hunn, D.K. "Measuring Performance in Policy Advice: A New Zealand Perspective." In *Performance Measurement in Government: Issues and Illustrations*,
ed. OECD, 25–37. Paris: OECD, 1994.

Huntington, S.P. "The Marasmus of the ICC: The Commissions, the Railroads
and the Public Interest." *Yale Law Review* 61, no. 4 (1952): 467–509. http://
dx.doi.org/10.2307/793586.

Huppes, G. "New Instruments for Environmental Policy: A Perspective."
International Journal of Social Economics 15, no. 3/4 (1988): 42–50. http://
dx.doi.org/10.1108/eb014102.

Hutter, B.M. "Variations in Regulatory Enforcement Styles." *Law & Policy*
11, no. 2 (April 1989): 153–74. http://dx.doi.org/10.1111/j.1467-9930.1989.
tb00024.x.

in't Veld, R.J. "The Dynamics of Instruments." In *Public Policy Instruments:
Evaluating the Tools of Public Administration*, ed. B.G. Peters and F.K.M. van
Nispen, 153–62. New York: Edward Elgar, 1998.

Ingram, H.M., and D.E. Mann. "Policy Failure: An Issue Deserving Analysis."
In *Why Policies Succeed or Fail*, ed. H.M. Ingram and D.E. Mann. Beverly
Hills, CA: Sage Publications, 1980.

Innvaer, S., G. Vist, M. Trommald, and A. Oxman. "Health Policy-Makers' Perceptions of their Use of Evidence: A Systematic Review." *Journal of Health
Services Research & Policy* 7, no. 4 (October 2002): 239–44. http://dx.doi.
org/10.1258/135581902320432778. Medline:12425783

Jackson, A., and B. Baldwin. "Policy Analysis by the Labour Movement in a
Hostile Environment." In *Policy Analysis in Canada: The State of the Art*, ed. L.
Dobuzinskis, M. Howlett, and D. Laycock. Toronto: University of Toronto
Press, 2007.

Jackson, P.M. "Making Sense of Policy Advice." *Public Money and Management*
27, no. 4 (2007): 257–64. http://dx.doi.org/10.1111/j.1467-9302.2007.00592.x.

Jann, W. "From Policy Analysis to Political Management? An Outside Look at
Public Policy Training in the United States." In *Social Sciences and Modern
States: National Experiences and Theoretical Crossroads*, ed. P. Wagner, B. Wittrock, and H. Wollman, 110–30. Cambridge: Cambridge University Press,
1991. http://dx.doi.org/10.1017/CBO9780511983993.004.

Jann, W., and K. Wegrich. "Theories of the Policy Cycle." In *Handbook of Public Policy Analysis: Theory, Politics and Methods*, ed. F. Fischer, G.J. Miller, and
M.S. Sidney, 43–62. Boca Raton, FL: CRC Press, 2007.

Jenkins-Smith, H.C., G.K. St. Clair, and B. Woods. "Explaining Change in Policy Subsystems: Analysis of Coalition Stability and Defection over Time."

American Journal of Political Science 35, no. 4 (1991): 851–80. http://dx.doi.org/10.2307/2111497.

Jennings, B. "Interpretation and the Practice of Policy Analysis." In *Confronting Values in Policy Analysis: The Politics of Criteria*, ed. F. Fischer and J. Forester, 128–52. Newbury Park, CA: Sage, 1987.

Jenson, J. "Commissioning Ideas: Representation and Royal Commissions." In *How Ottawa Spends 1994–95: Making Change*, ed. S.D. Phillips, 39–69. Carleton Public Policy Series #16. Ottawa: Carleton University Press, 1994.

Jentoft, S. "Legitimacy and Disappointment in Fisheries Management." *Marine Policy* 24, no. 2 (March 2000): 141–8. http://dx.doi.org/10.1016/S0308-597X(99)00025-1.

Johansson, R., and K. Borell. "Central Steering and Local Networks: Old-Age Care in Sweden." *Public Administration* 77, no. 3 (Autumn 1999): 585–98. http://dx.doi.org/10.1111/1467-9299.00169.

Johnston, R. *Public Opinion and Public Policy in Canada*. Toronto: University of Toronto Press, 1986.

Jones, B.D. "Bounded Rationality and Public Policy: Herbert A. Simon and the Decisional Foundation of Collective Choice." *Policy Sciences* 35, no. 3 (2002): 269–84. http://dx.doi.org/10.1023/A:1021341309418.

Jones, B.D. *Reconceiving Decision-Making in Democratic Politics: Attention, Choice and Public Policy*. Chicago: University of Chicago Press, 1994.

Jones, B.D., J.L. True, and F.R. Baumgartner. "Does Incrementalism Stem from Political Consensus or from Institutional Gridlock?" *American Journal of Political Science* 41, no. 4 (1997): 1319–39. http://dx.doi.org/10.2307/2960491.

Jordan, A.G. "Iron Triangles, Woolly Corporatism and Elastic Nets: Images of the Policy Process." *Journal of Public Policy* 1, no. 01 (1981): 95–123. http://dx.doi.org/10.1017/S0143814X00001379.

Jordan, A. G. "Policy Community Realism versus 'New' Institutionalist Ambiguity." *Political Studies* 38 (1990): 470–84. http://dx.doi.org/10.1111/j.1467-9248.1990.tb01082.x.

Jordan, A. G. "Sub-Governments, Policy Communities and Networks: Refilling the Old Bottles?" *Journal of Theoretical Politics* 2, no. 3 (1990): 319–38. http://dx.doi.org/10.1177/0951692890002003004.

Jordan, A. G., and Klaus Schubert. "A Preliminary Ordering of Policy Network Labels." *European Journal of Political Research* 21, no. 1–2 (1992): 7–27. http://dx.doi.org/10.1111/j.1475-6765.1992.tb00286.x.

Kagan, R.A. "Adversarial Legalism and American Government." *Journal of Policy Analysis and Management* 10, no. 3 (1991): 369–406. http://dx.doi.org/10.2307/3325322.

Kassim, H. "Policy Networks, Networks and European Union Policy Making: A Skeptical View." *West European Politics* 17, no. 4 (1994): 15–27. http://dx.doi.org/10.1080/01402389408425041.

Keeler, J.T.S. "Opening the Window for Reform: Mandates, Crises and Extraordinary Policy-Making." *Comparative Political Studies* 25, no. 4 (1993): 433–86. http://dx.doi.org/10.1177/0010414093025004002.

Kenis, P. "The Pre-Conditions for Policy Networks: Some Findings from a Three Country Study on Industrial Re-Structuring." In *Policy Networks: Empirical Evidence and Theoretical Considerations*, ed. B. Mann and R. Mayntz, 297–330. Boulder, CO: Westview Press, 1991.

Kernaghan, K. "Judicial Review of Administration Action." In *Public Administration in Canada: Selected Readings*, ed. K. Kernaghan, 358–73. Toronto: Methuen, 1985.

Kernaghan, K. "Partnership and Public Administration: Conceptual and Practical Considerations." *Canadian Public Administration* 36, no. 1 (Spring 1993): 57–76. http://dx.doi.org/10.1111/j.1754-7121.1993.tb02166.x.

Kerr, D.H. "The Logic of 'Policy' and Successful Policies." *Policy Sciences* 7, no. 3 (1976): 351–63. http://dx.doi.org/10.1007/BF00137628.

Kickert, W.J.M., E-H Klijn, and J.F.M. Koppenjan, eds. *Managing Complex Networks: Strategies for the Public Sector*. London: Sage, 1997.

King, D.C., and J.L. Walker. "An Ecology of Interest Groups in America." In *Mobilizing Interest Groups in America: Patrons, Professions and Social Movements*, ed. J.L. Walker, 57–73. Ann Arbor: University of Michigan Press, 1991.

King, G., M. Laver, R.I. Hofferbert, I. Budge, and M.D. McDonald. "Party Platforms, Mandates and Government Spending." *American Political Science Review* 87, no. 3 (1993): 744–50. http://dx.doi.org/10.2307/2938748.

Kingdon, J.W. *Agendas, Alternatives and Public Policies*. Boston: Little, Brown, 1984.

Kirschen, E.S., et al. *Economic Policy in Our Time*. Chicago: Rand McNally, 1964.

Klijn, E.H. "Analyzing and Managing Policy Processes in Complex Networks: A Theoretical Examination of the Concept Policy Network and Its Problems." *Administration & Society* 28, no. 1 (1996): 90–119. http://dx.doi.org/10.1177/009539979602800104.

Klijn, E.H., and J.F.M. Koppenjan. "Politicians and Interactive Decision Making: Institutional Spoilsports or Playmakers." *Public Administration* 78, no. 2 (Summer 2000): 365–87. http://dx.doi.org/10.1111/1467-9299.00210.

Klijn, E.H., and J.F.M. Koppenjan. "Public Management and Policy Networks: Foundations of a Network Approach to Governance." *Public Management* 2, no. 2 (2000): 135–58. http://dx.doi.org/10.1080/146166700411201.

Klijn, E. H., and G. R. Teisman. "Effective Policymaking in a Multi-Actor Setting: Networks and Steering." In Autopoiesis and Configuration Theory: New Approaches to Societal Steering, edited by R. In 'T Veld, L. Schaap, C. J. A. M. Termeer, and m J. W. Van Twist, 99–111. Dodrecht: Kluwer, 1991.

Knill, C. "European Policies: The Impact of National Administrative Traditions." Journal of Public Policy 18, no. 1 (1998): 1–28. http://dx.doi.org/10.1017/S0143814X98000014.

Knoke, D. "Networks as Political Glue: Explaining Public Policy-Making." In Sociology and the Public Agenda, ed. W.J. Wilson, 164–84. London: Sage, 1993.

Knoke, D. Political Networks: The Structural Perspective. Cambridge: Cambridge University Press, 1990. http://dx.doi.org/10.1017/CBO9780511527548

Kohler-Koch, B. "Catching up with Change: The Transformation of Governance in the European Union." Journal of European Public Policy 3, no. 3 (Fall 1996): 359–380. http://dx.doi.org/10.1080/13501769608407039.

Kooiman, J. "Governance and Governability: Using Complexity, Dynamics and Diversity." In Modern Governance, edited by J. Kooiman, 35–50. London: Sage, 1993.

Koppenjan, J., and E.H. Klijn. Managing Uncertainties in Networks: A Network Approach to Problem Solving and Decision Making. London: Routledge, 2004.

Kriesi, H., and M. Jegen. "The Swiss Energy Policy Elite: The Actor Constellation of a Policy Domain in Transition." European Journal of Political Research 39, no. 2 (2001): 251–87. http://dx.doi.org/10.1111/1475-6765.00577.

Kuhn, T.S. "Second Thoughts on Paradigms." In The Structure of Scientific Theories, ed. F. Suppe, 459–82. Urbana: University of Illinois, 1974.

Kuhn, T.S. The Structure of Scientific Revolutions. Chicago: University of Chicago Press, 1962.

Laforest, R., and M. Orsini. "Evidence-Based Engagement in the Voluntary Sector: Lessons from Canada." Social Policy and Administration 39, no. 5 (2005): 481–97. http://dx.doi.org/10.1111/j.1467-9515.2005.00451.x.

Landry, R., M. Lamari, and N. Amara. "The Extent and Determinants of the Utilization of University Research in Government Agencies." Public Administration Review 63, no. 2 (2003): 192–205. http://dx.doi.org/10.1111/1540-6210.00279.

Larsen, J.K. "Knowledge Utilization: What is it?" Knowledge, Creation, Diffusion, Utilization 14, no. 3 (1980): 267–90.

Lasswell, H.D. "Key Symbols, Signs and Icons." In Symbols and Values: An Initial Study, ed. L. Bryson, L. Finkelstein, R. M. MacIver, and Richard McKean, 77–94. New York: Harper, 1954.

Lasswell, H.D. A Pre-View of Policy Sciences. New York: American Elsevier, 1971.

Lasswell, H.D. The Decision Process: Seven Categories of Functional Analysis. College Park: University of Maryland, 1956.

Laumann, E.O., and D. Knoke. *The Organizational State: Social Choice in National Policy Domains.* Madison: University of Wisconsin Press, 1987.

Laux, J. Kirk, and M. Appel Molot. *State Capitalism: Public Enterprise in Canada.* Ithaca, NY: Cornell University Press, 1988.

Le Gales, P., and M. Thatcher, eds. *Les Reseaux de Politique Publique.* Paris: Editions L'Harmattan, 1995.

Leeuw, E.L. "Policy Theories, Knowledge Utilization, and Evaluation." *Knowledge and Policy* 4, no. 3 (1991): 73–91. http://dx.doi.org/10.1007/BF02693089.

Lehmbruch, G. "The Organization of Society, Administrative Strategies, and Policy Networks." In *Political Choice: Institutions, Rules, and the Limits of Rationality,* ed. R.M. Czada and A. Windhoff-Heritier, 121–55. Boulder, CO: Westview Press, 1991.

Leik, R.K. "New Directions for Network Exchange Theory: Strategic Manipulation of Network Linkages." *Social Networks* 14, no. 3–4 (1992): 309–23. http://dx.doi.org/10.1016/0378-8733(92)90007-T.

Lewis-Beck, M.S. *Economics and Elections: The Major Western Democracies.* Ann Arbor: University of Michigan Press, 1988.

Lindblom, C.E., and D.K. Cohen. *Usable Knowledge: Social Science and Social Problem Solving.* New Haven, CT: Yale University Press, 1979.

Lindblom, C.E. *Bargaining.* Los Angeles: Rand Corporation, 1951.

Lindblom, C.E. "The Science of Muddling Through." *Public Administration Review* 19, no. 2 (1959): 79–88. http://dx.doi.org/10.2307/973677.

Lindblom, C.E. "Policy Analysis." *American Economic Review* 48, no. 3 (1958): 298–312.

Lindblom, C.E. "Still Muddling, Not Yet Through." *Public Administration Review* 39, no. 6 (1979): 517–26.

Linder, S.H., and B.G. Peters. "Instruments of Government: Perceptions and Contexts." *Journal of Public Policy* 9, no. 1 (1989): 35. http://dx.doi.org/10.1017/S0143814X00007960.

Linder, S.H., and B.G. Peters. "Policy Formulation and the Challenge of Conscious Design." *Evaluation and Program Planning* 13, no. 3 (1990): 303–11. http://dx.doi.org/10.1016/0149-7189(90)90061-Z.

Lindquist, E.A. "New Agendas for Research on Policy Communities: Policy Analysis, Administration, and Governance." In *Policy Studies in Canada: The State of the Art,* ed. L. Dobuzinskis, M. Howlett, and D. Laycock, 266–98. Toronto: University of Toronto Press, 1996.

Lindquist, E.A. "Public Managers and Policy Communities: Learning to Meet New Challenges." *Canadian Public Administration* 35, no. 2 (1992): 127–59. http://dx.doi.org/10.1111/j.1754-7121.1992.tb00685.x.

Lindquist, E.A., and J. Desveaux. *Recruitment and Policy Capacity in Government*. Ottawa: Public Policy Forum, 1998.

Liu, L-M. "Box-Jenkins Time Series Analysis." In *BMDP Statistical Software Manual*, vol. 1, ed. W.J. Dixon, 429–82. Berkeley: University of California Press, 1988.

Lober, D.J. "Explaining the Formation of Business-Environmentalist Collaborations: Collaborative Windows and the Paper Task Force." *Policy Sciences* 30, no. 1 (1997): 1–24. http://dx.doi.org/10.1023/A:1004201611394.

Lowi, T.J. "Distribution, Regulation, Redistribution: The Functions of Government." In *Public Policies and Their Politics: Techniques of Government Control*, ed. R.B. Ripley, 27–40. New York: W.W. Norton, 1966.

Lowi, T.J. *The End of Liberalism: Ideology, Policy and the Crisis of Public Authority*. New York: Norton, 1969.

Lowry, R.C. "Foundation Patronage toward Citizen Groups and Think Tanks: Who Gets Grants?" *Journal of Politics* 61, no. 3 (August 1999): 758–76. http://dx.doi.org/10.2307/2647827.

Lustick, I. "Explaining the Variable Utility of Disjointed Incrementalism: Four Propositions." *American Political Science Review* 74, no. 2 (1980): 342–53. http://dx.doi.org/10.2307/1960631.

Lynn, L., Jr. *Knowledge and Policy: The Uncertain Connection*. Washington, DC: National Academy of Sciences, 1978.

MacFarland, A.S. "Interest Groups and Political Time: Cycles in America." *British Journal of Political Science* 21, no. 03 (1991): 257–85. http://dx.doi.org/10.1017/S0007123400006165.

MacRae, D., Jr. "Guidelines for Policy Discourse: Consensual versus Adversarial"." In *The Argumentative Turn in Policy Analysis and Planning*, ed. F. Fischer and J. Forester, 291–318. Durham, NC: Duke University Press, 1993.

MacRae, D., Jr. "Policy Analysis and Knowledge Use." *Knowledge and Policy* 4, no. 3 (1991): 27–40. http://dx.doi.org/10.1007/BF02693086.

MacRae, D., and D. Whittington. *Expert Advice for Policy Choice: Analysis and Discourse*. Washington, DC: Georgetown University Press, 1997.

MacRae, D., Jr., and J.A. Wilde. *Policy Analysis for Public Decisions*. Lanham, MD: University Press of America, 1985.

Majone, G. *Evidence, Argument, and Persuasion in the Policy Process*. New Haven, CT: Yale University Press, 1989.

Malloy, J.M. "Policy Analysts, Public Policy and Regime Structure in Latin America." *Governance: An International Journal of Policy, Administration and Institutions* 2, no. 3 (1989): 315–38. http://dx.doi.org/10.1111/j.1468-0491.1989.tb00095.x.

Manitoba. Office of the Auditor General [Jon Singleton]. *A Review of the Policy Capacity between Departments.* Winnipeg: Queen's Printer, 2001.

Mann, B., and R. Mayntz, eds. *Policy Networks: Empirical Evidence and Theoretical Considerations.* Boulder: Westview Press, 1991.

Manzer, R. "Policy Rationality and Policy Analysis: The Problem of the Choice of Criteria for Decision-Making." In *Public Policy and Administrative Studies,* ed. O.P. Dwivedi, 27–40. Guelph: University of Guelph, 1984.

Mar, B., and R. Mayntz, eds. *Policy Networks: Empirical Evidence and Theoretical Considerations.* Boulder, CO: Westview Press, 1991.

March, J.G. *A Primer on Decision-Making: How Decisions Happen.* New York: Free Press, 1994.

March, J.G. "Decision Making Perspective: Decisions in Organizations and Theories of Choice." In *Perspectives on Organization Design and Behaviour,* ed. A.H. van de Ven and W.F. Joyce. New York: Wiley, 1981.

March, J.G., and J. Olsen. "Organizational Choice under Ambiguity." In *Ambiguity and Choice in Organizations,* 2nd ed., ed. J. March and J. Olsen, 10–23. Bergen: Universitetsforlaget, 1979.

Marsh, D. "The Utility and Future of Policy Network Analysis." In *Comparing Policy Networks,* ed. D. Marsh, 185–98. Buckingham: Open University Press, 1998.

Marsh, D., and R.A.W. Rhodes. "Policy Communities and Issue Networks: Beyond Typology." In *Policy Networks in British Government,* ed. D. Marsh and R.A.W. Rhodes, 249–68. Oxford: Clarendon, 1992. http://dx.doi. org/10.1093/acprof:oso/9780198278528.003.0011

Marsh, D., and M.J. Smith. "There is More Than One Way to Do Political Science: On Different Ways to Study Policy Networks." *Political Studies* 49, no. 3 (2001): 528–41. http://dx.doi.org/10.1111/1467-9248.00325.

May, P.J. "Mandate Design and Implementation: Enhancing Implementation Efforts and Shaping Regulatory Styles." *Journal of Policy Analysis and Management* 12, no. 4 (Autumn 1993): 634–63. http://dx.doi. org/10.2307/3325344.

May, P.J. "Policy Learning and Failure." *Journal of Public Policy* 12, no. 4 (1992): 331–54. http://dx.doi.org/10.1017/S0143814X00005602.

May, P.J. "Reconsidering Policy Design: Policies and Publics." *Journal of Public Policy* 11, no. 2 (1991): 187–206. http://dx.doi.org/10.1017/S0143814X0000619X.

May, P.J., and R.J. Burby. "Coercive versus Cooperative Policies: Comparing Intergovernmental Mandate Performance." *Journal of Policy Analysis and Management* 15, no. 2 (Spring 1996): 171–201. http://dx.doi.org/10.1002/(SICI)1520-6688(199621)15:2<171::AID-PAM2>3.0.CO;2-G.

May, P.J., and J.W. Handmer. "Regulatory Policy Design: Co-operative versus Deterrent Mandates." *Australian Journal of Public Administration* 51, no. 1 (March 1992): 43–53. http://dx.doi.org/10.1111/j.1467-8500.1992.tb01454.x.

Mayer, I., P. Bots, and C. E. Van Daalen. "Perspectives on Policy Analysis: A Framework for Understanding and Design." *International Journal of Technology, Policy and Management* 4, no. 2 (2004): 169–91. http://dx.doi.org/10.1504/IJTPM.2004.004819.

Mayntz, R. "Legitimacy and the Directive Capacity of the Political System." In *Stress and Contradiction in Modern Capitalism*, ed. L.N. Lindberg, R. Alford, C. Crouch, and C. Offe, 261–74. Lexington, MA: Lexington Books, 1975.

Mayntz, R. "Modernization and the Logic of Interorganizational Networks." In *Societal Change Between Market and Organization*, ed. J. Child, M. Crozier, and R. Mayntz, 3–18. Aldershot: Avebury, 1993.

McArthur, D. "Policy Analysis in Provincial Governments in Canada: From PPBS to Network Management." In *Policy Analysis in Canada: The State of the Art*, ed. L. Dobuzinskis, M. Howlett, and D. Laycock, 132–45. Toronto: University of Toronto Press, 2007.

McCubbins, M.D., and A. Lupia. "Learning from Oversight: Fire Alarms and Police Patrols Reconstructed." *Journal of Law Economics and Organization* 10, no. 1 (1994): 96–125. http://dx.doi.org/10.1093/jleo/10.1.96.

McCubbins, M.D., and T. Schwartz. "Congressional Oversight Overlooked: Police Patrols versus Fire Alarms." *American Journal of Political Science* 28, no. 1 (1984): 165–79. http://dx.doi.org/10.2307/2110792.

McDonnell, L.M. and R.F. Elmore. *Alternative Policy Instruments*. Santa Monica, CA: Center for Policy Research in Education, 1987.

McKelvey, B. *Organizational Systematics: Taxonomy, Evolution, Classification*. Berkeley: University of California Press, 1982.

McWilliams, W.C. "On Political Illegitimacy." *Public Policy* 19, no. 3 (Fall 1971): 444–54.

Meltsner, A.J. "Bureaucratic Policy Analysts." *Policy Analysis* 1, no. 1 (1975): 115–31.

Meltsner, A.J. *Policy Analysts in the Bureaucracy*. Berkeley: University of California Press, 1976.

Meltsner, A.J. *Rules for Rulers: The Politics of Advice*. Philadelphia, PA: Temple University Press, 1990.

Merelman, R.M. "Learning and Legitimacy." *American Political Science Review* 60, no. 3 (September 1966): 548–61. http://dx.doi.org/10.2307/1952970.

Michaud, N. "Bureaucratic Politics and the Shaping of Policies: Can We Measure Pulling and Hauling Games?" *Canadian Journal of Political Science* 35, no. 2 (2002): 269–300. http://dx.doi.org/10.1017/S0008423902778244.

Mills, M., and M. Saward. "All Very Well in Practice, But What about Theory? A Critique of the British Idea of Policy Networks." *Contemporary Political Studies* 1 (1994): 79–92.

Milward, B.H., and K.G. Provan. "Governing the Hollow State." *Journal of Public Administration: Research and Theory* 10, no. 2 (2000): 359–80. http://dx.doi.org/10.1093/oxfordjournals.jpart.a024273.

Milward, B.H., K.G. Provan, and B.A. Else, "What Does the 'Hollow State' Look Like?" In *Public Management: The State of the Art*, ed. B. Bozeman, 309–23. San Francisco, CA: Jossey-Bass, 1993.

Mintrom, M. *People Skills for Policy Analysts*. Washington, DC: Georgetown University Press, 2003.

Mintrom, M. "The Policy Analysis Movement." In *Policy Analysis in Canada: The State of the Art*, ed. L. Dobuzinskis, M. Howlett, and D. Laycock. Toronto: University of Toronto Press, 2007.

Mintrom, M. "Policy Entrepreneurs and the Diffusion of Innovation." *American Journal of Political Science* 41, no. 3 (1997): 738–70. http://dx.doi.org/10.2307/2111674.

Mintz, A. "Applied Decision Analysis: Utilizing Poliheuristic Theory to Explain and Predict Foreign Policy and National Security Decisions." *International Studies Perspectives* 6, no. 1 (2005): 94–8. http://dx.doi.org/10.1111/j.1528-3577.2005.00195.x.

Mintz, A. "Foreign Policy Decision Making: Bridging the Gap between the Cognitive Psychological and Rational Actor Schools." In *Decision Making in War and Peace*, ed. N. Geva and A. Mintz, 16–34. Boulder, CO: Lynne Rienner, 1997.

Mintz, A., and N. Geva. "The Poliheuristic Theory of Foreign Policy Decision Making." In *Decision-Making in War and Peace: The Cognitive-Rational Debate*, ed. N. Geva and A. Mintz, 167–199. Boulder, CO: Lynne Rienner, 1997.

Mondak, J.J. "Institutional Legitimacy, Policy Legitimacy and the Supreme Court." *American Politics Quarterly* 20, no. 4 (October 1992): 457–77. http://dx.doi.org/10.1177/1532673X9202000406.

Moore, G. "The Structure of a National Elite Network." *American Sociological Review* 44, no. 5 (1979): 673–92. http://dx.doi.org/10.2307/2094520.

Morgan, M.G., and M. Henrion. *Uncertainty: A Guide to Dealing with Uncertainty Quantitative Risk and Policy Analysis*. Cambridge: Cambridge University Press, 1990. http://dx.doi.org/10.1017/CBO9780511840609

Mortensen, P.B. "Stability and Change in Public Policy: A Longitudinal Study of Comparative Subsystem Dynamics." *Policy Studies Journal: the Journal of the Policy Studies Organization* 35, no. 3 (2007): 373–94. http://dx.doi.org/10.1111/j.1541-0072.2007.00229.x.

Mucciaroni, G. "The Garbage Can Model and the Study of Policy Making: A Critique." *Polity* 24, no. 3 (1992): 459–82. http://dx.doi.org/10.2307/3235165.

Mueller, C. *The Politics of Communication: A Study in the Political Sociology of Language, Socialization and Legitimation.* New York: Oxford University Press, 1973.

Murray, C. "The Media." In *Policy Analysis in Canada: The State of the Art*, ed. L. Dobuzinskis, M. Howlett, and D. Laycock, 286–97. Toronto: University of Toronto Press, 2007.

Nachmias, D. *Public Policy Evaluation.* New York: St. Martin's Press, 1979.

Nelson, R.H. "The Office of Policy Analysis in the Department of the Interior." *Journal of Policy Analysis and Management* 8, no. 3 (1989): 395–410. http://dx.doi.org/10.2307/3324931.

New Zealand State Services Commission. *Essential Ingredients: Improving the Quality of Policy Advice.* Wellington: Crown Copyright, 1999.

Nice, D.C. "Incremental and Nonincremental Policy Responses: The States and the Railroads." *Polity* 20, no. 1 (1987): 145–56. http://dx.doi.org/10.2307/3234941.

Nilsson, M., A. Jordan, J. Turnpenny, J. Hertin, B. Nykvist, and D. Russel. "The Use and Non-Use of Policy Appraisal Tools in Public Policy Making: An Analysis of Three European Countries and the European Union." *Policy Sciences* 41, no. 4 (2008): 335–55. http://dx.doi.org/10.1007/s11077-008-9071-1.

Nordhaus, W. "The Political Business Cycle." *Review of Economic Studies* 42, no. 2 (1975): 169–90. http://dx.doi.org/10.2307/2296528.

Nova Scotia Policy Excellence Initiative. *Policy Excellence and the Nova Scotia Public Service.* Halifax: Policy Advisory Council and Treasury and Policy Board, 2007.

Nownes, A., and G. Neeley. "Toward an Explanation for Public Interest Group Formation and Proliferation: "Seed Money," Disturbances, Entrepreneurship and Patronage." *Policy Studies Journal: The Journal of the Policy Studies Organization* 24, no. 1 (Spring 1996): 74–92. http://dx.doi.org/10.1111/j.1541-0072.1996.tb00552.x.

Nunan, F. "Policy Network Transformation: The Implementation of the EC Directive on Packaging and Packaging Waste." *Public Administration* 77, no. 3 (1999): 621–38. http://dx.doi.org/10.1111/1467-9299.00171.

Nutley, S.M., I. Walter, and H.T.O. Davies. *Using Evidence: How Research Can Inform Public Services.* Bristol, UK: Policy Press, 2007.

O'Connor, A., G. Roos, and T. Vickers-Willis. "Evaluating an Australian Public Policy Organization's Innovation Capacity." *European*

Journal of Innovation Management 10, no. 4 (2007): 532–58. http://dx.doi.
org/10.1108/14601060710828817.

O'Toole, Jr., L.J. "Implementing Public Innovations in Network Settings." *Public Administration* 29, no. 2 (Summer 1997): 115–39.

O'Toole, Jr., L.J. "Research on Policy Implementation: Assessment and Prospects." *Journal of Public Administration: Research and Theory* 10, no. 2 (April 2000): 263–88. http://dx.doi.org/10.1093/oxfordjournals.jpart.a024270.

Oh, C.H. "Explaining the Impact of Policy Information on Policy-Making." *Knowledge and Policy* 10, no. 3 (1997): 22–55.

Olsen, J.P. "Garbage Cans, New Institutionalism, and the Study of Politics." *American Political Science Review* 95, no. 1 (2001): 191–8.

Ontario Executive Research Group. *Investing in Policy: Report on Other Jurisdictions and Organizations*. Toronto: Ministry of the Environment, 1999.

Packwood, A. "Evidence-Based Policy: Rhetoric and Reality." *Social Policy and Society* 1, no. 3 (2002): 267–72. http://dx.doi.org/10.1017/S1474746402003111.

Page, E.C., and B. Jenkins. *Policy Bureaucracy: Governing with a Cast of Thousands*. Oxford: Oxford University Press, 2005.

Painter, M., and J. Pierre. *Challenges to State Policy Capacity: Global Trends and Comparative Perspectives*. London: Palgrave Macmillan, 2005.

Pal, L.A. "Advocacy Organizations and Legislative Politics: The Effects of the Charter of Rights and Freedoms on Interest Lobbying of Federal Legislation, 1989-1991." In *Equity and Community: The Charter; Interest Advocacy and Representation*, ed. F.L. Seidle, 119–57. Montreal: Institute for Research on Public Policy, 1993.

Pal, L.A. *Beyond Policy Analysis: Public Issue Management in Turbulent Times*. Toronto: ITP Nelson, 1997.

Pal, L.A. *Interests of State: The Politics of Language, Multiculturalism, and Feminism in Canada*. Montreal, Kingston: McGill-Queen's University Press, 1993.

Pappi, F.U., and C.H.C.A. Henning. "The Organization of Influence on the EC's Common Agricultural Policy: A Network Approach." *European Journal of Political Research* 36, no. 2 (1999): 257–81. http://dx.doi.org/10.1111/1475-6765.00470.

Pappi, F.U., and C.H.C.A. Henning. "Policy Networks: More than a Metaphor." *Journal of Theoretical Politics* 10, no. 4 (1998): 553–75. http://dx.doi.org/10.1177/0951692898010004008.

Pappi, F.U., and D. Knoke, "Political Exchange in the German and American Labor Policy Domains." In *Policy Networks: Empirical Evidence and Theoretical Considerations*, ed. B. Mann and R. Mayntz, 179–208. Boulder, CO: Westview Press, 1991.

Patton, C.V., and D.S. Sawicki. *Basic Methods of Policy Analysis and Planning.* Englewood Cliffs, NJ: Prentice Hall, 1993.

Pawson, R. *Evidence-Based Policy: A Realist Perspective.* London: Sage Publications, 2006.

Pawson, R. "Evidence-Based Policy: In Search of a Method?" *Evaluation* 8, no. 2 (2002): 157–81. http://dx.doi.org/10.1177/1358902002008002512.

Pawson, R., T. Greenhalgh, G. Harvey, and K. Walshe. "Realist Review – A New Method of Systematic Review Designed for Complex Policy Interventions." *Journal of Health Services Research & Policy* 10, Suppl 1 (July 2005): 21–34. http://dx.doi.org/10.1258/1355819054308530. Medline:16053581

Payne, J.W., J.R. Bettman, and E.J. Johnson. *The Adaptive Decision Maker.* London: Cambridge University Press, 1993. http://dx.doi.org/10.1017/CBO9781139173933

Pemberton, H. "Policy Networks and Policy Learning: UK Economic Policy in the 1960s and 1970s." *Public Administration* 78, no. 4 (2000): 771–92. http://dx.doi.org/10.1111/1467-9299.00230.

Perl, A., and D.J. White. "The Changing Role of Consultants in Canadian Policy Analysis." *Policy and Society* 21, no. 1 (2002): 49–73. http://dx.doi.org/10.1016/S1449-4035(02)70003-9.

Perrow, C. *Normal Accidents: Living with High Risk Technologies.* New York: Basic Books, 1984.

Peters, B.G. *The Future of Governing: Four Emerging Models.* Lawrence: University Press of Kansas, 1996.

Peters, B.G. "Government Reorganization: A Theoretical Analysis." *International Political Science Review* 13, no. 2 (April 1992): 199–217. http://dx.doi.org/10.1177/019251219201300204.

Peters, B.G. *Managing Horizontal Government: The Politics of Coordination.* Ottawa: Canadian Centre for Management Development, 1998.

Peters, B.G. *The Policy Capacity of Government.* Ottawa: Canadian Centre for Management Development, 1996.

Peters, B.G. "Policy Instruments and Public Management: Bridging the Gaps." *Journal of Public Administration: Research and Theory* 10, no. 1 (January 2000): 35–47. http://dx.doi.org/10.1093/oxfordjournals.jpart.a024265.

Peters, B.G. "Policy Networks: Myth, Metaphor and Reality." In *Comparing Policy Networks*, ed. D. Marsh, 21–32. Buckingham: Open University Press, 1998.

Peters, B.G., and A. Barker. 1993. *Advising West European Governments: Inquiries, Expertise and Public Policy.* Edinburgh: Edinburgh University Press.

Peters, B.G., and J. Pierre. "Citizens versus the New Public Manager: The Problem of Mutual Empowerment." *Administration & Society* 32, no. 1 (March 2000): 9–28. http://dx.doi.org/10.1177/00953990022019335.

Peters, B.G., and J. Pierre. "Developments in Intergovernmental Relations: Towards Multi-Level Governance." *Policy and Politics* 29, no. 2 (2001): 131–5. http://dx.doi.org/10.1332/0305573012501251.

Peters, B.G., and J. Pierre. "Governance without Government? Rethinking Public Administration." *Journal of Public Administration: Research and Theory* 8, no. 2 (April 1998): 223–43. http://dx.doi.org/10.1093/oxfordjournals. jpart.a024379.

Peters, B.G. and F.K.M. van Nispen, eds., *Public Policy Instruments: Evaluating the Tools of Public Administration*. New York: Edward Elgar, 1998.

Phillips, S. "Meaning and Structure in Social Movements: Mapping the Network of National Canadian Women's Organizations." *Canadian Journal of Political Science* 24, no. 04 (1991): 755–82. http://dx.doi.org/10.1017/ S0008423900005655.

Phillips, S.D. "How Ottawa Blends: Shifting Government Relationships with Interest Groups." In *How Ottawa Spends 1991–92: The Politics of Fragmentation*, ed. F. Abele, 183–228. Carleton Public Policy Series #13. Ottawa: Carleton University Press, 1991.

Phillips, S.D. "Policy Analysis and the Voluntary Sector: Evolving Policy Styles." In *Policy Analysis in Canada: The State of the Art*, ed. L. Dobuzinskis, M. Howlett, and D. Laycock, 272–84. Toronto: University of Toronto Press, 2007.

Pierson, P. "Increasing Returns, Path Dependence, and the Study of Politics." *American Political Science Review* 94, no. 2 (2000): 251–67. http://dx.doi. org/10.2307/2586011.

Pierson, P. "When Effect Becomes Cause: Policy Feedback and Political Change." *World Politics* 45, no. 04 (1993): 595–628. http://dx.doi. org/10.2307/2950710.

Pollard, W.E. "Decision Making and the Use of Evaluation Research." *American Behavioral Scientist* 30, no. 6 (1987): 661–76. http://dx.doi. org/10.1177/000276487030006009.

Polsby, N.W. *Political Innovation in America: The Politics of Policy Initiation*. New Haven, CT: Yale University Press, 1984.

Preskill, H., and S. Boyle. "A Multidisciplinary Model of Evaluation Capacity Building." *American Journal of Evaluation* 29, no. 4 (2008): 443–59. http:// dx.doi.org/10.1177/1098214008324182.

Pressman, J.L., and A.B. Wildavsky. *Implementation: How Great Expectations in Washington Are Dashed in Oakland*. Berkeley: University of California Press, 1973.

Priestley, M.B. *Spectral Analysis and Time Series*, vol. 2: *Multivariate Series, Prediction and Control* . New York: Academic Press, 1981.

Prince, M.J. "Policy Advisory Groups in Government Departments." In *Public Policy in Canada: Organization, Process, Management*, ed. G.B. Doern and P. Aucoin, 275–300. Toronto: Gage, 1979.

Prince, M.J. "Soft Craft, Hard Choices, Altered Context: Reflections on 25 Years of Policy Advice in Canada." In *Policy Analysis in Canada: The State of the Art*, ed. L. Dobuzinskis, M. Howlett, and D. Laycock, 95–106. Toronto: University of Toronto Press, 2007.

Prince, M.J., and J. Chenier. "The rise and fall of policy planning and research units." *Canadian Public Administration* 22, no. 4 (1980): 536–50.

Pross, A.P., I. Christie, and J.A. Yogis, eds. *Commissions of Inquiry*. Toronto: Carswell, 1990.

Pross, P. *Group Politics and Public Policy*. Toronto: Oxford University Press, 1992.

Qureshi, H. "Evidence in Policy and Practice: What Kinds of Research Designs?" *Journal of Social Work* 4, no. 1 (2004): 7–23. http://dx.doi.org/10.1177/1468017304042418.

Radaelli, C.M. "The Role of Knowledge in the Policy Process." *Journal of European Public Policy* 2, no. 2 (1995): 159–83. http://dx.doi.org/10.1080/13501769508406981.

Radin, B.A. *Beyond Machiavelli: Policy Analysis Comes of Age*. Washington, DC: Georgetown University Press, 2000.

Radin, B.A. "Policy Analysis in the Office of the Assistant Secretary for Planning and Evaluation in the HEW/HHS: Institutionalization and the Second Generation." In *Organizations for Policy Analysis: Helping Government Think*, ed. C.H. Weiss, 144–60. London: Sage Publications, 1992.

Radin, B.A., and J.P. Boase. "Federalism, Political Structure, and Public Policy in the United States and Canada." *Journal of Comparative Policy Analysis* 2, no. 1 (2000): 65–89. http://dx.doi.org/10.1080/13876980008412636.

Rajan, S. C. "Legitimacy in Environmental Policy: The Regulation of Automobile Pollution in California." *International Journal of Environmental Studies* 42, no. 4 (Winter 1992): 243–58. http://dx.doi.org/10.1080/00207239208710800.

Rasmussen, K. "Policy Capacity in Saskatchewan: Strengthening the Equilibrium." *Canadian Public Administration* 42, no. 3 (1999): 331–48. http://dx.doi.org/10.1111/j.1754-7121.1999.tb01554.x.

Rein, M., and S.H. White. "Policy Research: Belief and Doubt." *Policy Analysis* 3, no. 2 (1977): 239–70.

Rhodes, R.A.W. "From Marketisation to Diplomacy: It's the Mix that Matters." *Australian Journal of Public Administration* 56, no. 2 (June 1997): 40–53. http://dx.doi.org/10.1111/j.1467-8500.1997.tb01545.x.

Rhodes, R.A.W. *Understanding Governance: Policy Networks, Governance, Reflexivity and Accountability.* Buckingham: Open University, 1997.

Rhodes, R.A.W., and D. Marsh. "New Directions in the Study of Policy Networks." *European Journal of Political Research* 21, no. 1–2 (1992): 181–205. http://dx.doi.org/10.1111/j.1475-6765.1992.tb00294.x.

Rice, R.E., and W.D. Richards. "An Overview of Network Analysis Methods and Programs." In *Progress in Communication Sciences*, vol. 6, ed. B. Dervin and M.J. Voight, 105–65. Norwood: Ablex, 1985.

Rich, R.F. "Measuring Knowledge Utilization: Processes and Outcomes." *Knowledge and Policy* 10, no. 3 (1997): 11–24. http://dx.doi.org/10.1007/BF02912504.

Richardson, J.G.G., and G. Jordan. "The Concept of Policy Style." In *Policy Styles in Western Europe*, ed. J.G.G. Richardson, 1–16. London: George Allen and Unwin, 1982. 1-16

Richardson, J.G.G. "Interest Groups, Multi-Arena Politics and Policy Change." In *The Policy Process*, ed. S.S. Nagel, 65–100. Commack, NY: Nova Science Publishers, 1999.

Riddell, N. *Policy Research Capacity in the Federal Government.* Ottawa: Policy Research Initiative, 1998.

Riker, W.H. *The Art of Political Manipulation.* New Haven, CT: Yale University Press, 1986.

Riker, W.H. "Political Theory and the Art of Heresthetics." In *Political Science: The State of the Discipline*, ed. A.W. Finifter, 47–67. Washington, DC: American Political Science Association, 1983.

Ripley, R.B., and G.A. Franklin. *Congress, the Bureaucracy, and Public Policy.* Homewood: Dorsey Press, 1980.

Roberts, N.C., and P.J. King. "Policy Entrepreneurs: Their Activity Structure and Function in the Policy Process." *Journal of Public Administration: Research and Theory* 1 (1991): 147–75.

Rochefort, D.A., and R.W. Cobb, eds. *The Politics of Problem Definition: Shaping the Policy Agenda.* Lawrence: University of Kansas Press, 1994.

Rochet, C. "Rethinking the Management of Information in the Strategic Monitoring of Public Policies by Agencies." *Industrial Management & Data Systems* 104, no. 3 (2004): 201–8. http://dx.doi.org/10.1108/02635570410525753.

Roots, R.I. "When Laws Backfire: Unintended Consequences of Public Policy." *American Behavioral Scientist* 47, no. 11 (2004): 1376–94. http://dx.doi.org/10.1177/0002764204265339.

Rose, R. "What is Lesson-Drawing." *Journal of Public Policy* 11, no. 1 (1991): 3–30. http://dx.doi.org/10.1017/S0143814X00004918.

Sabatier, P. "The Acquisition and Utilization of Technical Information by Administrative Agencies." *Administrative Science Quarterly* 23, no. 3 (September 1978): 396–417. http://dx.doi.org/10.2307/2392417. Medline:10297211.

Sabatier, P.A. "An Advocacy Coalition Framework of Policy Change and the Role of Policy-Oriented Learning Therein." *Policy Sciences* 21, no. 2–3 (1988): 129–68. http://dx.doi.org/10.1007/BF00136406.

Sabatier, P.A. "Knowledge, Policy-Oriented Learning, and Policy Change." *Knowledge: Creation, Diffusion, Utilization* 8, no. 4 (1987): 649–92.

Sabatier, P.A. "Political Science and Public Policy: An Assessment." In *Advances in Policy Studies since 1950*, ed. W.N. Dunn and R.M. Kelly, 27–58. New Brunswick, NJ: Transaction, 1992.

Sabatier, P.A. "Policy Change over a Decade or More." In *Policy Change and Learning: An Advocacy Coalition Approach*, ed. P.A. Sabatier and H.C. Jenkins-Smith, 13–40. Boulder, CO: Westview, 1993.

Sabatier, P.A., and H.C. Jenkins-Smith. "The Advocacy Coalition Framework: Assessment, Revisions, and Implications for Scholars and Practitioners." In *Policy Change and Learning: An Advocacy Coalition Approach*, ed. P.A. Sabatier and H.C. Jenkins-Smith. Boulder, CO: Westview, 1993.

Saint-Martin, D. "The New Managerialism and the Policy Influence of Consultants in Government: An Historical-Institutionalist Analysis of Britain, Canada and France." *Governance: An International Journal of Policy, Administration and Institutions* 11, no. 3 (1998): 319–56. http://dx.doi.org/10.1111/0952-1895.00074.

Salamon, L.M., ed. *Beyond Privatization: The Tools of Government Action.* Washington, DC: Urban Institute, 1989.

Salamon, L.M. "Rethinking Public Management: Third-Party Government and the Changing Forms of Government Action." *Public Policy* 29, no. 3 (Fall 1981): 255–75.

Salter, L., and D. Slaco. *Public Inquiries in Canada.* Ottawa: Science Council of Canada, 1981.

Sanderson, I. "Complexity. 'Practical Rationality' and Evidence-Based Policy Making." *Policy and Politics* 34, no. 1 (2006): 115–32. http://dx.doi.org/10.1332/030557306775212188.

Sanderson, I. "Evaluation, Policy Learning and Evidence-Based Policy Making." *Public Administration* 80, no. 1 (2002a): 1–22. http://dx.doi.org/10.1111/1467-9299.00292.

Sanderson, I. "Making Sense of 'What Works': Evidence Based Policymaking as Instrumental Rationality?" *Public Policy and Administration* 17, no. 3 (2002b): 61–75. http://dx.doi.org/10.1177/095207670201700305.

Savoie, D.J. *Governing from the Centre: The Concentration of Power in Canadian Politics.* Toronto: University of Toronto Press, 1999.

Saward, M. *Co-optive Politics and State Legitimacy.* Aldershot: Dartmouth, 1992.

Schaap, L., and M.J.W. van Twist. "The Dynamics of Closedness in Networks." In *Managing Complex Networks: Strategies for the Public Sector*, ed. W.J.M. Kickert, E.H. Klijn, and J.F.M. Koppenjan, 62–78.London: Sage, 1997.

Schaar, J.H. *Legitimacy in the Modern State.* New Brunswick, NJ: Transaction Books, 1981.

Scharpf, F.W. "Political Institutions, Decision Styles, and Policy Choices." In *Political Choice: Institutions, Rules and the Limits of Rationality*, ed. R.M. Czada and A. Windhoff-Heritier, 53–86. Frankfurt: Campus Verlag, 1991.

Scharpf, F.W. "Community and Autonomy: Multilevel Policy-Making in the European Union." *Journal of European Public Policy* 1 (1994): 219–42.

Scharpf, F.W. "Policy Failure and Institutional Reform: Why Should Form Follow Function?" *International Social Science Journal* 38, no. 2 (1986): 179–90.

Schmidt, M.G. "When Parties Matter: A Review of the Possibilities and Limits of Partisan Influence on Public Policy." *European Journal of Political Research* 30, no. 2 (1996): 155–83. http://dx.doi.org/10.1111/j.1475-6765.1996.tb00673.x.

Schmidt, V.A. "The Politics of Economic Adjustment in France and Britain: When Does Discourse Matter?" *Journal of European Public Policy* 8, no. 2 (2001): 247–64. http://dx.doi.org/10.1080/13501760110041578.

Schmitter, P.C., and W. Streeck. *The Organization of Business Interests: Studying the Associative Action of Business in Advanced Industrial Societies.* Cologne: Max Planck Institute for the Study of Societies, 1999.

Schneider, A.L., and H. Ingram. "Behavioural Assumptions of Policy Tools." *Journal of Politics* 52, no. 2 (May 1990): 510–29. http://dx.doi.org/10.2307/2131904.

Schneider, A.L., and H. Ingram. "Policy Design: Elements, Premises and Strategies." In *Policy Theory and Policy Evaluation: Concepts, Knowledge, Causes and Norms*, ed. S.S. Nagel, 77–102. New York: Greenwood, 1990.

Schneider, F., and B.S. Frey. "Politico-Economic Models of Macroeconomic Policy: A Review of the Empirical Evidence." In *Political Business Cycles: The Political Economy of Money, Inflation and Unemployment*, ed. T.D. Willett, 239–75. Durham, NC: Duke University Press, 1988.

Schneider, V. "The Structure of Policy Networks: A Comparison of the 'Chemicals Control' and 'Telecommunications' Policy Domains in Germany." *European Journal of Political Research* 21, no. 1–2 (1992): 109–29. http://dx.doi.org/10.1111/j.1475-6765.1992.tb00291.x.

Schudson, M. "The Trouble with Experts – and Why Democracies Need Them." *Theory and Society* 35, no. 5/6 (2006): 491–506. http://dx.doi.org/10.1007/s11186-006-9012-y.

Schulman, P.R. "The Politics of 'Ideational Policy'." *Journal of Politics* 50, no. 02 (1988): 263–91. http://dx.doi.org/10.2307/2131795.

Schultz, D. "Stupid Public Policy Ideas and other Political Myths." Paper presented to the American Political Science Association, Chicago, 2007.

Sciarini, P. "Elaboration of the Swiss Agricultural Policy for the GATT Negotiations: A Network Analysis." *Swiss Journal of Sociology* 22 (1986): 85–115.

Serdült, U., and C. Hirschi. "From Process to Structure: Developing a Reliable and Valid Tool for Policy Network Comparison." *Swiss Political Science Review* 10, no. 2 (2004): 137–55. http://dx.doi.org/10.1002/j.1662-6370.2004.tb00026.x.

Sharp, E.B. "Paradoxes of National Anti-Drug Policymaking." In *The Politics of Problem Definition: Shaping the Policy Agenda*, ed. D.A. Rochefort and R.W. Cobb, 98–116. Lawrence: University Press of Kansas, 1994.

Shaxson, L. "Is Your Evidence Robust Enough? Questions for Policy Makers and Practitioners." *Evidence and Policy* 1, no. 1 (2005): 101–12. http://dx.doi.org/10.1332/1744264052703177.

Shulock, N. "The Paradox of Policy Analysis: If It Is Not Used, Why Do We Produce So Much of It?" *Journal of Policy Analysis and Management* 18, no. 2 (1999): 226–44. http://dx.doi.org/10.1002/(SICI)1520-6688(199921)18:2<226::AID-PAM2>3.0.CO;2-J.

Simmons, A.B., and K. Keohane. "Canadian Immigration Policy: State Strategies and the Quest for Legitimacy." *Canadian Review of Sociology and Anthropology. La Revue Canadienne de Sociologie et d'Anthropologie* 29, no. 4 (November 1992): 421–52. http://dx.doi.org/10.1111/j.1755-618X.1992.tb02446.x.

Simon, H.A. "A Behavioral Model of Rational Choice." *Quarterly Journal of Economics* 69, no. 1 (1955): 99–118. http://dx.doi.org/10.2307/1884852.

Simon, H.A. "Bounded Rationality and Organizational Learning." *Organization Science* 2, no. 1 (1991): 125–34. http://dx.doi.org/10.1287/orsc.2.1.125.

Simon, H.A. *Models of Man, Social and Rational: Mathematical Essays on Rational Human Behavior in a Social Setting*. New York: Wiley, 1957.

Singer, O. "Policy Communities and Discourse Coalitions." *Knowledge: Creation, Diffusion, Utilization* 11 (1990): 428–58.

Singleton, J. 2001. *A Review of the Policy Capacity between Departments*. Winnipeg: Office of the Auditor-General.

Skogstad, G. "Interest Groups, Representation and Conflict Management in the Standing Committees of the House of Commons." *Canadian Journal of Political Science* 18, no. 04 (1985): 739–72. http://dx.doi.org/10.1017/S0008423900059564.

Smith, A. "Policy Networks and Advocacy Coalitions: Explaining Policy Change and Stability in UK Industrial Pollution Policy?" *Environment and Planning. C, Government & Policy* 18, no. 1 (2000): 95–114. http://dx.doi.org/10.1068/c9810j.

Smith, G., and D. May. "The Artificial Debate between Rationalist and Incrementalist Models of Decision-Making." *Policy and Politics* 8, no. 2 (1980): 147–61. http://dx.doi.org/10.1332/030557380782629005.

Smith, M.J. "Policy Networks and State Autonomy." In *The Political Influence of Ideas: Policy Communities and the Social Sciences*, ed. S. Brooks and A.G. Gagnon. New York: Praeger, 1994.

Smith, M.J. *Pressure, Power and Policy: State Autonomy and Policy Networks in Britain and the United States.* Aldershot: Harvester Wheatsheaf, 1993.

Smith, M.J., D. Marsh, and D. Richards. "Central Government Departments and the Policy Process." *Public Administration* 71, no. 4 (Winter 1993): 567–94. http://dx.doi.org/10.1111/j.1467-9299.1993.tb00992.x.

Smith, T.B. "Advisory Committees in the Public Policy Process." *International Review of Administrative Sciences* 43, no. 2 (June 1977): 153–66. http://dx.doi.org/10.1177/002085237704300210.

Speers, K. "The Invisible Public Service: Consultants and Public Policy in Canada." In *Policy Analysis in Canada: The State of the Art*, ed. L. Dobuzinskis, M. Howlett, and D. Laycock, 220–31. Toronto: University of Toronto Press, 2007.

SPSS. Spss Trends 6.1. New York: SPSS, 1994

State Services Commission. *Essential Ingredients: Improving the Quality of Policy Advice.* Wellington: New Zealand State Services Commission, 1999.

State Services Commission. *Review of the Purchase of Policy Advice from Government Departments.* Wellington: State Services Commission, 2001.

Steunenberg, B., and D. Schmidtchen. "The Comitology Game: European Policymaking with Parliamentary Involvement." In *Governance in Modern Society: Effects, Change and Formation of Government Institutions*, ed. O. van Heffen, W.J.M. Kickert, and J.J.A. Thomassen. Dordrecht: Kluwer Academic Publishers, 2000.

Stewart, K., and P.J. Smith. "Immature Policy Analysis: Building Capacity in Eight Major Canadian Cities." In *Policy Analysis in Canada: The State of the Art*, ed. L. Dobuzinskis, M. Howlett, and D. Laycock, 146–158. Toronto: University of Toronto Press, 2007.

Stillman, P.G. "The Concept of Legitimacy." *Polity* 7, no. 1 (1974): 32–56. http://dx.doi.org/10.2307/3234268.

Stimson, J.A. *Public Opinion in America: Moods Cycles and Swings*. Boulder, CO: Westview Press, 1991.

Stimson, J.A., M.B. Mackuen, and R.S. Erikson. "Dynamic Representation." *American Political Science Review* 89, no. 3 (1995): 543–65. http://dx.doi. org/10.2307/2082973.

Stokman, F.N., and E.P.H. Zeggelink. "Is Politics Power or Policy Oriented? A Comparative Analysis of Dynamic Access Models in Policy Networks." In *Evolution of Social Networks*, ed. P. Doreian and F.N. Stokman, 93–127. Amsterdam: Gordon and Breach Science, 1997.

Stritch, A. "Business Associations and Policy Analysis in Canada." In *Policy Analysis in Canada: The State of the Art*, ed. L. Dobuzinskis, M. Howlett, and D. Laycock, 242–59. Toronto: University of Toronto Press, 2007.

Stryker, R. "Rules, Resources and Legitimacy Processes: Some Implications for Social Conflict, Order and Change." *American Journal of Sociology* 99, no. 4 (January 1994): 847–910. http://dx.doi.org/10.1086/230366.

Suchman, M.C. "Managing Legitimacy: Strategic and Institutional Approaches." *Academy of Management Review* 20, no. 3 (July 1995): 571–610.

Sulitzeanu-Kenan, R., and C. Hood. "Blame Avoidance with Adjectives? Motivation, Opportunity, Activity and Outcome." Paper for ECPR Joint Sessions, Blame Avoidance and Blame Management Workshop, 14–20 April, Granada, Spain, 2005.

Suzuki, M. "Political Business Cycles in the Public Mind." *American Political Science Review* 86, no. 4 (1992): 989–96. http://dx.doi.org/10.2307/1964350.

Teisman, G.R. "Models for Research into Decision-Making Processes: On Phases, Streams and Decision-Making Rounds." *Public Administration* 78, no. 4 (2000): 937–56. http://dx.doi.org/10.1111/1467-9299.00238.

Tenbensel, T. "Does More Evidence Lead to Better Policy? The Implications of Explicit Priority Setting in New Zealand's Health Policy for Evidence-Based Policy." *Policy Studies* 25, no. 3 (2004): 189–207. http://dx.doi.org/10.1080/0 144287012000277480.

Thatcher, M. "The Development of Policy Network Analyses: From Modest Origins to Overarching Frameworks." *Journal of Theoretical Politics* 10, no. 4 (1998): 389–416. http://dx.doi.org/10.1177/0951692898010004002.

The Policy Excellençe Initiative. *Policy Excellence and the Nova Scotia Public Service*. Halifax, NS: Policy Advisory Council and Treasury and Policy Board, 2007.

Thissen, W.A.H., and P.G.J. Twaalfhoven. "Toward a Conceptual Structure for Evaluating Policy Analytic Activities." *European Journal of Operational Research* 129, no. 3 (2001): 627–49. http://dx.doi.org/10.1016/ S0377-2217(99)00470-1.

Thompson, P.R., and M.R. Yessian. "Policy Analysis in the Office of Inspector General, U.S. Department of Health and Human Services." In *Organizations for Policy Analysis: Helping Government Think*, ed. C.H. Weiss, 161–77. London: Sage Publications, 1992.

Thomson, R., F. Stokman, and R. Torenvlied. "Models of Collective Decision Making: Introduction." *Rationality and Society* 15, no. 1 (2003): 5–14. http://dx.doi.org/10.1177/1043463103015001037.

Thrall, T., and L. Engelman. "Univariate and Bivariate Spectral Analysis." In *BMDP Statistical Software Manual*, vol. 2, ed. W.J. Dixon, 971–1012. Berkeley: University of California Press, 1988.

Torgerson, D. "Between Knowledge and Politics: Three Faces of Policy Analysis." *Policy Sciences* 19, no. 1 (1986): 33–59. http://dx.doi.org/10.1007/BF02124483.

Trebilcock, M.J. "Regulating Service Quality in Professional Markets." In *The Regulation of Quality: Products, Services, Workplaces, and the Environment*, ed. D.N. Dewees, 83–108. Toronto: Butterworths, 1983.

Tsebelis, G. *Nested Games: Rational Choice in Comparative Politics*. Berkeley: University of California Press, 1990.

Tufte, E.R. *Political Control of the Economy*. Princeton, NJ: Princeton University Press, 1978.

Tuohy, C. *Policy and Politics in Canada: Institutionalized Ambivalence*. Philadelphia, PA: Temple University Press, 1992.

Tupper, A. "The State in Business." *Canadian Public Administration* 22, no. 1 (Spring 1979): 124–50. http://dx.doi.org/10.1111/j.1754-7121.1979.tb01807.x.

Tupper, A., and G.B. Doern. "Public Corporations and Public Policy in Canada." In *Public Corporations and Public Policy in Canada*, ed. A. Tupper and G.B. Doem, 1–50. Montreal: Institute for Research on Public Policy, 1981.

Turnpenny, J., M. Nilsson, D. Russel, A. Jordan, J. Hertin, and B. Nykvist. "Why Is Integrating Policy Assessment so Hard? A Comparative Analysis of the Institutional Capacity and Constraints." *Journal of Environmental Planning and Management* 51, no. 6 (2008): 759–75. http://dx.doi.org/10.1080/09640560802423541.

Tyler, T.R. *Why People Obey the Law*. New Haven, CT: Yale University Press, 1990.

Uhr, J. "Testing the Policy Capacities of Budgetary Agencies: Lessons from Finance." *Australian Journal of Public Administration* 55, no. 4 (1996): 124–34. http://dx.doi.org/10.1111/j.1467-8500.1996.tb02566.x.

Uhr, J., and K. Mackay, eds. *Evaluating Policy Advice: Learning from Commonwealth Experience*. Canberra: Federalism Research Centre, ANU, 1996.

Van Bueren, E.M., E.H. Klijn, and J.F.M. Koppenjan. "Dealing with Wicked Problems in Networks: Analyzing an Environmental Debate from a Network Perspective." *Journal of Public Administration: Research and Theory* 13, no. 2 (2003): 193–212. http://dx.doi.org/10.1093/jopart/mug017.

Van Bueren, E.M., E.H. Klijn, and J.F.M. Koppenjan. "Network Management as a Coupling Mechanism in Complex Decision and Implementation Processes: Facilitating Interaction and Learning Processes Regarding a Complex Environmental Problem." Paper for the Fifth International Research Symposium in Public Management, IRSPMV University of Barcelona, 9–11 April 2001.

Van Merode, F., A. Nieboer, H. Maarse, and H. Lieverdink. "Analyzing the Dynamics in Multilateral Negotiations." *Social Networks* 26, no. 2 (2004): 141–54. http://dx.doi.org/10.1016/j.socnet.2004.01.006.

Van Waarden, F. "Dimensions and Types of Policy Networks." *European Journal of Political Research* 21, no. 1–2 (1992): 29–52. http://dx.doi.org/10.1111/j.1475-6765.1992.tb00287.x.

Vedung, E. "Policy Instruments: Typologies and Theories." In *Carrots, Sticks and Sermons: Policy Instruments and Their Evaluation*, ed.M.L. Bemelmans-Videc, R.C. Rist, and E. Vedung, 21–58. New Brunswick, NJ: Transaction Publishers, 1997.

Verhoest, K., B.G. Peters, G. Bouckaert, and B. Verschuere. "The Study of Organisational Autonomy: A Conceptual Review." *Public Administration and Development* 24, no. 2 (2004): 101–18. http://dx.doi.org/10.1002/pad.316.

Vogel, D. *National Styles of Regulation: Environmental Policy in Great Britain and the United States*. Ithaca, NY: Cornell University Press, 1986.

Vogel, S.K. *Freer Markets, More Rules: Regulatory Reform in Advanced Industrial Countries*. Ithaca, NY: Cornell University Press, 1996.

Voyer, J. "Policy Analysis in the Federal Government: Building the Forward-Looking Policy Research Capacity." In *Policy Analysis in Canada: The State of the Art*, ed. L. Dobuzinskis, M. Howlett, and D. Laycock, 123–31. Toronto: University of Toronto Press, 2007.

Wagner, P., and H. Wollman. "Social Scientists in Policy Research and Consulting: Some Cross-National Comparisons." *International Social Science Journal* 110 (1986): 601–17.

Walker, J.L. "Setting the Agenda in the U.S. Senate: A Theory of Problem Selection." *British Journal of Political Science* 7, no. 04 (1977): 423–45. http://dx.doi.org/10.1017/S0007123400001101.

Waller, M. "Evaluating Policy Advice." *Australian Journal of Public Administration* 51, no. 4 (1992): 440–6. http://dx.doi.org/10.1111/j.1467-8500.1992.tb01092.x.

Waller, M. "Framework for Policy Evaluation." In *Evaluating Policy Advice: Learning from Commonwealth Experience*, ed. J. Uhr and K. Mackay, 9–20. Canberra: Federalism Research Centre, 1996.

Walters, L.C., J. Aydelotte, and J. Miller. "Putting More Public in Policy Analysis." *Public Administration Review* 60, no. 4 (July/August 2000): 349–59. http://dx.doi.org/10.1111/0033-3352.00097.

Warburton, R.N., and W.P. Warburton. "Canada Needs Better Data for Evidence-Based Policy: Inconsistencies between Administrative and Survey Data on Welfare Dependence and Education." *Canadian Public Policy* 30, no. 3 (2004): 241–55. http://dx.doi.org/10.2307/3552301.

Weatherford, M.S. "Political Economy and Political Legitimacy: The Link between Economic Policy and Political Trust." In *Economic Decline and Political Change: Canada, Great Britain, the United States*, ed. H.D. Clarke, M.C. Stewart, and G. Zuk, 225–51. Pittsburgh, PA: University of Pittsburgh Press, 1989.

Weaver, R.K. "The Politics of Blame Avoidance." *Journal of Public Policy* 6, no. 4 (1986): 371–98. http://dx.doi.org/10.1017/S0143814X00004219.

Weber, M. "Politics as a Vocation." In *From Max Weber: Essays in Sociology*, ed. H. Gerth and C. Wright Mills, 78. New York: Oxford University Press, 1958.

Weible, C.M. "Expert-Based Information and Policy Subsystems: A Review and Synthesis." *Policy Studies Journal: The Journal of the Policy Studies Organization* 36, no. 4 (2008): 615–35. http://dx.doi.org/10.1111/j.1541-0072.2008.00287.x.

Weimer, D.L., and A.R. Vining. *Policy Analysis: Concepts and Practice*. Saddle River, NJ: Prentice Hall, 1999.

Weimer, D.L., and A.R. Vining. *Policy Analysis: Concepts and Practice*. Upper Saddle River, NJ: Prentice Hall, 2004.

Weirich, P. *Realistic Decision Theory: Rules for Nonideal Agents in Nonideal Circumstances*. New York: Oxford University Press, 2004.

Weiss, A., and E. Woodhouse. "Reframing Incrementalism: A Constructive Response to Critics." *Policy Sciences* 25, no. 3 (1992): 255–73. http://dx.doi.org/10.1007/BF00138785.

Weiss, C.H. "Knowledge Creep and Decision Accretion." *Knowledge: Creation, Diffusion, Utilization* 1, no. 3 (1980): 381–404.

Weiss, C.H., ed. *Organizations for Policy Analysis: Helping Government Think*. London: Sage Publications, 1992.

Weiss, C.H. "Policy Research: Data, Ideas or Arguments?" In *Social Sciences and Modern States: National Experiences and Theoretical Crossroads*, ed. P. Wagner, B. Wittrock, and H. Wollman, 307–32. Cambridge: Cambridge University Press, 1991. http://dx.doi.org/10.1017/CBO9780511983993.014

Weiss, C.H. "Research for Policy's Sake: The Enlightenment Function of Social Science Research." *Policy Analysis* 3 (1977): 531–45.

Weiss, C.H., and M.J. Bucuvalas. *Social Science Research and Decision-Making*. New York: Columbia University Press, 1980.

Weiss, J.A., and M. Tschirhart. "Public Information Campaigns as Policy Instruments." *Journal of Policy Analysis and Management* 13, no. 1 (Winter 1994): 82–119. http://dx.doi.org/10.2307/3325092.

Weller, P., and B. Stevens. "Evaluating Policy Advice: The Australian Experience." *Public Administration* 76, no. 3 (1998): 579–89. http://dx.doi.org/10.1111/1467-9299.00118.

Wellman, B. "Structural Analysis: From Method and Metaphor to Theory and Substance." In *Social Structures: A Network Approach*, ed. B. Wellman and S.D. Berkowitz, 19–61. New York: Cambridge University Press, 1988.

Wellstead, A., R. Stedman, and E. Lindquist. "Beyond the National Capital Region: Federal regional policy capacity." In *Report Prepared for the Treasury Board Secretariat of Canada*. Ottawa: Public Works and Government Services Canada, 2007.

Whiteman, D. "The Fate of Policy Analysis in Congressional Decision Making: Three Types of Use in Committees." *Western Political Quarterly* 38, no. 2 (1985): 294–311. http://dx.doi.org/10.2307/448631.

Wildavsky, A.B. "Rescuing Policy Analysis from PPBS." *Public Administration Review* 29, no. 2 (1969): 189–202. http://dx.doi.org/10.2307/973700.

Wildavsky, A.B. *Speaking Truth to Power: The Art and Craft of Policy Analysis*. Boston: Little, Brown, 1979.

Wilkinson, L., M.A. Hill, and E. Yang. SYSTAT: Statistics, Version 5.2. Edition (Evanston: SYSTAT, 1992); and SPSS, SPSS Trends 6.1. Chicago: SPSS, 1994.

Williams, A. "Governance and Sustainability: An Investigation of the Role of Policy Mediators in the European Union Policy Process." *Policy and Politics* 32, no. 1 (2004): 95–110. http://dx.doi.org/10.1332/030557304772860076.

Wolfe, A.W. "The Rise of Network Thinking in Anthropology." *Social Networks* 1, no. 1 (1978): 53–64. http://dx.doi.org/10.1016/0378-8733(78)90012-6.

Wollmann, H. "Policy Analysis in West Germany's Federal Government: A Case of Unfinished Governmental and Administrative Modernization?" *Governance: An International Journal of Policy, Administration and Institutions* 2, no. 3 (1989): 233–66. http://dx.doi.org/10.1111/j.1468-0491.1989.tb00092.x.

Wood, B.D., and J.S. Peake. "The Dynamics of Foreign Policy Agenda-Setting." *American Political Science Review* 92, no. 1 (1998): 173–84. http://dx.doi.org/10.2307/2585936.

Woodside, K. "Policy Instruments and the Study of Public Policy." *Canadian Journal of Political Science* 19, no. 4 (December 1986): 775–93. http://dx.doi.org/10.1017/S0008423900055141.

Wraith, R.E., and G.B. Lamb. *Public Inquiries as an Instrument of Government.* London: George Allen and Unwin, 1971.

Young, K., D. Ashby, A. Boaz, and L. Grayson. "Social Science and the Evidence-Based Policy Movement." *Social Policy and Society* 1, no. 3 (2002): 215–24. http://dx.doi.org/10.1017/S1474746402003068.

Zahariadis, N.M., and C.S. Allen. "Ideas, Networks, and Policy Streams: Privatization in Britain and Germany." *Policy Studies Review* 14, no. 1–2 (1995): 71–98. http://dx.doi.org/10.1111/j.1541-1338.1995.tb00622.x.

Zahariadis, N.M. *States and Public Policy: Privatization in Britain and France.* Ann Arbor: University of Michigan Press, 1995.

Zelditch Jr., M., W. Harris, G.M. Thomas, and H.A. Walker. "Decisions, Non-decisions and Metadecisions." *Research in Social Movements, Conflicts and Change* 5 (1983): 1–32.

Zijlstra, G.J. "Networks in Public Policy: Nuclear Energy in the Netherlands." *Social Networks* 1, no. 4 (1978): 359–89. http://dx.doi.org/10.1016/0378-8733(78)90004-7.

Permission Credits

Chapter 6: "Policy Advice in Multi-Level Governance Systems: Sub-National Policy Analysts and Analysis." *International Review of Public Administration* 13, no. 3 (2009): 1–16.

Chapter 7: "Policy Analytical Capacity and Evidence-Based Policy Making: Lessons from Canada." *Canadian Public Administration* 52, no. 2 (2009): 153–75.